Realist Vision

Realist Vision

PETER BROOKS

YALE UNIVERSITY PRESS   NEW HAVEN & LONDON

Published with assistance from the foundation established in memory of Philip Hamilton McMillan of the Class of 1894, Yale College.

Designed by James J. Johnson and set in Joanna Roman types by Tseng Information Systems, Inc.
Printed in the United States of America.

Library of Congress Cataloging-in-Publication Data

Brooks, Peter, 1938–
    Realist vision / Peter Brooks.
        p.   cm.
    Includes bibliographical references (p.   ) and index.
    ISBN 0-300-10680-7 (clothbound : alk. paper)

1. English fiction—19th century—History and criticism. 2. Realism in literature. 3. French fiction—19th century—History and criticism. 4. Literature, Comparative—English and French. 5. Literature, Comparative—French and English. I. Title.
PR878.R4B76 2005
823'80912—dc22   2004029501

A catalogue record for this book is available from the British Library.

The paper in this book meets the guidelines for permanence and durability of the Committee on Production Guidelines for Book Longevity of the Council on Library Resources.

10 9 8 7 6 5 4 3 2 1

For Anna

Contents

Preface

Three years ago, as Eastman Visiting Professor at Oxford, I was instructed to present a series of public lectures, open to students and faculty, during Michaelmas Term. This daunting prospect prompted me to turn to what I know best, the English and French novels of the nineteenth-century realist tradition, and some painters in the same sphere, to try to offer a rethinking of books and problems that have been with me for many years. The following year, I was asked to give the William Clyde DeVane Lectures at Yale University, and took this as an opportunity to revisit and expand (a Yale term being longer than an Oxford term) my thinking on the subject. I have tried to maintain as much as possible the informality and generality of the lectures in moving to this book. My hope is to renew interest in the realist vision, but especially to invite rereading, reviewing, rethinking of some masterful works.

Realist Vision

Realism and Representation

I THINK WE HAVE A THIRST FOR REALITY. WHICH IS CURIOUS, SINCE WE HAVE too much reality, more than we can bear. But that is the lived, experienced reality of the everyday. We thirst for a reality that we can see, hold up to inspection, understand. "Reality TV" is a strange realization of this paradox: the totally banal become fascinating because offered as spectacle rather than experience—offered as what we sometimes call vicarious experience, living in and through the lives of others. That is perhaps the reality that we want.

More simply, we might ask ourselves: Why do we take pleasure in imitations and reproductions of the things of our world? Why do we from childhood on like to play with toys that reproduce in miniature the objects amid which we live? The pleasure that human beings take in scale models of the real—dollhouses, ships in bottles, lead soldiers, model railroads—must have something to do with the sense these provide of being able to play with and therefore to master the real world. The scale model—the *modèle réduit*, as the French call it—allows us to get both our fingers and our minds around objects otherwise alien and imposing. Models give us a way to bind and organize the complex and at times overwhelming energies of the world outside us. Freud suggests that the infant's play with a spool on a string— thrown out of its crib and pulled back—presents a basic scenario in mastering reality through play. The anthropologist Claude Lévi-Strauss speculates that the hobbyist's building of the scale model figures intellectual process in general, a way to understand through making. And Friedrich von Schiller long ago argued that art is the product of a human instinct for play, the *Spieltrieb*, by which we create our zone of apparent freedom in a world otherwise constricted by laws and necessities.

Let's suppose, then, that making models of the things of the world is a function of our desire to play, and in playing to assert that we master the world, and therefore have a certain freedom in it. For a child to push around a toy bulldozer is to imitate the work of the adult world, of course, and play with a dollhouse can imitate the child's entire environment. But the imitation brings with it the mastery the child otherwise doesn't have. Play is a form of repetition of the world with this difference that the world has become manageable. We are in charge, we control its creatures and things. The mode of "let's pretend" immediately transports children into a world of their own making. It is a world that can be wholly vivid and "real," though there can be a coexisting consciousness that it is only pretend. And surely that continues to be true of all forms of adult play, including that form of play we call literature, the creation and consumption of fictions.

Wallace Stevens suggests that fictions arise from the need to build a space or even a shelter for ourselves in an alien world. He writes in *Notes Toward a Supreme Fiction*:

> From this the poem springs: that we live in a place
> That is not our own and, much more, not ourselves
> And hard it is in spite of blazoned days.

If the world around us is not our own, more specifically if it is not human but rather a world of other species and inanimate objects, then the "poem," the artwork, becomes our counteraction, our attempt to humanize the world —pursued by an artist as self-aware as Stevens of course in full knowledge that the attempt is only fictional, carried on in a realm of the as-if. Fictions are what we make up in order to make believe: the word in its Latin root, *fingere, ficto,* means both to make, as in the model builder's activity, and to make up, to feign. Making in order to make up, to make believe, seems a reasonable description of literary fictions, and why we write them and read them.

Now, if what I've been saying applies to all fictions, in whatever medium, what may be specific to fictions that explicitly claim to represent the real world—"realist" art and literature—is its desire to be maximally reproductive of that world it is modeling for play purposes. It claims to offer us a kind of reduction—*modèle réduit*—of the world, compacted into a volume that we know can provide, for the duration of our reading, the sense of a parallel reality that can almost supplant our own. More than most other fictions, the realist novel provides a sense of play very similar to that given by the scale model. There is a novel from early in the tradition, Alain-René Le Sage's *Le Diable boîteux* (1707), that offers a striking image of the similarity. The benevolent devil Asmodée takes the novel's protagonist, Don Cléofas, up to the top of the highest tower in Madrid, then removes all the city's rooftops, to show what is going on in the rooms exposed (fig. 1). It is very much like playing with a dollhouse or with a toy city. Yet of course it is already a gesture from Honoré de Balzac or Charles Dickens, seeing through the roofs and facades of the real to the private lives behind and beneath.

Removing housetops in order to see the private lives played out beneath them: the gesture also suggests how centrally realist literature is attached to the visual, to looking at things, registering their presence in the world through sight. Certainly realism more than almost any other mode of literature makes sight paramount—makes it the dominant sense in our understanding of and relation to the world. The relative dominance and prestige given to the visual in the human grasp of the world reaches back to Greek philosophy, at least, and after that rarely is challenged in Western culture. Broadly speaking, Western arts are representational: different styles from the reproductive to the abstract play off the notion of representation. The claim of "realism" in both painting and literature is in large part that our sense of sight is the most reliable guide to the world as it most immediately affects us. The claim clearly owes much to John Locke and the rise of empiricism as a dominant, widely shared kind of thinking about mind and environment. The visual is not necessarily the end of the story—hearing, smell, touch may ultimately be just as or more important—but it almost of necessity seems to be the beginning of the story. Realism tends to deal in "first impressions" of all sorts, and they are impressions on the retina first of all—the way things look. It is not coincidental that photography comes into being along with realism, with the lens imitating the retina to reproduce the world. It is on the basis of first impressions that the greatest realists will go on to far more encompassing and at times visionary visions, ones that attempt to give us not only the world viewed but as well the world comprehended.

Let's say that realism is a kind of literature and art committed to a form of play that uses carefully wrought and detailed toys, ones that attempt as much as possible to reproduce the look and feel of the real thing. And this kind of fiction becomes in the course of the nineteenth century the standard mode

Fig. 1. Engraving of Asmodée and Don Cléofas from Alain-René Le Sage,
Le Diable boîteux (Paris, 1707)

of the novels we continue to think of as great, as classics. Once a radical gesture, breaking with tradition, realism becomes so much the expected mode of the novel that even today we tend to think of it as the norm from which other modes—magical realism, science fiction, fantasy, metafictions—are variants or deviants. That is, we eventually came to regard the styles of representing the world pioneered by such as Balzac, Dickens, Gustave Flaubert, George Eliot as standard, what we expected fiction to be. The novel in the airport newsstand will tend to be written from a repertory of narrative and descriptive tools that come from the nineteenth-century realists. What they are doing, and their radical pioneering in the novel, has ceased to astonish us. And yet when you go back to them, they are in fact astonishing, innovators seeking and finding new and radical ways to come to terms with and convey a reality that itself was constantly presenting radical new challenges.

Playing with the world seriously—in a form of play governed by rules of modeling, one might say—is a bold new enterprise for these novelists. They invent the rules as they go along and then refine them to the point that subsequent generations of novelists can find them codified in writing manuals. One premise of this serious play is that it includes dolls that are supposed to look and act like people—characters who ought to be recognizable in terms of not only dress and appearance but also social function and, beyond that, motive, psychology. Marcel Proust remarks on the genius of the first writer to understand that readers can be made to experience life through the eyes and mind of a fictional being. Whoever that originating writer may have been, the realist writers had the genius to understand the importance of making characters comparable to their supposed readers—situating them in ordinariness, as tokens of our own experience, though perhaps then moving them through more than ordinary experience, in order to make their adventures significant, even exemplary. Emma Bovary and Dorothea Brooke, Old Goriot and Nana—such characters have taken on an imaginative reality in their cultures, they are referred to as if they were real, or rather, more significant than the merely real, since they sum up and represent more fully certain choices of ways of being. They offer, in the best possible sense, criticisms of life: instances that lend themselves to discussion and debate, that pose important questions about our being in the world.

The difference of literary play from play with toys lies in the sign system used for modeling in literature: that is, language. Imitation in litera-

6 ture cannot, in the manner of painting or sculpture or film, present visual images that are immediately apprehended and decoded by the eye. Its representations are mediated through language. Language can itself be a thing or event in the world that can be literally reproduced in literary imitation—as in dialogue, which we can reproduce in the novel—and this gives what Plato would identify as the only complete form of *mimesis*. But this form of reproduction is fairly limited, and even dialogue tends to refer outside itself, to events and settings once again mediated through representation. Fictions need forms of telling and showing other than *mimesis*—what Plato labels as *diegesis*, and later writers have called "summary" or "narration" or a variety of other things. Fictions have to lie in order to tell the truth: they must foreshorten, summarize, perspectivize, give an illusion of completeness from fragments. Henry James said that of all novelists, Balzac pretended hardest. It is how you pretend that counts.

But here of course is a source of objection to attempts at realist representation: Why bother with such pretending, especially since we know that language does not coincide with the world? The lesson of much criticism and theory in the last decades of the twentieth century seemed to suggest that notions of representation, and especially representation that thinks of itself as an accurate designation of the world, are naive and deluded. Representation in the realist mode seemed to depend on a faulty understanding of the linguistic sign, which in fact does not transparently designate the world. Linguistic signs are used to compensate for the absence of the things they designate—use of a word stands in for the absent referent of the word, or perhaps creates the illusion that there is a referent for the word where some might doubt this to be the case (for example, "god" or "soul" or perhaps "honor"). Signs are slippery as well as creative: as Niccolò Machiavelli noted, language was given to men and women so they could lie. Realist fictions labor under the burden of accusation that they are lies that don't know it, lies that naively or mendaciously claim to believe they are truths. For experimental "new novelists" of the 1960s and after, as for some post-structuralist critics, the "Balzacian novel" became a kind of whipping boy, an example of blinded and bourgeois novelizing without any sophisticated critical perspective on sign-systems and on the illusions of the bourgeois society and its concepts—including the fully rounded and situated "character"—it was dedicated to representing.

This was, I think, a blinded view of Balzac and the realist tradition in general. But it of course picked up a very old line of critique of realism, reaching back at least to Plato. If to Plato art is an imitation of an imitation—that is, of shadows, appearances, rather than true reality—then the art that attempts to be most faithful to appearances, to surfaces, will be the lowest in value. And for many centuries of European art and especially literature, imitation of the everyday, of the real in the sense of what we know best, belongs to low art, and to low style: comedy, farce, certain kinds of satire. Erich Auerbach's magisterial history of the representation of reality in Western literature, *Mimesis*, tells the story of the emergence of a serious attention to the everyday real. It is not that there haven't been kinds of realism, and impulses toward realism, throughout history—see Chaucer, see Rabelais, see Pieter Bruegel the Elder, or American photorealism of the 1970s. The instinct of realist reproduction may be a constant in the human imagination (though at times it seems to be wholly dismissed or repressed, as in Byzantine art). What seems to change with the coming of the modern age—dating that from sometime around the end of the eighteenth century, with the French Revolution as its great emblematic event, and Jean-Jacques Rousseau and then the English Romantic writers as its flag bearers—is a new valuation of ordinary experience and its ordinary settings and things. This new valuation is of course tied to the rise of the middle classes to cultural influence, and to the rise of the novel as the preeminent form of modernity. What we see at the dawn of modernity—and the age of revolutions—is the struggle to emerge of imaginative forms and styles that would do greater justice to the language of ordinary men (in William Wordsworth's terms) and to the meaning of unexceptional human experience.

Keeping a register of what happens every day, Rousseau once described his one novel. This means finding a certain dignity in the ordinary, as in Wordsworth's strange cast of peasants. But it can also mean attention to the ugly, that which doesn't fit the standard definitions of the beautiful. George Eliot in *Adam Bede* famously compares her novel to Dutch genre painting, but even that kind of humble picturesqueness seems too prettified for what such late realists—or "naturalists"—as Emile Zola and George Gissing seek. Zola proposed that every writer saw life through a certain kind of screen. Whereas the Romantic screen gave rosy coloring to what was viewed through it, the

8   Naturalist screen was plainly transparent—yet, Zola admits, with a certain effect of graying, making more somber what was perceived through it. That is, Zola recognizes that the realist, in reaction against more idealized forms of art, seeks to show us a non-beautified world. Or perhaps more aptly: to show us the interest, possibly the beauty, of the non-beautiful. When the painting of Gustave Courbet first appeared on the Paris art scene, critics notably found it ugly. (See, for instance, in chapter 5, Courbet's *Burial at Ornans*, fig. 5, and *Bathers*, fig. 9.) "Vive le laid, le laid seul est aimable," they wrote, in parody of the critic Nicolas Boileau's famous line in praise of truth. In their obtuseness, these critics were on to something: the fascination of the non-conforming, that one finds in our own moment, for instance, in the work of Lucian Freud. This painting has the almost oxymoronic title of *Naked Portrait* (fig. 2): that it is a portrait makes a strong point, about its individualization, particularization, as opposed to the generalizing and idealizing tradition of the nude. Consider also Freud's *Naked Man with Rat* (fig. 3), with its kind of raw exposure. Freud, like Courbet before him, has claimed he can only paint what he sees; and the act of seeing is itself exposing, relentlessly stripping bare to a self that is not allowed to hide from the painter's gaze. Then there is Freud's repeated use of the huge model Leigh Bowery, as in determined violation of all the canons of beauty (see fig. 36, in chapter 12). Documentation of the modern city, in writing, painting, and photography, will also find a fascination in the ugly, as part of our created landscape (fig. 4). The ugly is often used here, as in Zola, as a call to attention: look, see. And of course when you do look with the intensity of Lucian Freud, the ugly ceases to be simply that, to become something full of interest. The discovery of the ugly is part of the process of disillusioning in which realism deals, but then beyond the loss of illusions something else seems to loom: something we find in Freud's painting, or in Flaubert's later work—the fascination of the banal and the ugly. We will want to explore further this problematic question of the ugly and what you might call its mode of existence.

Realism as the ugly stands close to realism as the shocking, that which transgresses the bounds of the acceptable and the representable. Flaubert and *Madame Bovary* are put on trial in 1857 for outrage to public morality; though acquitted, Flaubert is severely reprimanded by the presiding judge for exceeding the limits permitted to literature, and for proposing a "system" that, applied to art and literature, leads to "a realism which would be the nega-

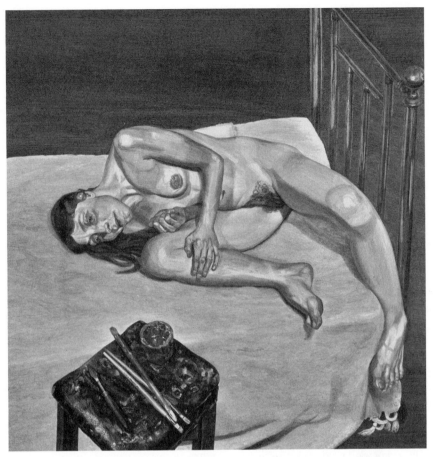

Fig. 2. Lucian Freud, *Naked Portrait*, 1972–73, oil on canvas. Tate, London.
© Lucian Freud. Photo: Tate Gallery, London / Art Resource, NY

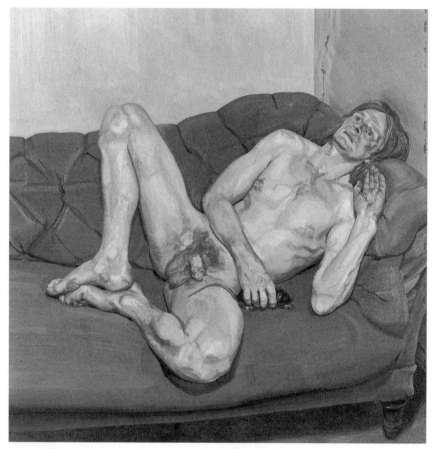

Fig. 3. Lucian Freud, *Naked Man with Rat*, 1977–78, oil on canvas. Collection, Art Gallery of Western Australia. © Lucian Freud

Fig. 4. Lucian Freud, *Factory in North London*, 1972, oil on canvas. Private collection. © Lucian Freud. Photo: © Christie's Images Inc. 2004

12 tion of the beautiful and the good." Zola translated into English—only late and cautiously—becomes the target of the National Vigilance Association and the subject of a parliamentary debate in 1888: "The Secretary of State for the Home Department (Mr. Matthews) (Birmingham, E.) said, that it was beyond doubt that there had been of recent years a considerable growth of evil and pernicious literature, and that its sale took place with more openness than was formerly the case. The French romantic literature of modern days, of which cheap editions were openly sold in this country, had reached a lower depth of immorality than had ever before been known." Zola's L'Assommoir and Nana were followed by his novel about peasants, La Terre. Even though translated in a bowdlerized version, that novel was the last straw for English middle-class morality—the word "bestial" keeps coming back in the comments—and in that same year, 1888, Zola's publisher, Henry Vizetelly, was made to suppress all three novels and promise to publish no more, was fined one hundred pounds, and was then sent to prison for three months. It is a curious reminder that the British, who had created the worst human squalor in their industrial cities, could find representation of poverty, misery, and sexuality dangerous. Being a realist or naturalist was risky business.

Realism as we know it, as a label we apply to a period and a family of works, very much belongs to the rise of the novel as a relatively rule-free genre that both appealed to and represented the private lives of the unexceptional—or rather, found and dramatized the exceptional within the ordinary, creating the heroism of everyday life. Ian Watt's story in The Rise of the Novel remains, despite critiques and modifications, generally accurate: the rise of the novel tracks the rise of the European bourgeoisie, it is tied to a new phenomenon of middle-class leisure time—especially for women—and a new concern with private lives and the psychology and morality of individual choices. Tied, too, of course to the expansion of printing, and the diffusion of multiple copies of the same work that, whether bought or rented from the lending library, can be read alone, at home, to oneself. Privacy is both the subject and the condition of the novel, though with this paradox that both subject and condition repose on an invasion of privacy, a promiscuous broadcast of the private. And tied also to the remarkable increase in literacy, perhaps most dramatically in France, where in 1820 about 25 percent of the population is literate, then by the 1860s, 65 percent, and by the end of the century around 90 percent. When Edmond and Jules de Goncourt, in the preface to their novel *Germinie Lacerteux* (1865), spoke of a "droit au roman"—a right to the novel of all social sectors and classes, including the proletariat—they were demonstrating one logic of the novel and of realism: that it was inevitably tied to a loosening of hierarchy and a spread of democratized taste.

With the rise of the realist novel in the nineteenth century, we are into the age of Jules Michelet and Thomas Carlyle, of Karl Marx and John Ruskin, of Charles Darwin and Hippolyte Taine: that is, an age where history takes on new importance, and learns to be more scientific, and where theories of history come to explain how we got to be how we are, and in particular how we evolved from earlier forms to the present. It is the time of industrial, social, and political revolution, and one of the defining characteristics of any realist writing is I think a willingness to confront these issues. England develops a recognizable "industrial novel," one that takes on the problems of social misery and class conflict, and France has its "roman social," including popular socialist varieties. Some English novelists address the issue Benjamin Disraeli, novelist as well as politician, labeled that of "the two nations," the owners and the dispossessed. If the Industrial Revolution comes to England far earlier than to France—and more visibly—political upheaval becomes a French specialty in the nineteenth century: the revolutions (and counter-revolutions) that punctuate modern French history starting in 1789 and its long aftermath concluding in restoration of the monarchy in 1815, then 1830, 1848, 1851, 1871—and one could refine on the list. Perhaps because modern French history is so well demarcated by the rise and overthrow of various regimes, it seems to have offered particularly grateful territory for the novelist who wanted to be the historian of contemporary society. Balzac and Zola, for instance, both write their principal works following a revolution that has put an endstop to the period they are writing about, and this gives them valuable perspective, enables them to see an epoch in its entirety. And it confronts them with the stark question: To whom does France belong?

The nineteenth century in the Western world is of course a time of massive change, much of it resulting from the industrial transformation of work and production, the creation of complex heavy machinery, the coming of the railroad—a true revolution in the experience of space and time—and the formation of the modern city, bringing with it the perception of glamour, entertainment, the variety and excitement of the urban crowd—but also the perception of threat from a newly constituted urban proletariat. The population of Paris doubles during the first half of the century, and similar changes occur in other major cities, even more dramatically in the new industrial cities such as Manchester. Such rapid urban growth strains the relations of social groups one to another—it makes class warfare something of a daily experience. It also makes the city a total environment that writers concerned with the contexts of life must come to terms with.

The nineteenth century also marks the emergence of the cash nexus as possibly underlying or representing all social relations. If Old Regime wealth was principally expressed and undergirded by ownership of land—the feudal, aristocratic model of wealth and of identity—this will be replaced by money in ways both liberating and terrifying. You inherit land, you make money: and the emergence of the cash nexus tracks a transition from inherited identity to achieved identity, that of the self-made man, or the speculator, the capitalist, the gambler—or the destitute genius—all familiar figures in the nineteenth-century novel. Marx noted that capitalist industrial production typically creates objects that are transitory, quickly used up and cast aside in the forward movement of progress: "All that is solid melts into air." Money represents the fluidity and vaporousness of things in an economy that can swiftly move from boom to bust and then recycle. Money indeed comes to represent representation itself: a system of signs for things. It's no accident that the founder of modern linguistics, Ferdinand de Saussure, often compares language as a system to money: meaning in both systems depends on exchange value, what you get in return for what you are offering. And the great realist novelists come to understand that words, like shillings or francs, are part of a circulatory system subject to inflation and deflation, that meanings may be governed by the linguistic economies and marketplaces of which they are part.

In a direct and literal way, the coming of modern modes of production will transform literature in the nineteenth century, propelling it toward what the French critic Charles-Augustin Sainte-Beuve called "industrial literature." Sainte-Beuve was reacting in particular to the creation of the *roman-feuilleton*, the serial novel running in daily installments on the front page of the newspaper. This was a French invention from the 1830s and 1840s that then caught on worldwide (and continues in some parts of the world today), and was an example of fiction financing fact. The serial novel allowed newspapers to reduce their subscription rates dramatically (there were no single-

issue sales at the time) and increase their circulation three- and fourfold. The
novelists who succeeded in the new form learned to segment melodramatic
plots into short episodes with cliff-hanging endings, followed by the sacramental line: "La suite à demain": Continued tomorrow. But the serial novel
is only the most flamboyant instance of literature in its industrial transformation, tied to the development of the steam press, cheap paper, the book-
seller, and the lending library. Writers now can attempt to live from sales of
their works—and sometimes succeed at it—rather than from noble or royal
patronage. We have the beginnings of an uneasy relation between high culture and the mass market, with the novel hovering ambiguously between:
a socially mobile form that can go popular, in an age of expanding readership, or upscale toward increasingly alienated artistic milieux, or in rare
cases appeal to the whole population.

"The age of property," E. M. Forster called the nineteenth century, and
there is much in these novels about property of all sorts, there are lots of
things, clutter, an apparent fear of emptiness. In Dickens's *Great Expectations*,
the law clerk Wemmick delivers to young Pip homilies on the importance of
"portable property." To Wemmick, anything of value is potentially portable
property. It should not be lost, squandered, allowed to slip away. It needs
to be accumulated, stored in one's home, considered as one's castle (and
Wemmick's home in the Walworth suburb of London, a miniature gim-
crack castle, literalizes the metaphor), turned into wealth. Balzac's usurer and
miser, Gobseck, probably appears in more novels of the *Comédie humaine* than
any other character: he is at the still center of the turning earth, trading in
property, lending money against things. By the end of his life, he can't get rid
of things fast enough: at his death his house is stuffed with decaying things
and rotting produce. At a time of nascent capitalism (which comes earlier in
Britain than in France), there is a fascination with investment, accumulation,
wealth—and of course their collapse in bankruptcy. If wealth and poverty
are, very explicitly for these novelists, questions of money—the ultimate
portable property—their overt expression most often is visible in objects,
things, bought and sold as part of one's declaration of success or failure.
Careers are played out between the gambling house and the pawnshop. The
property noted by Forster clutters up many of these novels, precisely because
it tells us so much about those who have accumulated it, in self-definition.
Balzac left us a remarkable unpublished non-novel: the inventory he labori-

16 ously wrote of the furnishings in his newly acquired, overstuffed house in Passy. It is more Balzacian than Balzac.

"Things" will in fact be a main theme in my exploration of the realist vision. Things, first of all, because they represent the hard materiality that one cannot get around in any non-idealist picture of the world: things in the sense of the stone that Dr. Johnson kicked in refutation of Bishop Berkeley's idealism. You cannot, the realist claims, represent people without taking account of the things that people use and acquire in order to define themselves—their tools, their furniture, their accessories. These things are indeed part of the very definition of "character," of who one is and what one claims to be. The presence of things in these novels also signals their break from the neoclassical stylistic tradition, which tended to see the concrete, the particular, the utilitarian as vulgar, lower class, and to find beauty in the generalized and the noble. The need to include and to represent things will consequently imply a visual inspection of the world of phenomena and a detailed report on it—a report often in the form of what we call description. The descriptive is typical—sometimes maddeningly so—of these novels. And the picture of the whole only emerges—if it does—from the accumulation of things. In fact, to work through the accumulation of things, of details, of particularities, could be considered nearly definitional of the realist novel. If lyric poetry, according to the linguist Roman Jakobson, typically uses and best represents itself in the figure of metaphor, narrative fiction of the realist type uses and represents itself in metonymy, the selected parts that we must construct sequentially into a whole.

Thing-ism, then, is our subject, in the context of the world looked at. For realism is almost by definition highly visual, concerned with registering what the world looks like. We tend to believe—and centuries of philosophical tradition stand behind the belief—that sight is the most objective and impartial of our senses. Thus any honest accounting for the real, in the sense of the appearances of the world, needs to call upon visual inspection and inventory. It needs to give a sense of the thereness of the physical world, as in a still-life painting. In fact, realism as a critical and polemical term comes into the culture, in the early 1850s, to characterize painting—that of Courbet in particular—and then by extension is taken to describe a literary style. It is a term resolutely attached to the visual, to those works that seek to inventory the immediate perceptible world. And then: to show that the immediate perceptible world and the systems it represents and implies constitute constraints on human agents attempting to act in the world, hard edges against which they rub up. And here we return to the importance of money, of the cash nexus, in realism: money becomes the representation of representation itself, of the systematic need to acquire things in self-definition. As Balzac's usurer Gobseck puts it, money is the lifeblood of modern civilization.

Visual inspection and inventory of the world mean, I noted, a large deployment of description, in what sometimes seems to us a misplaced faith that verbal pictures of the world are both necessary and sufficient to creating a sense of place, context, milieu that in turn explain and motivate characters, their actions and reflections. To understand how and what people are, and how they have become such, you need to understand their environment. There is a naturalist or zoological premise in realism, made explicit early on by Balzac, theorized by Taine in his famous "race, milieu, and moment" as the vectors of human history. It is what we might call the Bronx Zoo principle: you need to see the animals in their native habitats to understand them. Their adaptive mechanisms, their character traits, come from the need to hunt on the plains or seek refuge in the trees—and this applies to industrial Manchester and the *beaux quartiers* of Paris as well.

We may at this point want to recall Virginia Woolf in her famous essay "Mr. Bennett and Mrs. Brown" (retitled in one of its versions "Character in Fiction") on the practice of the novelists she calls "the Edwardians": "I asked them—they are my elders and betters—How shall I begin to describe this woman's character? And they said, 'Begin by saying that her father kept a shop in Harrogate. Ascertain the rent. Ascertain the wages of the shop assistants in the year 1878. Discover what her mother died of. Describe cancer. Describe calico. Describe—' But I cried, 'Stop! Stop!' And I regret to say that I threw that ugly, that clumsy, that incongruous tool out of the window." As readers of Balzac and Dickens we well know the kind of impatience with description that makes Woolf throw Arnold Bennett out the window—and may have provoked similar reactions in us. The invasion of narrative by this kind of discourse, what Roland Barthes would call the "cultural code" of the text—heavy in referential material, in names of places, people, things, in sociohistorical explanation—constitutes a kind of babble typical of the realist text, what can often seem most dated about it, least accessible. The descriptive imperative points to the primacy of the visual in realism, and for Woolf there is a need to go beyond the register of appearances. As Woolf also says in her essay, Mr. Bennett "is trying to hypnotise us into the belief that, because he has made a house, there must be a person living there." She rejects the premise that description of the habitat is the royal way to understanding persons. With the great modernists—with Woolf and James Joyce and Thomas Mann and Proust—the conception of character itself has undergone modification, in a inward turn of narrative that has often been described, perhaps most succinctly by Woolf herself when she says, "On or about December 1910 human character changed."

It seems to me that "postmodernism" has allowed us to relax a bit from the Woolfian strictures and that the history of the world since the high modernist moment has suggested that the inward turn of the European novel, its overriding concern with the workings of consciousness, had certain limitations—that the "environmentalism" of the realists matters in trying to understand alien cultures, for instance. We are perhaps more confused in our aesthetic appreciations than the high modernists, certainly more eclectic. As postmodernism in architecture may best illustrate, we have come to appreciate decoration, ornament, a certain elaboration of surfaces, not solely the sleek or stark functionalism of modernism. Our age is once again intensely visual, nourished on the museum and the media, and attuned to the enduring popular forms of fiction making—such as melodrama—that the media perpetuate as if they were platonic forms of the imaginary. And in literary studies, the renewal of an attention to historical and cultural context has made it possible, and important, to rethink what realism was up to. Behind cultural poetics in literary study stands the *Annales*-inspired history of the ordinary and the everyday: for example, the multivolume French undertaking, the *History of Private Life*, in which historians invade what had traditionally been the province of the novelist. Not only do such historians often turn to the novel, especially to Balzac, for their documentation, but they tend to write as novelists: for instance, the chapter by Alain Corbin in the nineteenth-century volume of the *History of Private Life* entitled "Backstage," which is about everything ostensibly hidden from sight by bourgeois society: about what the butler knew, or the washerwoman. This is precisely the world of the great realist novelists.

Balzac, Dickens, Flaubert, Eliot, Zola, Gissing, James, Woolf, along with Courbet, Edouard Manet, Gustave Caillebotte: this is essentially the selection

I will use to make the case for realism. There are omissions, of course, and disputed cases: Why have I left off Stendhal, consecrated as the first realist by Auerbach and possibly my favorite novelist? Too witty and worldly, too uninterested in the descriptive and the conditions of life, to be a true realist, in my view. I've actually sacrificed with more regret such novelists as Guy de Maupassant, Joris-Karl Huysmans, and Arnold Bennett—though they have not held up as well over time as the ones I've chosen. Gissing may appear distinctly of a lower rank than the other classics I've picked—but his claim as the only true English "naturalist" makes him interesting. Since I have with each writer chosen a single novel, there is further room for contest about the selections made. For all its shortcomings, the list has the advantage of including both French and English novels, which I would see as principally representative of the realist tradition—though a bit later the great Russians make their claim.

The two national traditions are not the same, in large part because of the greater self-censorship of the English novel, as of English culture in general. The French novel in the nineteenth century is well into adultery, casual fornication, prostitution, homosexuality, and all varieties of sexual obsession, tragic or kinky, at a time when sexual relations could barely be alluded to in the English novel. James, that American cosmopolitan who nourished himself on French just as much as English fiction, often objected that the English novel needed to grow up, to come out of its protracted adolescence, to break out of its "mistrust of any but the most guarded treatment of the great relation between men and women." The result of this mistrust, he says, has been "an immense omission in our fiction." Walter Scott and Dickens, for instance, represent fiction with "the 'love-making' left, as the phrase is, out." James, writing in 1899—a decade after Zola had been banned in Britain—believes that things have changed. "The novel is older, and so are the young": the young are demanding fiction no longer wholly anodyne. For James, the English novel has failed to acknowledge sufficiently the elasticity and freedom of the novel form. "There are too many sources of interest neglected—whole categories of manners, whole corpuscular classes and provinces, museums of character and condition, unvisited": the Goncourts' *droit au roman* has been singularly unused. And James goes on to notice in particular "the revolution taking place in the position and outlook of women"—with the result that "we may very well yet see the female elbow itself, kept in increasing activity by the play of the pen, smash with final resonance the window all this time most superstitiously closed." Prophetic words—except that James as admirer of Eliot, in particular, surely appreciated that windows had been broken before, even if not with the fracas of the French novelists. In fact, James more than anyone sees as well the strengths of the English tradition that may in part derive from its constraints: the more meditative and indirect approach to "the great relation." James in any event may be the best argument in favor of including English and French novelists as both indispensable. Studying, in this case, a single national tradition would be inadequate.

I think that we postmodernists (as I suppose we inevitably are) have come to appreciate again a certain eclecticism of styles, in which the realist discourse of things—its interpretation of realism in the etymological sense of res-ism, thing-ism—can again be enjoyed and valued. Of course as we pursue the works of such consummate fiction makers as these, we discover that any label such as "realism" is inadequate and that great literature is precisely that which understands this inadequacy, which sees around the corner of its own declared aesthetics, sees what may make its house of cards come tumbling down. Reading these novelists we are ever discovering both what it is like to try to come to terms with the real within the constraints of language, and how one encounters in the process the limits of realism, and the limits to representation itself. For these are among the most intelligent, inventive, aware—as well as the most ambitious—novelists in our history. And they are still—they are more than ever—part of our history, part of how we understand ourselves.

CHAPTER 2

Balzac Invents the Nineteenth Century

I BEGIN WITH BALZAC BECAUSE, AS OSCAR WILDE DECLARED, "THE NINE-teenth century, as we know it, is largely an invention of Balzac's." This is pro-foundly true, in that our conceptualization of the nineteenth century owes more to this reactionary who claimed to hate his time than to anyone else. Balzac was well-placed to invent a new century: born in 1799, he arrived— like so many of his young protagonists—from the provinces in Paris after the collapse of the Napoleonic epic, during the Bourbon Restoration that tried to turn back the clocks to Old Regime standard time but in the pro-cess only made it more evident that things had changed utterly. Monarchist and Catholic though he declared himself to be, Balzac nonetheless was fierce in his denunciation of the Restoration—which lasted from 1815 to 1830— as a time of narrow egotism when the ruling class sought only to restore its wealth and privileges, and forgot about the need to win the hearts and minds of the citizenry, and to recruit into its ranks the young intelligentsia—such as Balzac—who wanted to continue with the pen and the brain what Napo-leon had begun with the sword.

It is important to bear in mind that Balzac's major fiction was written fol-lowing the demise of the Restoration in the July Revolution of 1830, though it generally is *set* during the Restoration. In this sense, Balzac is able to make use of the lesson of the historical novel provided by Walter Scott, whom he prized above all other novelists. Balzac could be said to create the novel of modern society by decreasing the gap between the moment of writing (and reading) and the moment represented, making the historical gap a matter of a decade rather than some centuries. But even the retrospective of a decade allows him to see the France he represents as whole, as a complete society,

22   in the manner that Scott sees twelfth-century England, for instance. It must be said that the revolutions that punctuate French history from 1789 through 1830, 1848 (and 1851) to 1871 make French society particularly grateful terrain for the novelist: change and continuity, the struggle of order and adventure, are strongly marked. Each upheaval gives a viewing platform on history.

Balzac "invented" the nineteenth century by giving form to its emerging urban agglomerations, its nascent capitalist dynamics, its rampant cult of the individual personality. By conceptualizing, theorizing, and dramatizing the new—all the while deploring it—he initiated his readers into understanding the shape of a century. Because of his reactionary stance, he was able to perceive all the more sharply the decline of the landed gentry, the coming of the cash nexus, and the end of what he nostalgically saw as an ordered, organic society with each person in an assigned role. The new era was one of convulsive egotism, the exaltation of ungoverned individualism. His fictional philosopher, Louis Lambert, before he sinks into sullen madness formulates a "law of disorganization" that characterizes the new society. As Old Goriot raves on his deathbed, in Le Père Goriot, nothing matters anymore but money: money will buy you anything, even your unfaithful daughters. No wonder that, for all his reactionary views and his fear of the urban proletariat, he has ever been a favorite of Marxist critics, starting with Karl Marx and Friedrich Engels themselves.

The inevitable context of the new was the city—for Balzac, Paris, where he made his way in 1814, to study law, which he never practiced, preferring to write novels in a garret while he pursued various ill-fated get-rich-quick schemes, including a printing and publishing business that swiftly went bankrupt. Paris doubled in size during the first half of the century, mainly through immigration from the French provinces. If some of the new arrivals were ambitious young men like his own creations Eugène de Rastignac and Lucien de Rubempré—drawn to the sphere where talent could prosper and gain recognition—most contributed to the creation of a new sense of a dangerous urban underclass. Paris was becoming a jungle, and Balzac, an avid reader of James Fenimore Cooper, saw himself as its pathfinder. No novelist before Balzac made the city such a looming and living presence, and he offered a model for Dickens's London and Fyodor Dostoevsky's Saint Petersburg: cities as labyrinths, total environments where survival depends on your ability to read the signs, penetrate the appearances, and, for the ambitious, move out of the "valley of plaster" (where Rastignac begins his Parisian career) to the *beaux quartiers*.

Since Balzac's *Comédie humaine* counts some ninety novels and tales, and they are interlocked through the return of many of the same characters from one book to another, choice of a single representative text is not easy. *Le Père Goriot* and *Eugénie Grandet* are probably the most widely read of the novels. But on reflection, there is clearly one absolutely indispensable novel, which with its sequel makes up the backbone of the *Comédie humaine*. This is *Illusions perdues*—Lost Illusions—which, starting with its very title, stands as the seminal novel of the nineteenth century. The great Marxist critic Georg Lukács's claimed that this novel presents "the tragi-comedy of the capitalization of spirit," which seems a promising beginning for the study of realism. This exceptional and unwieldy novel was published in three parts over a long stretch of time (1837–43). It is part 2, "Un grand homme de province à Paris"— which we might translate loosely as "A provincial big shot comes to Paris"— that is of the most intense interest. But just a word needs to be said about part 1, and especially about the strange and arresting first paragraph:

> At the time when this story begins the Stanhope press and inking rollers were not yet functioning in small provincial printing offices. Despite the local paper-making that kept it in contact with Parisian printing, Angoulême was still using wooden presses, to which our language owes the phrase "to make the press groan," now no longer applicable. There, out-of-date printing made use of leather balls spread with ink to dab on the characters. The movable bed on which the form holding the letters is set, on which the sheet of paper is placed, was still in stone, justifying its name "the marble." The devouring mechanical presses of today have so made us forget this machinery—to which we owe, despite its imperfections, the fine books of such as Elzevir, Plantin, Aldi and Didot—that it's necessary to mention these old tools for which Jérôme-Nicholas Séchard had a superstitious affection, for they have a role to play in this great, though small, history. (*Illusions perdues*, 61) [*Lost Illusions*, 3]

We are certainly in the realm of the kind of descriptive material that Virginia Woolf would throw out the window. Why do we start with the detail of the "Stanhope press" (the kind of thing that now drives us to the footnotes), especially when we are told that this press wasn't yet functioning in the French provinces, including Angoulême, where part 1 is set?

24   That "not yet," *pas encore*, it seems to me, creates a dynamic that will drive the whole novel, in a process of catch-up. A couple of sentences later we encounter the *dévorantes presses mécaniques* that lie at the end of the not yet—at the "now" of the novel. When the narrator goes on to detail and explain the old equipment used by the elder Séchard in his print shop—equipment to which the printer brings a "superstitious affection"—it is in the mode of helpless nostalgia. This equipment will be devoured by the mechanical presses—and so will the lives of the characters presented to us, those "two poets" David Séchard and Lucien Chardon, and many others as well, and one might say poetry itself, as the new journalism made possible and necessary by the devouring mechanical presses eats up an older and better form of literature. And the very book we are reading contributes to and is a product of that devourment, literally in its mode of production, and thematically, since it has become subject to the forces put in play by journalism—as in the creation of the *roman-feuilleton*, the novel published in installments in the daily newspaper, which Balzac was the first to try his hand at, and never could succeed at. Balzac's prefaces to the three parts of the novel say it over and over again: poets, including novelists, are powerless before the rising tide of journalism. Their fictions are caught up in the dynamic that will project Lucien, in particular, from the not yet to the now, and subject him to devouring by the mechanical presses.

I will pass over the story of part 1 of the novel, which shows how the all-consuming ambition of the young poet Lucien, and his thus far platonic (though barely) liaison with the aristocratic Louise de Bargeton—herself ambitious for the grander social theater of Paris—produces the dynamic that will land them both in Paris, with the attendant consequence that Lucien will take out the first installment of what will eventually be a huge debt with his brother-in-law David and his sister Eve—the relation of the Paris episodes of the novel to the provinces will be largely one of debt, of bleeding those who stay behind to finance the Paris adventure. Part 1, as so often in Balzac's novels, is really an extended "motivation," in the sense given that term by the Russian formalists, for the Parisian adventure—a long explanation of the dynamic that makes the Parisian adventure necessary.

Paris itself is initially a lesson in things. "Lucien, like all newcomers, was much more concerned with things than persons," the narrator tells us (191) [159]. Baron du Châtelet, Mme de Bargeton's other admirer—Lucien's rival—explains the large principle governing things and their perception: "Wait and compare," he says to Mme de Bargeton—see how different things are in Paris, and how important. Lucien makes his own discovery when he takes his first walk in the Tuileries Garden, a great space for urban self-display—a walk that produces a kind of *cogito* of the self in relation to Parisian things, and a moment of severe self-judgment. He spends "two cruel hours in the Tuileries"—cruel, because he discovers by comparison the tastelessness, lack of stylishness, the defects and indeed the ugliness of his costume, all of which are detailed over several lines. The impression of being nightmarishly all wrong in his appearance is summed up, and confirmed, when he notices that the only cravat similar to the one he wears—embroidered for him by his sister Eve—adorns a grocer's delivery boy carrying a basket on his head. This gives Lucien a "blow in the chest." If you consider this a childish reaction, says the narrator, you could be wrong: "The question of costume is . . . of enormous importance to those who want to appear to have what they don't have; for it is often the best way to possess it later on" (196) [165].

The description of Lucien's stroll in the Tuileries then moves on to the desirable things that the beautiful people use for their "mise-en-scène."

> He saw ravishing studs on sparkling white shirts, his was rust-colored! All these elegant gentlemen wore marvelous gloves, and his were the gloves of a policeman! One of them toyed with a deliciously inlaid cane. Another wore a shirt with cuffs held by dainty gold links. Still another, speaking to a woman, twirled a charming riding-crop . . . . Another pulled from the pocket of his waistcoat a watch thin as a coin, and looked at it with the air of a man who has arrived too early, or too late, for a rendezvous. Looking at these pretty bagatelles that Lucien hadn't even suspected of existing, the world of necessary superfluities became apparent, and he shivered at the thought of the enormous capital necessary to exercise the profession of smart young fellow!" (197) [166]

I dwell on this moment of Lucien's first exposure to the world of Paris fashion because it seems to me exemplary: the discovery of how things define people, and how those things depend on the marketplace. The question of costume is paramount: without appearance, one is nothing; there is no way to "se faire valoir." A cravat that resembles that of the grocery boy puts one outside the social law. In studying the "mise-en-scène" of the person practiced by the Parisian dandies, Lucien discovers the "world of necessary superfluities." These are largely what we would call accessories: buttons, gloves,

26 the head of a cane, a riding crop, shining spurs, an elegant pocket watch. The thing as accessory represents the material world appropriated to human self-definition—furnishings, what humans use to "represent their manners," as Balzac puts it in the *Avant-Propos* of the *Comédie humaine*. The importance of things in this understanding lies in their representative value, what they tell you about the person who has acquired them and uses them as part of his self-presentation. The accessory is itself defined by market value: Lucien immediately understands that if intelligence is the lever to move this world, money is the fulcrum. When he gets himself outfitted by Staub a few pages later, the tailor tells him: "A young man in such clothes has only to take a stroll in the Tuileries, he'll marry a rich Englishwoman within two weeks" (214) [187]. Costume, appearance, accessory can in this manner *create* the substance they are supposed to represent. Rastignac's tailor in *Le Père Goriot* describes himself as a "hyphen," a *trait d'union*, between a young man's present and his future: create sufficiently the world of appearances, the signs of social prominence, affluence, and belonging, and the meaning that should underlie the signs will become a reality. In fact, Lucien's ultimate failure in his conquest of Paris will be caused by his inability to distinguish fully the sign from what it represents. Or perhaps more accurately, his failure to understand the ways in which signs can create meaning that is not unproblematically grounded in reference.

Before Lucien's metamorphosis at the hands of Staub—and Louise de Bargeton undergoes a parallel transformation at the hands of her cousin the Marquise d'Espard, who sits at the summit of Faubourg Saint-Germain society—there is the moment of exposure and disaster at the Opéra, when the Marquise whisks Louise out of their box rather than be caught with Lucien. His faults in Mme d'Espard's view are, first, appropriating a name that is not his—calling himself de Rubempré, after his mother's family— and, second, his clothing, which in and of itself *proves* his lack of the right to the name: "Cette mise de boutiquier endimanché prouve que ce garçon n'est ni riche ni gentilhomme," she says (209–10) [181]. Her judgment posits a connection between costume and name that Lucien will eventually come to believe in, to his undoing: that the aristocratic name, backed by an "ordonnance du Roi," which alone, she tells us, can authorize the passage of his mother's family name to him, makes all the difference. The whole sign-system of the novel suggests that this is nonsense: that costume is more important. Despite the claim of the Restoration to reproduce Old Regime hierarchies, with the royal Word ultimately controlling everything, we have really entered a circulatory system, that of the cash nexus, in which representation is up for grabs.

More on that in a moment. First I want to call attention to an episode that seems to me a locus classicus in understanding not only Balzac but the whole nineteenth-century novel: a passage, for instance, that Flaubert will rewrite in his L'Education sentimentale. It follows Lucien's night at the Opéra, when he goes to see his beloved Louise, only to be given a note by her maid, telling him she is obliged to stay with the indisposed Mme d'Espard and offering no further meetings. He senses the absolute rupture indicated by the cold and unsigned note, and wanders off to the Champs-Elysées in a state of distress. He is "étourdi"—astonished, bewildered, disoriented—by the spectacle of luxurious things that meets him on the grand avenue. The weather is fine, and on the Champs-Elysées the carriages of the rich and well born are on display, as are their occupants. In fact, some three to four thousand carriages crowd the avenue up to the unfinished (and at this point, in 1821, abandoned) construction site of the Arc de Triomphe—a reminder of that Napoleonic past the Restoration would like to bury. Dazzled by the luxury of the costumes and liveries, Lucien finally comes upon Mme d'Espard and Louise de Bargeton, by no means indisposed but decked out in their finest in a splendid calèche. Louise is metamorphosed by her new dress and coiffure and accessories, including an elegant perfume box, which she dangles from a finger. Lucien approaches the carriage to greet the great ladies, but they pretend not to see him. And all the elegant gentlemen in attendance refuse to acknowledge his existence: "This wasn't a verdict, but rather a denial of justice. A mortal chill seized the poor poet when de Marsay stared at him through his lorgnette; that Parisian lion then let his lorgnette fall in such a way that it seem to Lucien that it was the fall of the blade of the guillotine. The carriage passed by. Rage, a desire for vengeance took hold of this man disdained: if he had held Madame de Bargeton, he would have slit her throat. He made himself Fouquier-Tinville to give himself the pleasure of sending Madame d'Espard to the scaffold" (212–13) [185]. Lucien's momentary identification with Antoine-Quentin Fouquier-Tinville, Jacobin public prosecutor during

28   the Reign of Terror, marks his instant of extreme alienation and class warfare. This reaction will immediately be revised by the desire to have what
has been refused to him: "'My God! gold at any cost!' Lucien said to himself, 'gold is the only power that can make this society fall to its knees. . . .
My God, why am I here? but I'll triumph! I'll roll down this avenue in a carriage with a footman! I'll have some Marquise d'Espards!"

Note how these pages move from Lucien's initial bewilderment to his
final desire for possession. The presentation of desirable things, luxurious
accessories, and their denial to the subject, leads to the subject's overwhelming desire for possession: "je passerai dans cette avenue en calèche à chas-
seur! j'aurai des marquises d'Espard!" The "Jacobin," revolutionary, class-
war reaction is momentary; it is succeeded by the desire, not to destroy
or to wreak vengeance, but to have, to acquire the appurtenances of Mme
d'Espard's world—including some generic version of Mme d'Espard herself.
When Flaubert rewrites this passage according to the life of his own protagonist, Frédéric Moreau, it is precisely to demonstrate the deficits of desire
in his character. Flaubert's version highlights the nature of the Balzacian subject as a desiring machine, related to the outside world by a phallic drive for
possession and perhaps even more by a primitive oral need to devour. Like
those devouring presses at the outset of the novel.

All these initial scenes of Parisian initiation concern representation, especially self-representation, and the things one needs to acquire as signs of
what one is, or wants to be. The problem is played out across all the major
registers of the novel, in all its subcultures and plots. The obscure, honest
labor of Daniel d'Arthez and his literary *cénacle*, for instance, is all about re-
nouncing self-representation and its signs in a wager on the future power
of the literary sign. But the triumph of d'Arthez is projected forward into a
future beyond the confines of this novel. What we see of literature in Lucien's
experience is its commodification, as represented by Dauriat, Doguereau,
and the other bookseller-publishers, its dependence on exterior signs of success as defined by publicity. Successful novelists, Lucien discovers, are on
their knees before the booksellers, who are in turn on their knees before the
book reviewers. Books become part of the plot of things. Consider in this
context the telling passage when Lucien visits the digs of his new compan-
ion, Lousteau, who initiates him into the twin worlds of journalism and the
theater. Lousteau, who has bid farewell to poetry to become a journalist,

takes Lucien to a room that at once evokes a contrast with the "clean, decent misery" of d'Arthez's garret. Lousteau's misery is "sinister":

> A walnut bed without curtains, at its foot a shabby second-hand rug; in the windows, curtains yellowed by the smoke of a chimney that didn't draw and cigar smoke as well; on the mantel, a Carcel lamp, a present from Florine which so far had escaped the pawnshop; then, a chest of drawers in discolored mahogany, a table overloaded with papers, two or three ragged quill pens on it and no other books but those brought in the evening before or during the day: such was the furniture of this room devoid of objects of value, but which offered an ignoble assemblage of broken-down boots yawning in a corner, old socks reduced to the state of lace; in another corner, cigar butts, dirty handkerchiefs, shirts in two volumes, cravats that had reached their third edition. In sum, it was a literary bivouac furnished with negative things and of the strangest nudity that one can imagine. (269–70) [253–54]

The paragraph continues, in description of this room where there is essentially nothing worth describing, to tell us that "this room at once dirty and depressing announced a life without repose and without dignity." Note that this detailed descriptive passage—it interrupts the narrative flow for more than a page—insists on the valuelessness of what it describes. Lousteau's room is "dénuée d'objets de valeur." It is crowded with objects, but they are "choses négatives": kinds of antimatter, that suggest a failure to represent.

Lousteau himself is aware of the failure: he makes a joke to mask "le nu du Vice": "Here's my kennel, my show-place is in the rue de Bondy, in the new apartment that our druggist has furnished for Florine, which we're house-warming tonight." We sense here that "vice" is understood precisely as nudity, as the lack of valuable things, things that fetch a price on the marketplace. And Lousteau's joke indeed concerns his "grande représentation," which consists in the apartment furnished by Matifat, the official lover and keeper of Lousteau's mistress, the actress Florine. So that representation here explicitly entails both theatrical mise-en-scène and prostitution, and both are closely tied to the book trade and to journalism.

One can trace the plot of things—of furnishings and accessories—throughout the novel. To take just one example: Lucien goes to bed with the actress Coralie in the apartment furnished by Camusot, her lover and keeper, with the richest materials he can find, full of "costly bagatelles," rugs of swan and marten, slippers of velvet and silk (328) [323]. But Coralie will

30   ruin herself in furnishings—after dismissing Camusot—and in providing
Lucien with the very accessories he admired during his first stroll in the Tuileries: "marvelous canes, a charming lorgnette, buttons of diamond, rings
for his morning cravats, cavalier's rings, and splendiferous waistcoats in sufficient number to match them to the colors of his costume" (389) [396–97].
Lucien becomes a dandy who competes in the world of de Marsay and the
others who snubbed him, and as such he is the object of flattering attentions
from the very Marquise d'Espard who denied his right to exist. But Coralie's
bedecking of her lover leads to the inevitable dénouement, when her credi-
tors seize all the furnishings of her apartment: "There was no longer in the
household any object of gold or silver, nor any other intrinsic value; but
everything was moreover represented by receipts from the pawn shop form-
ing a small octavo volume full of instruction" (404) [414–15]. Lack of things
is the immediate precursor of death, for Coralie, and exile, for Lucien.

    The witty courtesan Suzanne du Val-Noble remarks, in showing off her
"magnificent apartments": "Voilà les comptes des Mille et Une Nuits!"—
punning on *comptes*, accounts, in the place of *contes*, tales (402) [412]. The
accounts of A Thousand and One Nights of prostitution naturally, in this
world, are represented by furnishings. La Val-Noble's remark forces us to see
the nexus of love, money, prostitution, furnishings, all in a marketplace that
is both financial and libidinal, and whose exchanges are the source of story.
This is the Arabian Nights of protocapitalist Paris.

    Coralie is a woman of the theater (in Balzac's world, as in the contem-
porary Parisian reality, the world of theater and of prostitution are barely
distinct, since girls displayed onstage are all fair game for the male spectators). Lucien's initiation into the theater is of course all about representation—here, representation as illusion, a world where "impossible things
appear true" (308) [299]. He is initiated into the double nature of the theater: the illusion on the stage and the backstage mechanisms that create it.
"After having seen in the Galeries de Bois the strings controlling the book
trade and the kitchen where glory is prepared, after strolling in the wings
of the theatre, the poet perceived the underside of consciences, the play of
the cogwheels of Parisian life, the machinery behind it all" (303) [293]. The
backstage metaphor returns frequently in Balzac: this is the hidden region,
both ugly and more deeply erotic and fascinating, where the spectacle of appearing is prepared and controlled. To penetrate to the backstage and be in

control of the drops and the prompts: this is to be the master of things, comparable to one of those obscure supermen banded together in the society known as Les Treize who perform so many extraordinary acts in the course of the *Comédie humaine,* or comparable to those figures of the *oeuvres philosophiques* who seek to understand the very principles that cause societies to behave as they do.

The experience of the theater in *Illusions perdues* is merely a threshold to the experience of journalism, which might be defined as the most theatrical— illusionistic, mendacious, prostituted—use of signs imaginable. It's following his first night at the theater that Lucien writes his first review, beds his first actress—and then wakes up to find himself famous. The newspaper, explains the veteran journalist Claude Vignon during this memorable evening, is a "boutique" where one sells the public words in the color the public wants. Soon enough, he predicts, all newspapers will be "cowardly, hypocritical, shameless, lying, homicidal" (320) [314]. "We all know . . . that newspapers will go further than kings in ingratitude, further than the filthiest commerce in speculations and manipulations, that they will devour our brains to sell every morning their mental rotgut; but we'll all write there, like miners in a quicksilver mine, knowing that we'll die from it" (322) [316]. The German diplomat present at this post-theater party recalls Field Marshal Blücher's supposed comment when contemplating a conquered Paris from the heights of Montmartre in 1814: when his second-in-command proposed burning Paris, Blücher replied: "Don't you dare, France will die only from *that!*" Paris and its intelligentsia seduced into journalism represent self-destruction. Journalists would in fact be in vanguard of the Revolution of 1830, in protest at the monarchy's new severe censorship law. And the Revolution of 1830, which in many ways blessed Balzac's career, always seemed to him another step toward social chaos.

It must be said that the power of the newspaper presented in *Illusions perdues* may be slightly anachronistic, representing a situation more characteristic of the 1830s than the 1820s. It was in the 1830s that newspapers began cutting their subscription prices drastically and making up for the lost revenue with paid advertising. And, to create a vastly increased circulation, printing fiction as well as fact on the front page—creating the roman-feuilleton which was mastered by Balzac's arch-rival Eugène Sue far more adeptly and profitably than Balzac ever could. It was really the coming of mass-circulation journalism and the roman-feuilleton that created what the critic Sainte-Beuve would dub "industrial literature." The world of Dauriat and Doguereau and Blondet and Nathan and Vignon is still proto-industrial. In fact, the power of the book and theater reviewers derives in part from the lack, in the 1820s, of paid advertising: a book or a play was invisible without notice from the reviewers.

In Balzac's diagnosis, journalism is the very nonprinciple of anti-authority, a manifestation of that "law of disorganization" that his fictional philosopher Louis Lambert declares to be the fate of modern society. If the Restoration failed to recruit the young intelligentsia into its ranks, they passed to the opposition less from political conviction than from the logic of journalism itself: that was where the readers were to be found. Journalists became a new priestly caste without a Sacred. And it follows, in Balzac's demonstration, that they understand the linguistic sign wholly in terms of its effect on readers rather than as referential. What matters is, not the representation of fact, but a simulacrum that the reading public will consume as true.

Lucien is instructed in the nature of the journalistic sign by way of the articles he is ordered to write on Nathan's new novel. Told by Lousteau to demolish the book—in order to take revenge on the publisher Dauriat, who has pronounced Lucien's collection of sonnets unsalable—Lucien protests that he can't, that the book is good. "Learn your trade," replies Lousteau. "A journalist is an acrobat." He proceeds to explain how Lucien can turn the book's beauties into faults, positing a literary "system" that it violates. (And incidentally demonstrating that the opposition newspaper at the this moment in history is liberal, classic, and anti-Romantic—since the early French Romantics tended to be monarchist, Catholic, medievalist.) A dozen pages later, Lousteau suggests that Lucien avoid making an enemy of Nathan— that it's time for an article praising the same book. Now Lucien replies that he can't find anything good to say about it. Hector Merlin is astonished: "You believed what you wrote?" Emile Blondet then takes over: "My boy, I thought you were made of sterner stuff!"

Blondet proceeds with the second lesson: there are always two sides of any question. "Everything is bilateral in the realm of thought. Ideas are binary. Janus is the myth of criticism and the symbol of genius." Lucien has only to reverse all the negatives of his first article into positives, and publish in Merlin's right-of-center paper. Then he can write still a third article, magisterially judging the two others. It's Coralie who at once gets the point: "Aren't I going on as an Andalusian tonight, and tomorrow night as a Bohemian, and still another night dressed as a man? Do like me, give them disguises for their money, and let's live happy" (372) [376]. In response, Lucien is "taken with the paradox," and writes two more brilliant articles; he discovers "the beauties born of contradiction." The "paradox" is Denis Diderot's *Paradoxe sur le comédien*, proving that the actor is most effective when he is most distanced from his role—when he perceives his act not from his perspective but from that of the spectator. In exactly the same way, the journalist must understand the linguistic signs he uses from the perspective of the reader—that alone counts. And when Lucien has mastered the paradox, he gains "the fantastic power granted the desires of those who possess talismans in Arabian tales" (373) [377–78]. Like Raphaël de Valentin in Balzac's *La Peau de chagrin*, he wields phantasmatic power.

Notice how the journalistic sign in this understanding is fully comparable to money in the emergent capitalist economy: tied to no referent (such as land), it is defined only by its exchange-value, by its circulation. This suggests the problem of a world where sign and referent stand in no stable relation. Balzac portrays a world in which representation is on everyone's mind—where self-representation is a central project—but where the signs used to represent are highly unstable. The linguistic sign, money, the accessory things purchased by money, and the desire that subtends things, money, and signs, appear to belong to an overheated libidinal economy that is ever on the verge of crash. It is the paradox of Balzac's realism that the world he describes in such impassioned detail seems, like the inflationary economy, menaced with collapse, mined from within by the threat of non-meaning. Balzac insists in a number of the fragmentary essays destined for his never-completed "Pathology of Social Life" that the nineteenth century, where everyone wears black and tries to look middle class, has lost the traditional social semiotics of the Old Regime, where who one was could be known immediately, by visual inspection. Thus the need for self-representation in the nineteenth century, and for the creation of miniscule signs that carry large significations: the cut of one's trousers, the way one knots a cravat. In Balzac's overt

34   declarations, the nineteenth century is a semiotic disaster area—as it is a disaster politically and spiritually. But it is precisely this fluidity and instability of signs that give the novelist his opportunity.

Lucien's crash is exemplary. It marks a collapse of his libidinal economy, quite explicitly from too much sex. "Coralie a perdu cet enfant-là," des Lupeaulx will comment. If we ask why Coralie receives the blame for Lucien's undoing, the narrator gives us several explicit hints. Lucien is "heureux tous les jours" (382) [388], which is the classic litotes meaning he is having sex every day. And "he had, like an ogre, tasted fresh flesh" (396) [405] —Coralie's—which makes him indifferent to the blandishments of Louise de Bargeton, who wishes to repair their rupture, and who could offer him a solid footing in the world. The "spring" of his will is softened, he loses the necessary lucidity and coolness of intellect to understand the psychosexual dynamics of the aristocratic salons. Balzac seems to have inherited from his father the belief that male sexual potency is a limited commodity, to be stored—in the manner of largely chaste and long-lived misers of the *Comédie humaine*—or else dissipated in a pleasurable but short existence, as most flamboyantly represented in *La Peau de chagrin*. Lucien no longer is able to invest libidinal energy into making his way in the world. Desire satisfied is no longer predatory and acquisitive.

Balzac gives us to understand that Lucien's condition is representative of a generation of young "viveurs": young men of talent who wasted it in eating, drinking, and the ferocious exercise of wit. It is a condition for which the rulers of France are directly responsible: "No other set of facts underlines so starkly the serfdom to which the Restoration had condemned youth." Here again is Balzac's repeated plaint (most fully developed in several pages of the novella *La Duchesse de Langeais*): that the Restoration, ruled by a gerontocracy, old men born into the values of the Old Regime and unaware of the new rules of the game, never made a place for the youthful intelligentsia—and thus drove it into a mocking opposition that eventually helped to destabilize the monarchy. This youth, the narrator claims in *Illusions perdues*, "wanted a place, and politics didn't give it one anywhere." Along with lost illusions, the novel gives us a strong sense of loss, waste, the frittering away of talent and passion and will to power of all sorts. The Restoration, like Lucien, was doomed through a failure to harness energies into a useful dynamic.

Lucien also never quite learns the lesson taught him by his journalist colleagues: he never quite understands the undetermined circulatory system of signs. He comes more and more to believe in the power of the name: curiously, the power of his mother's name. If only he can obtain the right to name himself de Rubempré, by royal decree, all, he believes, will be well. His enemies understand this excessive belief in the name, and play on it. Lucien changes political camps, passing from the left opposition to the ultraroyalists, without reassuring his old pals that it's pure expediency—he acts as if he believes in his new allegiances. As Finot tells him, he's shown the "innocence of a lamb in this affair" (439) [456], believing in a referentiality that the wolves had long since discarded. His ultimate discomfiture comes when this same Finot tricks him into writing articles mocking the Garde des Sceaux, who is pretending to be at work obtaining his change of name. He is everywhere baffled and stymied by a language he claimed to be master of.

It is just after the "loss" of the change of name—of the fiction of the change of name, since the royalists never intended to make Lucien one of their own—and his bitter task of having to attack his friend d'Arthez's masterpiece in a book review, that Lucien, "stunned like a man who has been hit on the head with a club" (hébété: recall how he was étourdi during his first Parisian misadventures), wanders through the streets and comes upon a lending library announcing the publication of his novel, the ci-devant *Archer de Charles IX*, given "a bizarre title, completely unfamiliar to him," with the author's name listed as M. Lucien Chardon de Rubempré—itself a kind of unstable sign. The scene will culminate with one of the Cénacle, Michel Chrestien, spitting in Lucien's face, challenging him to a duel over the d'Arthez review—not knowing that d'Arthez himself has revised and legitimated that review. The scene forcefully presents that alienation of the products of mind from their creators that Lukács finds so brilliantly demonstrated in *Illusions perdues*. The novel under its bizarre title has become a commodity, spirit has entered the marketplace. But since the newspapers have maintained a conspiracy of silence about the publication of the book, it has no place in the circulatory system. It's like Lucien and Coralie's naked apartment, divested of all its rich accessories. Self-representation is finished—and Lucien returns to Flicoteaux, the greasy student restaurant where he spent his early evenings in Paris.

Coralie dies—victim of the anti-Lucien cabal; Lucien is obliged to write Bacchic songs to pay for her funeral, and buries her in Père-Lachaise without

36   any of the dramatic gestures toward future conquest that Rastignac performs
after burying Old Goriot. It takes the prostitution of the maid Bérénice to
provide him with pocket money to travel back to the night of the provinces,
to Angoulême—and he bears this final act of prostitution, fittingly, as the
"last stigmata" of la vie parisienne.

Of part 3, which Balzac finally managed to complete some four years
after "Un Grand homme de province à Paris," I will say little. Its return to
Angoulême chronicles the monstrous effects of Lucien's attempted representations in Paris on his exploited relatives; and in David Séchard's search for
a cheap substitute for the rag content of paper, it continues the saga of the
devouring presses, here in the very material of the newspapers that Lucien
first conquers and then is destroyed by. From the modes of production we
have returned to the means of production. One senses, though, that Balzac,
faced with the need to complete his novel—and he had already published
parts of its sequel—has recourse to somewhat traditional and conventional
devices and characters to jump-start the action. The plots and counterplots
around David's bankruptcy and imprisonment, and Lucien's deluded effort
to free him (again depending on his self-representation in finery and accessories he's cadged from his Parisian friends), are a bit ready-made—though
they demonstrate Balzac's extraordinary ability to create the novelistic account from the financial account: that compte de retour on Lucien's bad debt
that becomes a compte fantastique. That the circulation of this bill, and the plus
values added to it, appears somewhat arbitrary and gratuitous suggests again
the disturbingly unstable and ungrounded production of wealth and meaning in this excessively fluid world.

What is not at all conventional is the scene Marcel Proust found so
breathtaking for its coded representation of homoerotic desire: the meeting
of Lucien, on the verge of suicide, with the Spanish priest Carlos Herrera,
alias Vautrin, alias Jacques Collin, on the road from Angoulême to Paris. This
brings the explosion of something new in the novel—something that will
require a lengthy new novel to play itself out: the vast and sprawling Splendeurs et misères des courtisanes, its four parts published from 1838 to 1847. That
novel makes good on the promises exchanged between Lucien and Carlos
Herrera–Vautrin–Collin at the end of Illusions perdues, where Lucien tells his
sister that he has sold his life, and Vautrin arranges his Parisian resurrection.
"I'll be the playwright, you'll be the drama," Vautrin tells Lucien, literalizing

the theatrical metaphor of *Illusions perdues*, foregrounding the very process of representation itself. Lucien, the self-indulgent poet who loves appearances, and appearing, explicitly becomes the vehicle for enactments managed from backstage, by the ugly put powerful and utterly devoted Vautrin.

The "author's" plot for his creature is tellingly scabrous. In order to gain aristocratic respectability, win back the de Rubempré name, and marry Clotilde de Grandlieu—fine flower of the Faubourg Saint-Germain nobility—Lucien needs to buy back the ancestral Rubempré estates, which will cost a round million. Vautrin therefore plans to sell Lucien's mistress, the redeemed prostitute Esther, to the banker Nucingen, whose many millions derive from the most dubious speculations. Note what this means: money of the most sordid origin will be laundered through its reinvestment in land in order to legitimate Lucien as a member of the aristocracy, and to marry him into one of the leading families of France. Even were the plot to succeed, it would indicate the deep corruption of a society on the brink of collapse (and the novel contains a number of references to the impending Revolution of 1830). It doesn't succeed; it instead becomes enmeshed in a spiderweb of plots and counterplots, police agents and private spies and counterspies, a sordid underworld lovingly displayed by Balzac. Esther, *fille sublime*, allows herself to be sold out of love for Lucien—but after granting Nucingen one night of bliss, kills herself, leaving 750,000 francs under her pillow for Lucien. The servants steal the money, but suspicion falls on Lucien. In a further irony, Esther without knowing it is the heiress to the fortune of her uncle the usurer Gobseck, recently deceased—a fortune of 7 million, possibly the most considerable of the *Comédie humaine*. That fortune from a lifetime of money lending then passes by Esther's will to Lucien—again too late, since he has been arrested and has hung himself in prison. ("The saddest day of my life," Oscar Wilde said of Lucien's suicide.) Tracing how Gobseck's fortune dissipates across the *Comédie humaine* once again gives a sense of the arbitrariness of value in the cash nexus.

The last two sections of the novel center on the prison, on convicts and their slang, on intense homosexual relations among them, on the subornation of justice by political ambition and manipulation, and on the strong man's ability to efface the truth and put fictions in its place. As Vautrin works to save the reputation of a number of very grandes dames of the Faubourg Saint-Germain compromised by Lucien's life and death, and chief Crown

38 prosecutor the Comte de Grandlieu abets his destruction of evidence and alteration of the records, we are given to understand that social history as well as justice are thoroughly malleable sign-systems. Herrera–Vautrin, now returned to his "real" name of Jacques Collin, passes to the police in a breath-taking moment — and goes on to be a pillar of this corrupt state, as head of the Sûreté. If Collin emerges as the key figure for knowing and controlling this society — for understanding how it is ordered, who runs it, how its sign-systems signify, and how they can be manipulated — the lesson seems to be that society as we know it is merely an epiphenomenon, since its deep structures are managed by invisible mafiosi. Collin at the end describes himself as a somewhat more benevolent power broker than Nucingen. Modernity seems to be the work of the corrupt and ruthless banker-speculator and the crime boss become police chief. The latter parts of the novel contain several allusions to a coming effort by King Charles X to reestablish true royal authority, instituting tight press censorship and abrogating La Charte, the constitution of the Restoration — an allusion to the "ordonnances" of July 1830, which promptly provoked the revolution that sent this final Bourbon king into exile. That revolution in Balzac's view would lead, not to any social regeneration, but to the victory of the Nucingens and the Collins. "Enrichissez-vous," get rich, Prime Minister François Guizot would tell the French; and the new industrial and financial bourgeoisie led France into modern market capitalism.

Part of that market capitalism, I mentioned, was the new newspaper publishing industry: a new economics based on advertising revenue rather than circulation. This new economics speculated on fiction, the daily front-page roman-feuilleton. Balzac provided the first example with La Vieille Fille in 1836 but never adapted comfortably to the form. He was too discursive and expansive, and too dilatory. But he published the last two parts of Splendeurs et misères as a feuilleton in La Presse, no doubt in order to rival the extremely popular and successful Eugène Sue, who had exploited the Paris underworld in the two-year serial run of Les Mystères de Paris (1842–44). So that this set of novels that Balzac referred to as the "backbone" of the Comédie humaine begins in the overt critique of journalism and the new "industrial literature," and ends up a product of industrial literature, absorbed by its means and modes of production, and thematically complicit with the needs and desires of its readership. To which one can perhaps most pertinently say: of course. And

Balzac, like those workers toiling in the quicksilver mine evoked by Claude
Vignon in *Illusions perdues*, knows that he is victim of his source of livelihood,
and that the writer cannot escape the material history of his time. This is after
all a writer who early in his career set up a print shop, in an effort to control
the means of production of literature. Balzac knows that the material conditions of "poetry"—as it is designated at the outset of *Illusions perdues*—are
changing, changing inevitably, and that you must adapt even as you protest.
Historians of the political right and the political left are in agreement: Balzac
understood better than anyone the contradictions and the deep structures
of modernizing France.

In conclusion, let me call attention to Lucien's testamentary letter to
his sister, where he speaks of a young woman who was "malade de son
père," sick from her father, and goes on to generalize about "family mala-
dies" (579) [630]. The novel presents a France that is in Balzac's view "malade
de son père," in the sense that it has never recovered from its killing of the
father-monarch during the Revolution, the regicide of 1793. France in the
nineteenth century lacks a father, lacks any true principle of authority, any
authorized system of signs and representations. It is headed toward chaos.
Before chaos comes, this world offers splendid opportunities for the individual gesture of self-representation, the usurpation of apparent authority.
But any such gesture is subject to an overheated circulatory system that can
quickly go from boom to bust, since it has no underlying system of value.
"Constant revolutionising of production, uninterrupted disturbance of all
social conditions, everlasting uncertainty and agitation distinguish the bourgeois epoch from all earlier ones," wrote Karl Marx. "All fixed, fast-frozen
relations, with their train of ancient and venerable prejudices and opinions, are swept away, all new-formed ones become antiquated before they
can ossify. All that is solid melts into air." Balzac is positively feudal in his
thinking—which, as Marx and the Marxist critics recognized, is what makes
him such a clear-sighted analyst of nascent capitalism and the emergent cash
nexus.

CHAPTER 3

Dickens and Nonrepresentation

BALZAC'S AMBIVALENT ADVENTURES IN THE NEW INDUSTRIAL LITERATURE MAY stand as some sort of odd preface to the Dickens of *Hard Times* (1854). I say the Dickens of *Hard Times* because this novel seems to me—as to many critics before me—oddly different from any other of his novels, and in that sense a bad choice to talk about, yet by its subject or, more accurately, its *project*, the inevitable choice if you want to talk about Dickens in the context of realism. I am of course not sure that it is right to talk about Dickens in the context of realism at all, since so much of Dickens appears as the avoidance or suppression of realism. To what extent can a text published in a journal called *Household Words*—Dickens's own journal, his contribution to the literature industry—be "realist" in the sense that the French had begun to attach to that term, a few years before the publication of *Hard Times?* Isn't there an incompatibility in the realist's claim to name the harshest realities and the context of self-censorship generally accepted by the Victorian novel, and surely by *Household Words?* I can recall my first adult re-reading of *Oliver Twist,* first read as a child, and the discovery that Nancy Sykes is a prostitute—something that had of course eluded me during childhood (a childhood in a less knowing era), and one that the adult reader must intuit from various murky signs, since Dickens certainly is not going to say it outright. This at the very moment Balzac was disserting on the various classes and categories of prostitutes, on their costumes and their language, in *Illusions perdues, Splendeurs et misères,* and a host of other texts. Nancy Sykes has no "comptes des Mille et une nuits" to recount—though it may also be true that the criminal operation of which she is a part is more soberly and realistically presented than its highly colored counterparts in Balzac.

So to *Hard Times*, this unusually spare and in some ways reticent Dickens novel, so interesting I think in its failures as well as its successes, and because these occur in a context of a very explicit choice to address the issue of the "two nations"—as Benjamin Disraeli stated the problem in his novel of 1845, *Sybil, or The Two Nations*—and the moral meanings of industrial England. *Hard Times for These Times* states the title page, as if preparing us for a moral tract or a parliamentary report—two genres that will be mocked in the course of the novel. And well before we get to any description of Coketown, the mills, the workers, we of course have the schoolroom, the scene of education, of *Bildung*, of de-formation of minds. We begin with Facts, in what has often been read as a critique of utilitarianism but seems to me more importantly about the mendacities of systems of representation—as in Bitzer's definition of the horse: "Quadruped. Graminivorous. Forty teeth, namely twenty-four grinders, four eye-teeth and twelve incisive," and so on, which is at once flawless and hopeless, and of course sealed with Gradgrind's approval. "Now girl number twenty . . . . You know what a horse is." Sissy Jupe's attempts to define her father's occupation—"He belongs to the horse-riding, if you please, sir"—is rejected by Grandgrind in favor of other language: "He is a veterinary surgeon, a farrier and horse-breaker." When we reach the question of wallpaper, it is clear that what's at issue is representation: "Now, let me ask you girls and boys, Would you paper a room with representations of horses? . . . Would you use a carpet having a representation of flowers upon it?" (13). The answer he expects, and insists on, is no; system has trumped not only fancy but also experience.

That Grandgrind and M'Choakumchild consider the schoolchildren as "little vessels, then and there arranged in order, ready to have imperial gallons of facts poured into them until they were full to the brim" (9), allows the narrator by the end of the scene to evoke the story of Ali Baba and the Forty Thieves. This points to what will be the repeated procedure in *Hard Times*: the positing on one hand of a world of fact and definition that claims to refuse metaphor, fancy, and the language of the senses, and on the other hand the narratorial use of a language that constantly rings figural changes upon that other world. This is no doubt Dickens's practice throughout his fiction, a procedure whereby descriptive details—Jaggers's handwashing, Wemmick's postbox of a mouth—become memorably emblematic. But in *Hard Times* its

42 use seems to result in a particularly curious process of representation of the conditions of industrialism and its population.

Consider in this context the famous description of Coketown:

> It was a town of red brick, or of brick that would have been red if the smoke and ashes had allowed it; but, as matters stood it was a town of unnatural red and black like the painted face of a savage. It was a town of machinery and tall chimneys, out of which interminable serpents of smoke trailed themselves for ever and ever, and never got uncoiled. It had a black canal in it, and a river that ran purple with ill-smelling dye, and vast piles of building full of windows where there was a rattling and a trembling all day long, and where the piston of the steam-engine worked monotonously up and down, like the head of an elephant in a state of melancholy madness. It contained several large streets all very like one another, and many small streets still more like one another, inhabited by people equally like one another, who all went in and out at the same hours, with the same sound upon the same pavements, to do the same work, and to whom every day was the same as yesterday and tomorrow, and every year the counterpart of the last and the next. (28)

It is a brilliant passage that works by the play of the metaphorical and metamorphic imagination on the details selected: the red brick blackened to become the face of a savage; the coils of smoke which become serpents, and never can get themselves uncoiled; and especially that piston that becomes the head of an elephant in a state of melancholy madness. By its play on the streets and surfaces and engines of Coketown, the narratorial prose upholds that ideal evoked in the allusion to the *Arabian Nights*: the play of fancy, of metaphor, of magic and the counterfactual. The narratorial language is constantly saying to Coketown, as to Grandgrind and company, I am not prisoner of your system, I can transform it, soar above it, though the imaginative resources of my prose. One can almost sense in the final sentence of the passage quoted, on the tedious routine of workers' lives in Coketown, the satisfaction of the successful writer and bohemian who is thankfully free of such constraints.

It's worth noting what we don't get in the passage. For instance:

> In one of these courts there stands directly at the entrance, at the end of the covered passage, a privy without a door, so dirty that the inhabitants can pass into and out of the court only by passing through foul pools of stagnant urine and excrement. . . . The view from this bridge, mercifully concealed from mortals of small stature by a parapet as high as a man, is char-

acteristic for the whole district. At the bottom flows, or rather stagnates, the Irk, a narrow, coal-black, foul-smelling stream full of débris and refuse, which it deposits on the shallower right bank. . . . Above the bridge are tanneries, bonemills, and gasworks, from which all drains and refuse find their way into the Irk, which receives further the contents of all the neighbouring privies. It may be easily imagined, therefore, what sort of residue the stream deposits. Below the bridge you look upon the piles of débris, the refuse, filth, and offal from the courts on the steep left bank; here, each house is packed close behind its neighbour and a piece of each is visible, all black, smoky, crumbling, ancient, with broken panes and window frames. The background is furnished by old barrack-like factory buildings. . . . in the rear of this, the Workhouse, the "Poor-Law Bastille" of Manchester, which, like a citadel, looks threateningly down from behind its high walls and parapets on the hilltop, upon the working-people's quarter below.

Thus Friedrich Engels describing the working-class sections of Manchester in The Condition of the Working Class in England in 1844—an indictment published in German in 1845, which Dickens did not know but which was preceded by a number of official and other inquiries into the question published in England, some of them Engels's source material. Engels's insistence on refuse, residue, offal, excrement, on the shit of industrialism, gives a sense of what Dickens can't do, what he avoids seeing or speaking about. Though Dickens had visited the Midlands, especially the industrial town of Preston, in preparation for writing Hard Times, we have very little of what we will get in Zola's Germinal, for instance, in its exhaustive descriptions of the organization, machinery, and workings of the coal mine, or even in Elizabeth Gaskell's descriptions of the Manchester-like city she calls "Milton-Northern" in her novel North and South (first published in Dickens's Household Words, shortly after Hard Times). There is no attempt to tell us what is manufactured in Coketown, and how. There is no attempt to show us the workers at work, the gestures of their labor at the looms—which we guess to be contained in those redbrick factories, though the narrator never lets on. If, in my argument, realism tends to be intensely visual, concerned with seeing and registering, and therefore has frequent recourse to the descriptive, here one could tax Dickens with a certain refusal to see, an avoidance of the inventories of the real that we normally associate with realism. This to be sure is to set up a criterion for judgment that Dickens is free to refuse—and does in fact refuse.

But it may give us some insight into his repeated procedure in Hard Times, in both its successes and its limitations: the procedure of turning all issues, facts, conditions, into questions of style. *Hard Times* becomes, even more than Dickens's other novels, a drama of opposed styles, presided over by the quicksilver agility of the narrator's styles. Consider here the case of the noble Stephen Blackpool. Stephen is introduced by way of another paragraph of brilliantly inventive descriptive prose on the "innermost fortifications of that ugly citadel" of Coketown and its inhabitants known generically as "the Hands": "a race who would have found more favour with some people, if Providence had seen fit to make them only hands, or, like the lower creatures of the seashore, only hands and stomachs" (68). Again, we have the metamorphic play of the narratorial style, metamorphosing the hands into strange clams or oysters that would better suit the preferences of the factory owners. Stephen himself is largely his verbal style, which is written out as a kind of Lancashire accent (Dickens apparently had on his desk a book on Lancashire dialect while composing the novel). It is hard for us today to judge the effects of Stephen's verbal style as presented in the novel: we don't tend to declaim novels aloud, and that is what it would take to make the graphic deformations in which Dickens renders Stephen's speech come alive—and even then, one would have to be able speak Lancaster-ese. Certainly the written presentation of his manner of speaking makes his voice, in a nearly operatic way, distinctive in its timbre and resonance, and inflects his highly biblical speech with a kind of prophetic portent. Yet it almost allies him with the Sleary world of the circus—Slearly himself is represented in a lisp—as wearing a kind of verbal greasepaint, not altogether different from that painted face of a savage the narrator sees in the walls of Coketown, or the Whelp's—Tom Grandgrind's—blackface disguise near the end of the novel.

Stephen is a linguistic performance, and his great scene with Bounderby in book 2, chapter 5, is a linguistic confrontation, where Stephen's rough eloquence provokes Bounderby's wrath and punishment but also offers the highest statement of conscience in the novel:

> "Sir, I canna, wi' my little learning an' my common way, tell the genelman what will better aw this—though some working men o' this town could, above my powers—but I can tell him what I know will never do't. The strong hand will never do't. Victory and triumph will never do't. Agreeing fur to mak one side unnat'rally awlus and for ever right, and toother side unnat'rally awlus and for ever wrong, will never, never do't. Nor yet lettin alone will never do't. Let thousands upon thousands alone, aw lead-

ing the like lives and aw faw'en into the like muddle, and they will be as one, and yo will be as anoother, wi' a black unpassable world betwixt yo, just as long or short a time as sitch-like misery can last. Not drawin nigh to fok, wi' kindness and patience an' cheery ways, that so draws nigh to one another in their monny troubles, and so cherishes one another in their distresses wi' what they need themseln—like, I humbly believe, as no people the genelman ha' seen in aw his travels can beat—will never do't till th' Sun turns t'ice. Most o' aw, rating 'em as so much Power, and reg'latin 'em as if they was figures in a soom, or machines; wi'out loves and likeins, wi'out memories and inclinations, wi'out souls to weary and souls to hope—when aw goes quiet, draggin on wi' 'em as if they'd nowt o' th' kind, and when aw goes onquiet, reproachin 'em for their want o' sitch humanly feelins in their dealins wi' yo—this will never do't, Sir, till God's work is onmade."
(154–55)

Stephen gets himself fired for this speech; Bounderby even perverts Stephen's refusal to join the union into a sign that he is a universal pariah.

Stephen's charge to Bounderby is a reproach to the nation for allowing Coketowns to go on as they do. "Look how we live, an wheer we live, an in what numbers, and by what chances, an wi' what sameness," says Stephen a moment earlier. "Look how this ha growen and growen, sir, bigger an bigger, broader an broader, harder an harder, fro year to year, fro generation unto generation. Who can look on't, sir, and fairly tell a man 'tis not a muddle?" (153). Here is the linguistic dramatization of the protest of conscience, of Carlyle and Ruskin and so many others, against the Industrial Revolution and what it has done to the conditions of life of the sometime English yeoman. It is a moving cry from the dispossessed nation to those that have power.

But note also that for Stephen it is a muddle for others to sort out. And though Stephen avers that some workingmen of Coketown could better express the problem than he, when we come to the only other attempt in the novel to articulate the problem of the industrial working class we encounter the voice of the union organizer Slackbridge. He comes to us first as a voice, introducing chapter 4 of part 2. Listen to him:

"Oh my friends, the down-trodden operatives of Coketown! Oh my friends and fellow-countrymen, the slaves of an iron-handed and a grinding despotism! Oh my friends and fellow-sufferers, and fellow-workmen, and fellow-men! I tell you that the hour is come, when we must rally round one another as One united power, and crumble into dust the oppressors that too long have battened upon the plunder of our families, upon the sweat of our brows, upon the labour of our hands, upon the strength of our sinews, upon the God-created glorious rights of Humanity, and upon the holy and eternal privileges of Brotherhood!" (141)

Many in the audience cry "Good!" and "Hear, hear!" and "Hurrah"; and I am inclined to join them. But the narrator has already made it clear that this is not the right reaction, that Slackbridge's verbal style is pretentious, tendentious, semi-educated, demagogic. He calls his audience "the prostrate sons of labour," he uses words like "subornation," he reaches for bombastic allusions to Brutus and the Spartan mothers. The description of Slackbridge on the following page underscores what we have heard in his verbal style. Compared to the men he is addressing, "he was not so honest, he was not so manly, he was not so good-humoured; he substituted cunning for their simplicity, and passion for their sage solid sense. An ill-made high-shouldered man, with lowering brows, and his features crushed into an habitually sour expression, he contrasted most unfavourably, even in his mongrel dress, with the great body of his hearers in their plain working clothes" (142). The "mongrel dress" may be the real giveaway: Slackbridge is not a purebred English workingman, he slips dangerously through the nets of classification, like Bounderby he's snuck upwards on the social ladder.

The representation of Slackbridge seems to me what is hardest to excuse in Dickens's novel. Everything in the conditions of Coketown—as in the Preston strike, which Dickens had visited before writing the novel— cry out for organization of the workers, for unionization as the sole tool to use on Bounderby. For Dickens to turn Slackbridge into a sinister emblem of seduction and misrule, and to do it through his pretentious inflation and misappropriation of the English language, and to make part of Stephen's heroism his refusal to join the union—this seems to me perverse beyond words. It's of course a standard middle-class reaction of the time, and indeed well beyond Dickens's time: even Zola has trouble with unions and strikes, he is visibly shaken by the "vision rouge de la révolution" that Etienne Lantier bears away from the strike at the end of *Germinal*. Still, it would seem within the logic of the very world he is portraying that collective action is the only way out of Stephen's "muddle." But Dickens won't go there. And his working-class hero is instead a pariah and a martyr persecuted and crucified not only by the mill owners but by his fellow hands as well.

The attention given to Slackbridge's "mongrel dress" may be one more clue that the whole novel is playing itself out as a question of dramatized styles around the questions posed by Coketown. One senses that this is a brilliantly Dickensian solution to an intractable problem. It's similar to the problem that will be recognized by Flaubert: that of faithful representation of an ugly, monotonous world that does not fall too much into the imitative fallacy, that preserves a certain implied play of ironic intelligence on the world represented without explicitly parting company with that world. Dickens is no Flaubert; his solution is less subtle, but very much of his own devising. The play of narratorial linguistic invention is among other things a way of giving greater tonal unity to the disparate worlds and material of the novel. Consider, for instance, the place of Mrs Sparsit in the Bounderby world:

> Mr Bounderby's first disquietude, on hearing of his happiness [his engagement to Louisa Gradgrind], was occasioned by the necessity of imparting it to Mrs Sparsit. He could not make up his mind how to do that, or what the consequences of the step might be. Whether she would instantly depart, bag and baggage, to Lady Scadgers, or would positively refuse to budge from the premises; whether she would be plaintive or abusive, tearful or tearing; whether she would break her heart, or break the looking-glass; Mr Bounderby could not at all foresee. (106)

This becomes positively Popean in its zeugmas (as in *The Rape of the Lock*: "Or stain her honor or her new brocade"); one can almost hear it in couplets. Mrs Sparsit's nose and her mittens become stylistic features on which the narrator can ring changes from the literal to the metaphorical and back again:

> "Why don't you mind your own business, ma'am?" roared Bounderby. "How dare you go and poke your officious nose into my family affairs?"
> This allusion to her favourite feature overpowered Mrs Sparsit. She sat down stiffly in a chair, as if she were frozen; and, with a fixed stare at Mr Bounderby, slowly grated her mittens against one another, as if they were frozen, too. (261)

Against the world of imposture and pretence represented by Bounderby, Sparsit, and associates, Stephen is the real thing, the authentic Englishman. Note that in the scene where Louisa Gradgrind goes to offer assistance to Stephen in his lodgings—after Bounderby has sacked him—it is the style with which he takes the two pounds (all he'll accept) that merits the narratorial commentary: "He was neither courtly, nor handsome, nor pictur-

48   esque, in any respect; and yet his manner of accepting it, and of expressing his thanks without more words, had a grace in it that Lord Chesterfield could not have taught his son in a century" (163). Compare not only Bounderby, compare Slackbridge. If there is hope for an England divided into two nations, it lies in the simplicity, honesty, and decency of Stephen Blackpool. The evocation of Lord Chesterfield suggests that Stephen is a natural, and authentic, working-class "gentleman."

The extent to which the worlds of *Hard Times* are known, dramatized, judged in terms of style—the extent to which style of representation and self-representation is key, and representation itself, whether with Stephen or the factories of Coketown, is made out to be largely a question of style— may make us ask whether Dickens hasn't made the questions posed by industrialism too much into a trope. It's as if the initial problem presented in the schoolroom—that of definition, designation, reference, and representation—has been spun out into a series of mis-definitions and abusive representations, where all is imposture or pretense or some other attempt to mislead, be it the Bounderby type of fakery or the Slackbridge type of demagogy or the Whelpish theft and false accusation. The narrator's own style, and the styles he underwrites with his approval—Stephen's, Rachel's—seem to be offered as the moral baseline for judging a world gone off course. If Stephen and Rachel are what the novel offers in opposition to the forces generated by Coketown, there is little ground for an optimistic reading.

The scene of Louisa's benevolent visit to Stephen is of course also a scene of betrayal: she is accompanied by her brother, Tom, who here hatches the scheme that will falsely implicate Stephen in the bank robbery Tom is plotting. Stephen will leave Coketown, never to return alive, and the novel turns to its other plotlines: the exposure of the imposter Bounderby, Louisa's near-seduction by Harthouse, her return to her father with a broken and changed heart—and the beginnings of her father's change of heart, too—while Sissy Jupe in her great and good innocence routs Harthouse and sends him off to Egypt, and then the denouement of the bank robbery plot in the exposure and exile of the Whelp. The novel takes a turn—not unfamiliar in Dickens— into moral melodrama or even allegory. The social issues of Coketown seem to be largely forgotten in the personal drama. Louisa's conversion is to be sure very much a commentary on the Grandgrindian philosophy and educational system propounded in the opening scenes, and the emergence of Sissy Jupe as the moral standard of the Grandgrind household an effective transvaluation of values. Louisa in her near-seduction is I think quite a remarkable creation, a portrait of someone faced with something new welling up in her that she cannot fully understand, nor control, but knows she must recognize. If Louisa were a character in a French novel, she would of course yield to Harthouse, and discover her broken and reformed heart only at the end of the affair. She would not be so far from Emma Bovary — though Emma's education was conventual and frivolous rather than utilitarian. As it is, she looks less toward Emma Bovary than toward one of D. H. Lawrence's Midland heroines brought to new consciousness by sexual passion — which is here of course painfully but thoroughly repressed.

The return of Stephen, and all he represents, will be by way not of the mill but of the mine — those black pits that scar the green countryside where Sissy and Rachel go walking of a bright Sunday morning. Stephen has fallen victim to the dangerous byproduct of industrialism, to its waste. (Though he can't do Engels's Manchester privies, Dickens has a sharp sense for the meaning of waste, most memorably rendered in the dust heaps of *Our Mutual Friend*). And in the rescue of what is left of Stephen, Dickens I think brings to bear, in this sinister pockmarked landscape, what he sees as the best in the English working class. The rescue of Stephen requires ingenuity, strength, courage, character. Led by "the drunken man whom the news had sobered and who was the best man of all" (268–69), the workers quickly organize themselves, rig a scaffold to hold bucket and pulley, test the air in the pit, then "the sobered man" and another get in and order "Lower away!" The sobered man returns alone, to tell of having found Stephen, alive but gravely wounded. Then the men build a stretcher, and back the sobered man goes with it.

There are three or four pages (269–72) that offer a fine, taut, suspenseful, and sober narrative — a kind of relatively unadorned account that Dickens is capable of at moments of climactic action. It is evident that the narrator takes pleasure in the recounting of the action here, perhaps because it is handwork, tough and ingenious, not industrial work. The machines it uses are simple and handmade, the qualities it tests and brings to the surface are not rote movements but skilled uses of hand and body. I won't cite the several pages; let me give as an inadequate example just a short paragraph, as the sobered man—now the pitman—prepares to make the crucial trip down to bring up Stephen:

> When all was ready, this man, still taking his last hurried charges from his comrades and the surgeon after the windlass had begun to lower him, disappeared into the pit. The rope went out as before, the signal was made as before, and the windlass stopped. No man removed his hand from it now. Every one waited with his grasp set, and his body bent down to the work, ready to reverse and wind in. At length the signal was given, and all the ring leaned forward.
>
> For, now, the rope came in, tightened and strained to its utmost as it appeared, and the men turned heavily, and the windlass complained. (271)

Here is the real heroism of the English workingman—his capacity to work intelligently, freely, cooperatively, with his hands. I sense in this passage a contribution to that long history of resistance to industrialism, on the part of middle-class observers, that takes the form of exalting handwork. (And I note that "handwork" may be, as Walter Benjamin suggests in his essay "The Storyteller," the best description of the craft of writing. The writer's reaction to industrialism, holding up handwork as its antidote, may be heavily predetermined.)

Stephen raised from the pit—but critically injured—speaks in indictment of the pit as a central site of the crime of industrialism:

> I ha' fell into th' pit, my dear, as have cost wi'in the knowledge o' old folk now livin, hundred and hundreds o' men's lives—fathers, sons, brothers, dear to thousands an thousands, an keepin 'em fro' want and hunger. I ha' fell into a pit that ha' been wi' the' Fire-damp crueller than battle. I ha' read on't in the public petition, as onny one may read, fro' the men that works in pits, in which they ha' pray'n and pray'n the lawmakers for Christ's sake not to let their work be murder to 'em, but to spare 'em for th' wives and children that they loves as well as gentlefok loves theirs. When it were in work, it killed w'out need; when 'tis let alone, it kills wi'out need. See how we die and no need, one way an another—in a muddle—every day! (272–73)

This is eloquent, and it places the indictment squarely before "the lawmakers," to take action against an industry where work is murder to the workers. But it ends once again not in revolt but in a sense of the "muddle."

And Stephen's final message is not one of revolt but of reconciliation: "I ha' seen more clear, and ha' made it my dyin' prayer that aw th' world may on'y coom toogether more, an get a better understan'in o' one another, than when I were in't my own weak seln." Here may lie the essential weakness of most nineteenth-century middle-class responses to the chasm separating the "two nations": that the solution is to be sought only in reconciliation and harmony, not in struggle, combat, and the political vindication of rights. Stephen's story tends toward no "vision rouge de la révolution," not even toward a strike on the part of the Coketown hands, but toward personal forgiveness and redemption, guided by the star he contemplates from deep in the pit. "The star had shown him where to find the God of the poor; and through humility, and sorrow, and forgiveness, he had gone to his Redeemer's rest" (275). Death scenes are usually pretty insufferable in Dickens. Stephen's death is no exception, only blessedly shorter than some.

Stephen's death effectively purges from the novel what had appeared to be its central social problem, and leaves the remainder of the novel for "whelp-hunting" and then the final wrap-up. This trivial business permits a return of Bitzer, of the horse-definition, and a demonstration that he has become a model of the original Grandgrindian philosophy, who believes in the "catechism" of self-interest. (Grandgrind's appeal to Bitzer to have a heart is answered with: "No man, Sir, acquainted with the facts established by Harvey relating to the circulation of the blood, can doubt that I have a heart.") But Bitzerian self-interest is routed at the last by the disguises and dodges of Sleary's circus, and particularly its horses and dogs, and Tom is saved from justice. The reintroduction of the circus people of course allows Sleary to have the last word on the affair: "Don't be croth with uth poor vagabonth. People muth be amuthed" (292). Sleary's envoi echoes the line with which the narrator introduced the early chapter that presented Stephen Blackpool: "I entertain a weak idea that the English people are as hard-worked as any people upon whom the sun shines. I acknowledge to this ridiculous idiosyncrasy, as a reason why I would give them more play" (67–68).

"More play": the admonition stands as a justification of the narratorial style of Hard Times, which takes its stands with the circus people, with what David Lodge identified as the "pantomime model" represented by Sleary and associates, a model ever dear to Dickens. More precisely, the performance of the narrator's prose in the novel uses the circus and a variety of other traditional amusements—the Arabian Nights, nursery rhymes, fairy tales—to present its own antics as the antidote to dreary utilitarianism and the hard facts of Coketown. The brilliant linguistic performance of the narrator in the novel is amusement with a purpose, making a statement about a better approach to education and life in general than those provided by the dominant characters of Coketown. The narrator on the last page of the novel makes it explicit that the life of imaginative literature is the necessary antidote to the grim statistics of Coketown. He evokes a future Louisa's benevolence toward Sissy's children, "trying hard to beautify their lives of machinery and reality with those imaginative graces and delights, without which the heart of infancy will wither up, the sturdiest physical manhood will be morally stark death, and the plainest national prosperity figures can show, will be the Writing on the Wall" (298). In the end, it is not so much that this novel represents Coketown as that it stands as a counteraction against Coketown, and an alternative to it. The novel versus the life of machinery.

That is no doubt a worthy mission, and it would be unfair to tax Dickens for not finding the means adequately to represent Coketown and the issues it raises when his prose so often is aimed in the other direction: at nonrepresentation of Coketown in favor of something else, a representation of imaginative process at work, a representation of transformative style at play on the world. Coketown in Dickens's view must be metamorphosed, and his prose does just that. Still, it is worth registering that *Hard Times* does not quite make good on the "droit au roman" of the industrial proletariat that the Goncourt brothers would call for, ten years later, in France. Ruskin thought this the finest of Dickens's novels, and it is indeed Ruskinian in its argument that beauty is the truth to oppose to the bleak shabbiness of industrial production. No one who spends his life professing literature could disagree with that. But at the same time that we find it just, we may find it inadequate.

George Bernard Shaw was a partisan of *Hard Times*, which he sees as marking a turning point in Dickens's fiction. Shaw says: "*The Old Curiosity Shop* was written to amuse you, entertain you, touch you; and it succeeded. *Hard Times* was written to make you uncomfortable; and it will make you uncomfortable (and serve you right) though it will perhaps interest you more, and certainly leave a deeper scar on you, than any two of its forerunners." I can't quite decide whether Shaw is right or not. I wish *Hard Times* made us more uncomfortable, or perhaps I mean, more uncomfortable in the ways that would seem to suit better with an effective political response, that would answer better to the issues the novel raises. But Shaw is certainly right in detecting an element of discomfort in reactions to Hard Times ever since its publication. The discomfort arises from the sense of its being too un-Dickensian, its lacking the comic amplitude of the other novels. I'm not certain Shaw has it right that Hard Times marks a shift in Dickens's social attitudes, a turn from amusement to anger. It still seems to me to stand apart in his work, a different kind of project from most of the other novels, a project not wholly mastered or even wholly understood by its author but nonetheless full of interest.

I will end without trying to resolve the puzzlements that the novel provokes, in me at least. The easiest thing, in the context I have set for this study, would simply be to rule it out of the canon of the realist novel—whatever that canon may be—which would be simple enough to do, since it cannot be counted a persuasively full effort to represent industrial England. Gaskell could be said to try harder. Nonetheless, that gesture of exclusion would solve nothing except the literary historian's need for categories and classifications. Hard Times for These Times: read together, the title and subtitle make the case for the novel as a tract for the times. "Dear reader!" the narrator says at the very end, "It rests with you and me, whether, in our two fields of action, similar things shall be or not." He is talking here about Louisa's education of Sissy's children, not about the mills or Stephen's lot or the union. We may feel that is a pity—that the reader at the end should be summoned instead to build Jerusalem among the dark satanic mills. Yet the novel does in a more general sense summon the reader. Its very incoherences and failures of representation in its attempts to take on a very big subject make it a pest of a novel, a kind of disruption in smoother understandings of Dickens, and that surely is a good thing.

CHAPTER 4

Flaubert and the Scandal of Realism

I SOMETIMES THINK THAT MADAME BOVARY IS THE ONE NOVEL, OF ALL NOVELS, that deserves the label "realist." Even Flaubert's own later fiction, which I find in some ways more weird and interesting than Madame Bovary, may be less clearly realist: L'Education sentimentale, and then Bouvard et Pécuchet, are so intent to dismantle the structures, forces, and meaning-systems of the traditional novel that their project seems to lie more in this cosmic housewrecking than in the painstaking attention to the detail of the real. Flaubert didn't like the label "realist," and hated being constrained to the kind of attention it required. Over and over again he complains to his correspondents about the meanness and tedium of the task he has set for himself. His preference for the exotic subject matter of Salammbô and La Tentation de Saint-Antoine is well known. Yet for all the ungratefulness of the material, the need to document detestable provincial ways, mœurs de province, he sticks to what he is doing. And it may be precisely in this disciplining of his imagination to something he loathes that the arduous perfection of Madame Bovary is forged. There is nothing natural about this novel. It is absolutely the most literary of novels, Henry James said—which he did not mean entirely as praise. There is indeed something labored about the novel, its characters, plot, milieux are all constructed with effort. Everything, as Flaubert understands it, depends on the detail.

The initial presentation of Emma comes with Doctor Charles Bovary's visits to attend her father at his farm, in the form of glimpses, noticings of details of gesture and appearance. She pricks her fingers while sewing and puts them in her mouth to suck them. When she drinks a glass of liqueur, "the tip of her tongue, from between her perfect teeth, licked delicately over the bottom of the glass" (70) [17]. We learn of the whiteness of her fingernails, her pink cheeks, how the tip of her ear emerges from her hair, the sound of her clogs on the scrubbed floor, the little drops of sweat on her bare shoulders. One day when Charles says good-bye to her at the door, she goes to fetch her parasol because of the melting snow. "The parasol, made of iridescent silk, with the sun shining through it, lighted with shifting colors the white surface of her face. She smiled in the moist warmth of its shade; and you could hear the drops of water, one by one, falling on the taut silk" (65) [13]. In retrospect, you can say that these glimpses of Emma all suggest her sensuous nature—the extent to which she will live, and die, by her senses. But as we read them they are details that we have yet to recover for meaning—to recuperate, as the French would say. They are simply there, as precise notations of what has been seen.

Emma's husband and her lovers seem to know her by way of the details and the accessories of her beauty. For instance, Charles in the early days of their marriage: "He couldn't stop himself from continually touching her comb, her rings, her scarf" (84) [26]. And Emma with Rodolphe: "It was for him that that she filed her nails with the care of a metalsmith, and there was never enough cold cream on her skin, or enough patchouli in her handkerchiefs. She loaded herself with bracelets, rings, necklaces" (261) [151]. As for Léon, "He admired the exaltation of her soul and the lace of her petticoat" (350) [215]. For the narrator as well, looking at Emma tends to fix on such details, rather than giving an image of the whole. On her wedding day, for instance, we are treated to a full page of description of the wedding guests, and a paragraph on the wedding cake created by the ambitious local pâtissier, but just this on Emma: "Emma's dress, too long, dragged a bit on the ground; from time to time she stopped to lift its hem, and then, delicately, with her gloved fingers picked out the weeds and burrs" (76) [21].

One could multiply the examples. There seems to be a problem of vision or perspective in this intensely visual novel, in that the central object of vision, Emma as a physical presence, never quite seems to cohere into a whole. We may read this as a comment on the limits of seeing, suggested to me in a moment following the ball at the Château de La Vaubyessard—a turning point in Emma's aspirations to a more glamorous life—when Emma opens the window of the room in the château where she and Charles are sleeping: "She gazed for a long time at the windows of the château, trying to figure out which were the rooms of the people she had noticed during the evening. She would have liked to know their lives, to get into them, to become part of them" (107) [42]. Windows are always important in realist fiction, as in realist painting. Here, the window is doubled: Emma is looking out from one, and trying to look in through another—and by looking in, to know the lives of others, to penetrate into them, to become part of them ("y pénétrer, s'y confondre"). The moment suggests both the ambitions and the limitations of sight, the kind of knowledge it would like to gain but the blockages it encounters—blockages that then can provoke the compensatory, and error-prone, play of the imagination.

The limitations of vision may point as well to a problem in the desire subtending the gaze. The seeming fragmentation of Emma in the novel's field of vision might be ascribed to the mediocrity of the men who admire and look at her. Thus Léon: "She was the beloved of all the novels, the heroine of all the plays, the vague *she* of all the volumes of poetry. He rediscovered on her shoulders the amber color of the 'Bathing Odalisque'; she had the deep bosom of feudal noblewomen; she looked like 'The Pale Lady of Barcelona'; but above all she was the Angel!" (350) [215]. Léon sees only in clichés, in preformed images. More radically, when Charles attempts to stare into her eyes—into those "mirrors of the soul"—he uncovers nothing about her; he sees instead the observer: "His own eye became lost in these depths, and he saw himself in miniature to the shoulders, with the kerchief tied around his head and the top of his nightshirt unbuttoned" (83) [25–26]. In the lack of a coherent embrace of Emma by her lovers' gazes, we have a kind of fetishization of details of her person and accessories of her femininity. The stable boy Justin sets the tone here, with the undergarments Emma's maid, Félicité, is ironing: "He gazed avidly at these women's things spread around him: damask petticoats, little lace shawls, collars, knickers with draw-strings, voluminous around the hips and gathered at the knee" (261) [151]. Then Justin goes to clean Emma's boots—a traditional fetish object.

This is classic fetishism, the investment of accessory and ancillary objects—objects metonymically associated with the body—with desire. A key instance occurs when Rodolphe is leading Emma into the clearing in the woods where he will become her lover: she lifts the hem of her dress, and "Rodolphe, walking behind her, noticed, between the black cloth and the black boot, the delicacy of her white stocking, like a bit of her nakedness" (228) [128]. The moment of seduction itself calls attention to the materials of the clothes they wear: "The wool of her dress caught on the velvet of his jacket. She stretched back her white throat, which filled with a sigh, and swooning, all in tears, with a deep shudder, hiding her face, she yielded" (230) [129]. The drama of the novel seems so often to come to us in bits and pieces of this sort, as if the world could only be known in detail, in what the eye and the touch single out to be known. Another example, Emma rushing to undress to join Léon in bed: "She undressed brutally, tearing at the delicate lace of her corset, which whipped around her thighs like a slithering adder" (369–70) [229–30]. Here a moment of high arousal is entirely focused in that corset lace.

Fetishization seems to be at work throughout the novel, as one of the principal ways in which things are invested with meaning. Consider the Vicomte's green silk cigar case, which Charles finds along the wayside as he and Emma leave La Vaubyessard after the ball, and which Emma takes out from time to time in her erotic reveries: "A sigh of love had passed into the fabric of the work; each stitch of the needle had fixed a hope or a memory, and all these interwoven silk threads were the continuation of the same speechless passion" (110) [44]. The very woven fabric of the cigar case is a kind of net that has caught forever the passion invested in its making; it is, like all fetishes, a hypersignificant accessory, one that means far beyond itself, that means more than meaning itself, in that the fetish, in classic psychoanalytic doctrine, is a substitute for meanings—such as "castration"—that cannot be faced. If foot fetishism is the best-known instance, this is given a savage ironic twist in Hippolyte's club foot and Charles's botched attempt to correct it, which then results in amputation—and eventually an expensive prosthetic leg that Hippolyte can't bring himself to wear, except on festive occasions. This is a fetish of a fetish. And the failure of Charles's operation, which Emma had counted upon to make his reputation, and renew her love for him, results in her throwing herself back into the "bad ironies of adultery triumphant" (259) [150].

But I really want to suggest that the object or accessory become fetish does more than evoke the limitations of Emma's spectators and admirers; it offers a clue to the larger importance of the object and the detail in the novel. It suggests the extent to which details carry the plot and meaning of the novel. Roman Jakobson in a famous essay claimed that while lyric poetry is characterized by the trope of metaphor, narrative prose of the real-

ist mode is characterized by metonymy: the use of details, of partial representations, the creation of totalities of meaning only through the accumulation of details along the "axis of combination." In Jakobson's prime example,
it is Anna Karenina's handbag that the narratorial eye follows as she throws
herself under the onrushing train. In this sense, one could say that the way
details are picked out by the characters and by the narrator in Madame Bovary
instances its status as realist narrative: it works by the detail, through a foregrounding of the thinginess of the world. Meaning is not to be thought of—
it is not created—independently of the objects amid which we live.

Yet things in this novel, and their use, strike me as very different from
those things that clutter Balzac's described rooms and places. Things in Balzac
are usually indexical: they point to character traits of those people who wear
them, live amid them, endure them. Things are known primarily through
their market value, and by other kinds of sentimental or psychic value. They
promote an intelligent decipherment of their meaning, they are clues to the
legibility of persons, and of the world. Rhetorically, I suppose you would
call all those riding crops and cravats and shirt buttons in Balzac's world
synecdoches: they are parts that stand for an intelligible whole. In Flaubert's
world, however, they seem more like *apparent* synecdoches, in that often the
whole is never given, never quite achieved. While Emma is frequently described, we never quite see her whole. She and her world never quite cohere.
Perhaps we should read this as one sign, among several, that she does not
cohere as a person: that one result of her *Bovarysme*, of her perpetual dissat-
isfaction with things as they are, her constant search for a life in fantasy, is
her failure to be a full, coherent, autonomous person.

This is undoubtedly true, and a legitimate, even necessary way to understand the atomization of her person as described. Yet there seems to be a
more general, and more radical, failure of the world to cohere in the novel.
It is as if the parts of the world really are what is most significant about it—
the rest may simply be metaphysics. Consider in this context the famous cab
ride during which Léon presumably seduces Emma. It is one of the passages
that the editors of the *Revue de Paris*, where the novel was serialized, found so
shocking that they censored it—without the author's permission—and one
of the passages singled out for indignant reprobation by the imperial prosecutor, Maître Ernest Pinard, when Flaubert and his novel were put on trial
for outrage to public morality. What is curious about these reactions is that

one sees precisely nothing of what is going on inside the cab as it meanders through Rouen and the surrounding countryside: the curtains are drawn. Only once during the ride do we see a hand emerge from the curtains to scatter the torn fragments of Emma's letter of rupture, now no longer relevant. It is "une main nue"—literally, a naked hand. We don't usually—we don't any more, at least—think of a hand without covering as naked. "Unclad hand," Geoffrey Wall translates, which is good. But Flaubert didn't simply write "a hand" or even "une main dégantée," a hand without its glove. He says "a naked hand," and it carries this force. It is in a naked hand that you find the meaning of the scene. And in this sense, Prosecutor Pinard got it right.

Another passage that enraged the prosecutor describes Emma embellished by adultery, and it is worth dwelling on for a moment:

> Never had Madame Bovary been so beautiful as at this time. She had that indefinable beauty that comes from joy, enthusiasm, success, and which is only the harmony of temperament with circumstances. Her desirings, her troubles, the experience of pleasure and her illusions, still fresh, had worked upon her as manure, rain, the wind and the sun work to germinate flowers, and she bloomed at last in the fullness of her nature. Her eyelashes seemed formed expressly for long amorous gazes where the pupil sank into depths, while a deep breath opened her delicate nostrils and lifted the corners of her ripe lips, shadowed by a bit of dark down. It was as if an artist skilled in corruption had disposed on the nape of her neck the coils of her hair: they were rolled negligently in a heavy tress, according to the chances of adultery, which undid them every day. Her voice now took on softer modulations, her figure as well. Something subtle that took hold of you wafted from the very folds of her dress and the curve of her foot. Charles, as in the first days of their marriage, found her delicious and completely irresistible. (269–70) [157]

In reaching for organic imagery, comparing Emma's beauty to that of flowers fed on manure, rain, wind, and sun, and in positing a harmony of temperament and circumstance, the description is proto-Zola, claiming a naturalist origin for what the right-minded think of as moral conditions. Adultery is simply good fertilizer for a woman's beauty. And as that beauty is described, it is all in details of her face, voice, and body. Emma is not so much a character here, as the Victorian novel understood character, as a kind of biological product, a particularly successful collection of human traits. That "artist skilled in corruption" of course too much resembles Flaubert. As the prosecutor exclaims: "What the author shows us is the poetry of adultery, and I ask you once again if these lascivious pages be not of a profound im-morality!!!"—a sentence that ends with three exclamation points. Flaubert compounds the immorality by having his description of how Emma is im-proved by her adulterous passion for Rodolphe end with the beguiled gaze of the deceived husband, who finds her "delicious and irresistible."

Let me offer just one further instance of fetishization. When Rodolphe turns to the task of writing a letter of rupture to Emma, he opens the biscuit tin in which he keeps the souvenirs of his mistresses, old letters, miniatures, dried bouquets, a garter, pins, and locks of hair. The box opened gives off an odor of mildew and faded roses. These fetishes have lost their power to arouse; the different women blend confusedly in Rodolphe's memory. And when he sets to the composition of his letter to Emma, it is stitched together of clichés like the objects in his box, mildewed and faded words and phrases that mean nothing to him, though their effect on the addressee of the letter will be devastating.

It is Emma's protestations of impassioned love to an increasingly indif-ferent Rodolphe that provoke one of the most interesting and revealing mo-ments of narratorial commentary in the novel. The whole paragraph needs to be read.

> He had heard these things said so often that they didn't have any originality left. Emma resembled all mistresses; and the charm of novelty, slipping from her bit by bit like a piece of clothing, laid bare the eternal monotony of passion, which always has the same forms and the same language. This experienced ladies' man couldn't distinguish the difference of sentiments concealed by the similarity of expressions. Because libertine or venal lips had whispered similar words to him, he had no great belief in the candor of these. One ought to discount them, he thought, exaggerations of speech hiding lukewarm affections; as if the fullness of the soul didn't overflow at times into the emptiest of metaphors, since no one, ever, can give the exact measure of his needs, or his thoughts, or his sufferings; since, too, human speech is like a cracked kettle on which we beat out tunes for bears to dance to, when we would wish to move the stars to pity. (265–66) [154]

It's not easy to construe this passage. Rodolphe's worldweariness makes Emma's expressions banal, clichés of passion, which "always has the same forms and the same language." But the narrator suggests that the sameness of language does not always point to a sameness of the emotions it is trying to express; and Rodolphe as expert reader of the language of passion seems in fact to be a limited reader of Emma, since he cannot decipher what lies behind her words, distinguish true passion under the banal linguistics of passion. But here the narrator appears to offer a comment, beginning with a "comme si," "as if," and dissimulating his hidden presence in the form of the general aphorism—an aphorism that suggests that "la plénitude de l'âme," the soul overfull of passion, sometimes overflows into the most empty metaphors. And this situation is then made a kind of law of the ratio of passion to language: "since no one, ever, can give the exact measure of his needs, nor of his ideas nor his sufferings." The problem here seems to be the inadequate expressivity of language. But then this sentence—run on beyond its "normal" length and rhythm—reaches for its own metaphor, one that seems to generalize still further, and to refers to "us": "human speech is like a cracked cauldron on which we beat out melodies for dancing bears, when we would wish to move the stars to pity." Here, the problem seems to be attributed to language itself: a cracked and inadequate instrument that produces effects other than what we would intend.

On a radical reading of this passage, language fails as an expressive instrument. It is a medium that cannot adequately give an account of human passion and aspiration, one that deforms the music that the soul would sing. On a more radical reading, however, the problem is not one of expression, and Flaubert, unlike Balzac, cannot be said to subscribe to an expressionist understanding of language. Language may well be a cracked cauldron, but it is all we have. In this sense, Rodolphe is not so much an obtuse reader as simply a ploddingly literal reader, one who cannot imaginatively fill in the gaps of language. I propose this more radical understanding of the cracked cauldron because the novel suggests over and over again that there is no beautiful soul to be found behind language—that the soul's beauty, and passion, is linguistically predetermined. Remember Emma in the first disappointment of her marriage, wondering what has become of "the happiness that ought to have resulted from" love and marriage. "Emma sought to find out what exactly one meant in life by the words *happiness, passion* and *rapture,* which had seemed so beautiful to her in books" (84) [27]. Emma seeks the meaning of words.

This line ends chapter 5 of part 1; the next chapter details those books which are the source of her understanding of the words—books that, as many a critic has noted, have given her a distorted view of reality, similar to the deluded state induced in Don Quixote by his reading of the *Amadis de Gaul*. But again, I think the problem presented in Flaubert's novel is more radical. Consider the start of chapter 7—immediately following the retrospect on her reading—and Emma's reveries of honeymoon:

> She used to reflect at times that these ought nonetheless to be the best days of her life, the honeymoon as it was called. In order to taste its sweetness, no doubt one would have had to travel to those countries with melodious names, where the newly-married state has more exquisite languors! In a post-chaise, under a blue silk canopy, you climb slowly up the precipitous roads, listening to the coachman's song, echoing through the mountains along with goat bells and the deep roar of the waterfall. At sunset, you breathe at the bay's edge the odor of lemon trees; then, at night, on the villa terrace, alone and with fingers enlaced, together you look at the stars while making plans for the future. It seemed to her that certain places on earth must produce happiness, like a plant native to a particular soil that would wither elsewhere. If only she could rest her elbows on the balcony rail of a Swiss chalet or take refuge with her melancholy in a Highland cottage, with a husband wearing a long-skirted black velvet coat, and soft leather boots, a cocked hat and ruffles at his cuffs! (91) [31]

Emma's reveries on "ces pays à noms sonores" has all the authenticity of a travel brochure. And yet, her creation of an inauthentic exoticism is an act of imaginative creation that we mock at our peril, since the alternative the novel presents is Charles, whose language is "flat like a pavement." Emma's delusions are at least that, attempts to reformulate a flat reality into aspiration. "Madame Bovary, c'est moi," in Flaubert's famous phrase, and we can see her as the protonovelist. Think in this regard of the young Marcel, in Proust's *Recherche*, and his reveries on "Balbec" and other place names. It is in the imaginings afforded by language that reflection and self-reflection begin. To be aware, to aspire: these, Flaubert suggests, are imaginative acts that begin in a linguistic *cogito*, by asking what the names of states of being mean. These imaginative acts of course lead straight to unhappiness as well. When after yielding to Rodolphe, she exclaims to herself, "J'ai un amant! un amant!" then summons up all the adulterous heroines of novels she has read, she is, I think, both pathetic and persuasive. It is only in its conceptualization—"I have a lover! A lover!"—that an experience makes sense. That Emma's conceptualizations come from reading novels may be sad and delusive—but it is not clear that any other source would solve the problem of language as defined by language. Those who perish by language—by believing too much in the promises of those "sonorous names"—also live by language. The imaginative ones, like Emma, may live more fully than the Charleses, whose cells in the prison house of language are at least as narrow.

I am becoming a bit too metaphorical. I want to suggest that if this novel proposes that language is a cracked instrument for the expression of human passion, it also relentlessly intimates that the limitations language places on passion are absolute boundaries since there is no passion outside language: that the very notion of passion, the concept of passion, is a linguistic invention. In that sense, Emma, like Flaubert, can only struggle with the language she is born into. Language is trans-individual, and each person who comes to consciousness in the world must find his or her place in it, discover how to speak it and, in a stage of further self-reflection that Emma at least initiates, how it speaks us. I think one could demonstrate on every page of *Madame Bovary* Flaubert's ultimate refusal of—despite some tempting steps in the direction of—an expressionist view of language. And his later work, culminating in *Bouvard et Pécuchet* and the "sottisier" or *Dictionnaire des idées reçues,* the compendium of clichés and stupidities that was to be part of its second volume, certainly confirms a fully disabused, or deconstructed, understanding of language. In *Madame Bovary,* there is of course the well-known case of Monsieur Homais, who is constructed of nothing but clichés. Homais is to Flaubert such a detestable character because he uses his clichés, his commonplaces and banalities, in entire good faith. Thinker as he supposes himself to be, and ultimately a reporter and writer, he never gives any sign of linguistic self-doubt.

One of the most celebrated episodes of *Madame Bovary* is constructed entirely from a game of linguistic banalities—the scene of the agricultural fair, the *comices agricoles.* As we move into the evocation of the comices, we have a long description of the animals before we come to the people. The animals indeed are lovingly detailed, in all their animality, whereas the following paragraph concerns "des messieurs," indistinguishable frock-coated men, who subsequently are largely referred to by the generic "*on.*" Rodolphe's seductive discourse to Emma is pursued against the background of pompous, empty, cliché-filled speeches by the invited notables, which has the effect of underlining the banalities of Rodolphe's own language. As we reach the climactic moments of the scene, the counterpoint of two systems of

64   cliché is played out in the dramatic exchange of one-liners the Greeks called
     stichomythia. Rodolphe has been evoking magnetism and elective affinities:

> And now he took her hand; she didn't take it back again.
> —Prize for general farming! shouted the chairman.
> —Just now, for instance, when I came to see you . . .
> —To Monsieur Bizet, of Quincampoix.
> —Did I know that I would be escorting you?
> —Seventy francs!
> —A hundred times I wanted to leave, and I followed you, I stayed.
> —Manures!

And so on, until we reach:

> —Oh! no, surely, I will be somewhere in your thoughts, in your life?
> —Swine category, prize shared by Monsieur Leherissé and Monsieur
> Cullembourg, sixty francs!
> Rodolphe gripped her hand, and he felt it warm and trembling like a
> captive turtle dove that strives to take wing again . . . (216–17) [119–20]

This is a world both saved by language and condemned to language.
And it's notable that the most moving moment of the agricultural fair—
one of the most touching moments of the novel—comes with the award of
a prize to the peasant woman Catherine Leroux for fifty years of servitude
on the same farm. Catherine Leroux is practically wordless. "Living close to
the animals, she had assumed their wordless placid state of being"—"leur
mutisme." Catherine Leroux looks forward to the Félicité of *Un Cœur simple* (*A
Simple Heart*), who also progressively becomes deaf and mute, almost like the
bêtes close to whom she lives her life—and who suggests that beyond irony
in Flaubert there is what you might call *bêtise*, stupidity, which is perhaps
finally the right relation to language, since you can never outwit it, only—
as Flaubert would suggest while working on *Bouvard et Pécuchet*—regurgitate
it, vomit it.

     Flaubert in that final novel seems to take pleasure in ruining language,
and already in *Madame Bovary* there are moments where we sense that language is deployed in ways that are self-defeating, that render the world, the
actions, the people it names and describes nonsignifying: language directed,
it seems, to the demonstration of its own futility. Charles Bovary's famous
cap, in the opening scene of the novel, has some of these qualities: it is described in great detail, too great detail, as essentially indescribable. Emma's

wedding cake is a slightly different example, an object that is so elaborately trivial and grotesque that the baroque description of it confounds understanding: What is meant by telling us of this overelaborated confection, with its lakes of jam and nutshell boats? Let me dwell on still another example, Binet at his lathe, at the moment when Emma comes begging for money:

> He was alone in his attic, in the process of imitating in wood one of those indescribable ivories which are composed of crescents, of spheres carved one within another, the whole thing standing up like an obelisk and not serving any purpose whatever. He was beginning the last piece, the end was in sight! In the chiaroscuro of his workshop, blond dust flew from his lathe like a shower of sparks from the hooves of a galloping horse; the twin wheels spun, hummed; Binet was smiling, his chin lowered, his nostrils wide open, indeed he seemed lost in one of those complete happinesses that doubtless only come with mediocre occupations, which amuse the mind with facile difficulties, and satisfy it in an achievement beyond which there is no place for dreaming. (396) [249]

Binet is busy making an imitation, a reproduction in another medium, of something essentially indescribable, and entirely useless. It's very like the kind of objects Bouvard and Pécuchet build in their garden, claiming to follow the instructions of their garden architecture manual, but producing something grotesque that eludes its designs and intentions. Binet is wholly absorbed in this useless absurdity, in a "mediocre" pursuit that amuses the intellect with "facile difficulties," that satisfy it with "an achievement beyond which there is no place for dreaming." We may wonder why Flaubert bothers with this reproduction of Binet's useless reproduction, and just what he means by this perplexing last phrase (Geoffrey Wall's "an achievement that quite dulls the imagination" closes the door on the question a bit too stolidly). It's as if Flaubert wants to insist upon the uselessness of artisanal reproduction, on the insignificance of what can be accomplished by hand and mind. And here we may irresistibly be reminded of the practice of writing the world, as if to say that representation of the world in language is by its nature useless, an achievement that forecloses dreaming, and perhaps most of all shows up language itself as mediocre. There is, as Gérard Genette has pointed out, a tendency of the Flaubertian text toward silence: the mutism of Catherine Leroux and Félicité, and the ruin of language in elaborate reproductions of reality that take one no closer to understanding.

It is less anything that Emma does that constitutes the scandal of *Madame*

66 *Bovary* than the way what she does is said. The prosecutor clearly sensed this: his *réquisitoire* is mainly the quotation of phrases from the novel, followed by indignant exclamations. Or sometimes he can merely repeat the quoted phrase, adding exclamation points. Such is the case with what may indeed be the most shocking phrase of the novel: "Emma was rediscovering in adultery all the platitudes of marriage": "Emma retrouvait dans l'adultère toutes les platitudes du mariage" (379) [236]. The phrase shocks by its aphoristic generality, also by the "retrouvait," finding again in adultery those platitudes of marriage, and of course by the conclusive panache of that "platitudes of marriage"—recall Charles's talk, flat as a pavement: there is a kind of etymological literalness to "platitudes" here. Note also how what is so shockingly at the core of Emma's experience of would-be passion is a term we normally apply to language use: platitude. Emma rediscovers in the adventure of adultery (recall: "I have a lover! a lover!") the same clichés that define marriage. Language is ruined, and it has ruined passion with it.

Any character in any novel is of course first of all, and literally, a linguistic structure, a set of signs that we imaginatively decipher and construct as "a character." Emma is surely one of the most memorable "characters" of the novels we have read, we want to construct her fully as a person, we live with her aspirations, delusions, disappointments. Yet we repeatedly are given to understand that as a living, breathing character-construction, Emma is a product of language—of her reading, and her reveries on her reading, and of the sociolects that define her world. If she is deluded by language it is because language is delusive. If she falls back into platitude, it is because language is in essence platitude. Complaints about Emma's inauthenticity, her false consciousness and superficiality, are accurate—but perhaps themselves deluded, based on an assumption that we can, some of us, escape to a kind of outside of language as platitude, become once again romantics of the word. *Madame Bovary* may allow us to hover in a zone of ambiguity on this question, and to feel a certain ironic superiority to all the characters of the novel. Flaubert's later work I think will chip away at this zone, pushing especially the cosmic misadventures of his two copyists, Bouvard and Pécuchet, toward a stupidity that lies beyond irony. He no longer allows us to feel superior. The goal of the *Dictionnaire des idées reçues* is after all to "write" a book—in fact composed entirely of citations—written in such a manner "que le lecteur ne sache pas si on se fout de lui, oui ou non": the reader will not know if he is being mocked or not, will not know how to take it. His copyists ruin everything they undertake, from gardening to child rearing. But it is not just their operations that are stupid, it is also the books from which they have copied them.

I have said little about the plot and movement of the novel, how Emma's desertion by Rodolphe leads to prostration, illness, then a phase of religious fervor, and then there is a resurgence of desire provoked by Romantic opera, Gaetano Donizetti's *Lucia di Lammermoor* (text by Walter Scott, of course), in a performance at Rouen where she re-finds Léon, which allows passion to reemerge because it is bathed in this melodramatic fiction. But I won't dwell on Emma and Léon and their movement from enchantment to platitude, because I want to come to the end of the novel, or close to it. Emma's debts mount—and note that they are largely debts for accessories of clothing and other such appurtenances, for herself or for Rodolphe, ordered through Lheureux—and Emma's things are eventually seized, as in any Balzac novel. The bailiff and his crew come to inventory the things that have so much defined her: "They examined her dresses, the linen, the bathroom; and her existence, down to its most intimate secrets, was completely exposed, like a cadaver autopsied, to the eyes of these three men" (384) [240]. Inventorying her clothes and things is like an autopsy: these are after all the things by which we have known her, they constitute what she is. Death is on the horizon, and without any of the poetry Balzac could find in the deaths of some of his sublime women, such as Coralie and Esther. Flaubert dutifully read up on arsenic and its effects, and gives us a detailed and horrible rendition of Emma's painful end.

Consider for a moment the priest's administration of the last rites:

> Then he recited the *Misereatur* and the *Indulgentiam*, dipped his right thumb in the oil and began his unctions: first on the eyes, which had so coveted worldly luxuries; then on the nostrils, avid for warm breezes and the smells of love; then on the mouth, which had opened to lie, which had moaned with pride and cried out in pleasure; then on the hands, which had taken delight in soft touches, and finally on the soles of the feet, once so quick when she ran to the satisfaction of her desires, and which now would walk no more. (418) [265]

We have at this last a final representation of Emma's body as "morselized," as rendered in pieces, in parts of the body explicitly, and erotically, fetishized. Each body part is the occasion for a lyrical evocation of its sensuous, sensual, and erotic uses. The paragraph is of course also a kind of travesty of the extreme unction, suggesting not absolution for the sins of the flesh but regret for their cessation. When, immediately following, Emma dies, it is to the accompaniment of the obscene ditty of the blind beggar, outside her window. Emma begins to laugh, with a horrible, frenetic, desperate laugh, "believing she saw the hideous face of the wretch, who rose up in the eternal shadows like a spectre" (420) [265]. The blind beggar, a kind of dark version of a Shakespearean fool, a figure of de-signification and nothingness, appears to be her last perception of life.

In the aftermath of her death, we are made witness to the ascension of Homais to the status of Writer, and his award of the Legion of Honor, and after Charles's death, bankrupt, his and Emma's daughter, Berthe, sent to work in the cotton mill. Charles, having discovered Emma's affair with Rodolphe, pardons his rival, even wishes he could be him. And when he and Rodolphe meet, Charles speaks his last words in the novel, ascribing all blame to fate: "C'est la faute de la fatalité" (445) [285]—in fact echoing Rodolphe's letter of rupture to Emma: "Est-ce ma faute? O mon Dieu! non, non, n'en accusez que la fatalité!" (278) [163]. Thus the men in Emma's life conspire to articulate her life and death in platitudes, in commonplaces. The lieu-commun, as Sartre noted, is a place where we can all come together, protected from perception and the risk of insight by the platitude of common ground. Flaubert keeps leading us back to the lieu-commun, possibly to suggest that language as our common ground—where we meet and exchange our perceptions—is inherently commonplace. Or more precisely: that the commonplace, the platitude and cliché, especially characterizes language, gives us its essence. Writing was such a slow and painful process for Flaubert because he had to make something new, strange, and beautiful out of a language in essence commonplace. Proust asserts that there is not a single beautiful metaphor in Flaubert's work. He may be right: that is not the kind of beauty Flaubert seeks. Flaubert's sort of beauty comes from the exact placement and alignment of the banal, something akin to Marcel Duchamp's readymades—the urinal, for instance—carefully installed in the space of an art gallery.

All great art is impersonal, it involves an "extinction of personality," as T. S. Eliot famously said, and the doctrine derives directly from Flaubert.

Part of his impersonality—the choice to be a hidden god in his universe, everywhere present but nowhere visible—lies in this respect for the everyday and its habitual things. Flaubert in his correspondence most often rails against the difficulty and servitude of writing. But there are rare moments where he speaks of its pleasure, which is precisely the pleasure of negative capability, of ceasing to be oneself because one enters into other people, animals, things. "It is a delicious thing to write," he says in a letter to Louise Colet when in the midst of creating Emma's seduction by Rodolphe in the woods, "to be no longer yourself but to move around in the whole of one's own creation. Today, for instance, as both man and woman, at the same time lover and mistress, I rode horseback in a forest on an autumn afternoon under the yellow leaves, and I was the horses, the leaves, the wind, the words my people uttered, and the red sun that made them almost close their love-drowned eyes." This alienation of the self in representation of the world may allow us to overcome the kind of contradiction I feel between my insistence on Flaubert's preoccupation with language and my claim that *Madame Bovary* is the indisputable realist novel.

That claim is ratified by his investment in the things of the world, in its detailed surface, in that materiality which displaces authorial personality, to give us a world objectified. But that investment in things also means, to Flaubert, an obsession with the *names* of things: the famous *mot juste*. In its obsession with things, and its laborious descriptive construction of things— Charles's cap, the wedding cake, Binet's useless object—it works to make us see even as it may drain any certain meaning from the thing: that is, we may *see* more purely when we leave meaning to one side. The preoccupation with things and their naming, their linguistic presentation, effectively takes the place of any postulation of interiority—any Romantic soul for Emma. What Roland Barthes would stigmatize as the "cœur romantique des choses" is effectively evacuated by Flaubert (which is why he is the hero of postmodernism). Emma is like the horses and the leaves and the wind: she is a material fact to be rendered in the most precise language you can find.

In an ethical language, we may want to say that Emma is superficial, hollow at the core. And that has been a source of objections to the novel throughout its existence: Henry James, for instance, found Emma "too small an affair," and objected that she and Frédéric (in *L'Education sentimentale*) were such "limited registers and reflectors" of experience. Yes, and James is right on his own terms—which are essentially the terms of the Balzacian novel. James wonders if Flaubert might be incapable of addressing the complicated human soul. Probably Flaubert stands guilty as charged: he's not capable of such, no doubt because he doesn't believe in the existence of complicated souls. Emma's hollowness is a limitation to James, but it is also no doubt part of Flaubert's "point." The kind of "character" we find in James's novels, or in George Eliot, or Proust, even, though more crudely, in Balzac belongs to a different kind of novel from Flaubert's, indeed to another view of what constitutes the human. The misunderstanding between James (whom I take of course as representative of a class of readers) and Flaubert is irreconcilable.

Even James was willing to concede that for what it is, *Madame Bovary* is perfectly done; and that the beauty of its doing makes it a classic. James's language is a bit vague here, but one seems to know what he means. Emma's story and the world in which it unfolds are in their own terms perfectly complete, everything is perfectly rendered. As in a Bruegel painting, nothing is missing. The more you look at it, the more you find that all the details are in place. I might end by circling back to the title: *Madame Bovary*. Flaubert has at the outset brilliantly robbed his heroine of her given name, made her merely Charles Bovary's wife. (Note that she is in fact the third Madame Bovary to appear in the novel, after Charles's mother and his first wife.) The title insists, already, on the conditions of existence that Emma will face, on the constraints on her personhood, and on the overwhelming importance of marriage in the nineteenth-century's stories—especially its importance for women, told to find fulfillment in marriage, and in marriage alone. Adultery is the novelistic master plot for women in the nineteenth century: it is in transgression that Emma, like Anna Karenina and so many others, becomes narratable, becomes an interesting figure to follow. In calling his novel *Madame,* not *Emma Bovary,* Flaubert again finds the right detail, in the right name—the name that robs Emma of her identity, or, rather, that affirms her woman's identity as always already in a state of being not hers.

CHAPTER 5

Courbet's House of Realism

MY UNDERSTANDING OF REALISM TURNS CRUCIALLY ON ITS VISUALITY: ITS primary attention to the visible world, the observation and representation of persons and things. It becomes important, then, to turn to the visual arts, all the more important in that the term *realism*—as critical and polemical label—seems to have been applied, in a consistent way, first of all to painting, most tellingly that of Gustave Courbet. Courbet became the focal figure in the controversies over realism, and he assumed that place largely with relish, accepting with a certain bravado the label he claimed was imposed on him and setting up his own art exhibit under the banner "Pavillon du Réalisme"—House of Realism—in 1855. It is the years around 1850 that are crucial in producing the label "realist"—though you can find a number of scattered uses of the term before then—and the sense of a new movement to take the place of a long-since moribund Romanticism. Since Balzac died in 1850, this makes him a realist only posthumously; but it was in fact in discussion of Balzac that the term *realism* makes some of its earliest appearances: in English, in the *Westminster Review* in 1853, for instance.

Its advent in France surely has much to do with the Revolution of 1848, which overthrew the "bourgeois monarchy" of Louis-Philippe and led to a brief period of a progressive republic—extinguished by Louis-Napoléon Bonaparte in his coup d'état of 2 December 1851, then the declaration of the Second Empire a year later, with this new Bonaparte become Emperor Napoléon III. The year 1848 sparked movements for the "democratization" of art; it conferred on realism an ideological and political identity and urgency, a context in which "the people" was a subject for celebration, as well as for concern, and fear. Courbet's images of the people brought strong reactions.

He was sometimes accused of creating socialist art. (T. J. Clark in *Images of the People* discusses the class references of Courbet's painting.) I don't think 1848 created realism—it was on its way before that—but it provided the context in which realism had to be taken seriously, by its partisans and its detractors.

In France, the label quickly became a rallying cry, a banner, and gave birth to the short-lived journal *Réalisme*, edited by Edmond Duranty, in 1856, and then the volume of his collaborator Champfleury (pseudonym of Jules Husson), under the same title. It is Champfleury's "Sur M. Courbet—Lettre à Madame Sand," which appeared in *L'Artiste* on 2 September 1855, and later as a chapter in his book, that is often considered the "manifesto" of realism.

The occasion of Champfleury's essay was the exhibit on the avenue Montaigne, just a short walk from the Exposition Universelle of 1855, that had over the entrance a sign reading "Du Réalisme. G. Courbet. Exposition de quarante tableaux de son œuvre." Courbet had done well under the Second Republic, following the Revolution of 1848, and the early years of the Second Empire. He had a notorious, noisy, controversial success in the Salon of 1850–51. But by the mid-1850s things were becoming more restrictive. The Exposition Universelle, designed as the showcase of Second Empire glory, included eleven of his paintings, but his vast *L'Atelier du peintre* (*The Painter's Studio*) was turned down by the jury. So in an audacious gesture he set up his own exhibit, making "a direct appeal to the public," as Champfleury puts it—using the plebiscite, you might say, in somewhat the manner of his enemy the Emperor Napoléon III. In the catalogue he composed for the exhibit, Courbet offers a brief polemical statement, claiming that the title of realist was imposed on him and arguing that what he really wants to do is paint the "manners, ideas, and appearance of my time as I see them, in a word, to make living art." But as so often has been the case with labels originally applied by hostile critics—"Impressionism," "Fauvism," and so on—that of realism is taken up with a certain stubborn arrogance, typical of Courbet, and displayed over the entrance to his show.

Champfleury's article suggests that there are by this date four successive scandals in Courbet's career (more would come): the three paintings, *A Burial at Ornans, The Young Ladies of the Village,* and *The Bathers,* and the Pavillon du Réalisme itself. I will come back to some of Champfleury's remarks in discussion of the paintings. Let me first note briefly, before turning to the paintings, that Champfleury's essay provoked Charles Baudelaire's intent to respond—

an intent not realized, but Baudelaire did leave notes for the article he intended to write, under the title *Puisque réalisme il y a* — meaning more or less: since it's there, I have to deal with it. Here he takes the view that Champfleury was guilty of a bad joke in coining the term, and that he "intoxicated" Courbet himself with the notion. Courbet, says Baudelaire, became "the maladroit Machiavelli of this Borgia." Once the canard was launched, Courbet had to believe in it. "Prometheus has his vulture," writes Baudelaire, implying that the idea he had to be a realist became a torturing punishment for Courbet. For Baudelaire, all true artists are "realists" — but their reality is of another world. *Puisque réalisme il y a* turns out to be a kind of Platonist reproach to his friends Champfleury and Courbet — whose paintings he liked — to have misunderstood the nature of art, or at least: to have mistakenly enrolled art to a false ideology. And as we look at Courbet's paintings, it is useful to keep in view both Champfleury's puffery and Baudelaire's perverse dissent.

Courbet came from Ornans, in the Franche-Comté — born in 1819, thus almost an exact contemporary of Flaubert — and made his way to Paris in 1839, and by 1844 he had his first acceptance in the salon. His *After Dinner at Ornans* (*L'Après-Dînée à Ornans*) won a medal at the Salon of 1849, and was purchased by the state, permitting future open entry to the annual salon. The Salon of 1849 was the artist-juried exhibit held during the Second Republic, a short-lived period of political liberalism and also a moment of artistic ferment. Courbet's notoriety dates from the Salon of 1850–51 (postponed because of political unrest, it opened only in December 1850), where he displayed nine works, including three major ones: *The Peasants of Flagey Returning from the Fair, The Stonebreakers,* and *A Burial at Ornans*. The paintings created an outcry and an uproar, especially the *Burial*.

The *Burial* — in its full original title, *Tableau de figures humaines, historique d'un enterrement à Ornans* — is huge, approximately ten by twenty-two feet (fig. 5). Its immense size was to contemporaries part of its scandalous quality. It is on a heroic scale usually reserved for the grandeur of history painting — the highest form of painting, that traditionally prized in the academies and the competitions — yet its subject matter is humble, or worse: low, vulgar, a bunch of villagers who don't even have the dignity of peasants dressed in traditional regional garb, who are on the contrary done up in their Sunday best (like Flaubert's Norman peasants and bourgeois *notables* at the famous agricultural fair of *Madame Bovary*). Nor are they represented in the traditional gestures of

Fig. 5. Gustave Courbet, *L'Enterrement à Ornans*, 1849, oil on canvas. Musée d'Orsay, Paris. Photo: Scala / Art Resource, NY

peasant life (as, for instance, in Jean-François Millet's *Sower* [see fig. 7] or his *Gleaners*), but at this local funeral, which seems to have no particular claim to the spectator's attention—yet by its heroic dimensions demands attention. As Champfleury put it in his "Lettre à Madame Sand," "Monsieur Courbet is a troublemaker on account of having represented in good faith bourgeois, peasants, and village dames in full size." What's most to the point here is the perception that the scandal of the *Burial* derives both from subject and treatment, and principally the treatment of this subject.

Most of all, reactions to the *Burial* stressed its ugliness. "Vive le laid, le laid seul est aimable!" ("Long live ugliness! Only she is lovable") wrote Champfleury in parody of a famous line in praise of the beauty of truth from the neoclassical poetician Nicolas Boileau. The manner of the painting was seen as ugly: this unfocused linear structure with its straggling line of figures, its horizontality emphasized by the line of the chalk cliff, the *causse*, in the background. The space of the painting seems both crowded and disorganized. To the extent that there is any focal point to which the eye is led, it appears to be the grave itself, the gaping hole foreground center. As Michael Fried notes (in a complex reading of the painting to which I will not attempt to do justice), that grave virtually cuts the ground out from under the viewer's feet: as we stand before the painting, we feel we might fall into this newly dug hole.

The referents of the painting seem clear enough: those middle- and peasant-class inhabitants of Ornans who have come to the burial and whose faces are particularized in the manner of portraits from life (and they were in fact portraits done by Courbet from his fellow townspeople). The original full title of the painting, with its phrase "historique d'un enterrement à Ornans," suggests a specificity of event, the recording of *a* burial. Yet why this one? Whose burial is it, and why does it warrant commemoration, in the manner of earlier representations of the interment of saints and aristocrats? That question is never answered by the painting. And indeed, as Fried points out, the apparent preoccupation with the specificity of the individuals portrayed, noted by many commentators, seems largely subverted by the painting as a whole, which draws attention rather to the massing of figures, their generic quality as mourners, and their nature as crowd—since they seem to be too many for the space they occupy.

The meanings of the painting, then, are enigmatic. Like its composition, what it intends to say to us appears heterodox and unspecifiable. What's its point, why this heroic consecration of what is at most deserving of treatment in a modest *tableau de genre*? A contemporary critic, Prosper Haussard, asked what one was to make of

> this long file of ludicrous masks and deformities copied from life, this village cleric and his priceless acolytes; those two churchwardens with noses as crimson as their robes; this joker with the funny hat and turned-up moustaches who carries the coffin, this brawny grave-digger who poses solemnly on one knee at the graveside; this seriousness and this buffoonery, these tears, these grimaces, this Sunday-best mourning, in black coat, in smock, in beguine cap, all adding up to a funeral from some carnival, ten yards long, an immense ballad in painting, where there is more to laugh at than to make you cry?

The problem has been well summarized in an essay by Françoise Gaillard: objections to the painting concerned at once the objects *represented* in the painting, considered ugly, inappropriate, shocking; the manner of *representation*, seen as inept, unharmonious, badly composed and painted; and even the very notion of the *representable*: what one should or even could show, the sense of generic violation caused by the size of the painting, the claim to attention it made. One might see here a perception that Courbet's tableau works a kind of "desymbolization," similar to that wrought by Flaubert: there is no transformation of an ugly reality in the process of its representation, no rhetoric of sentimentality to redeem it, no promise of transfiguration. One might ask, finally, what might be the *place* of such a painting? In what literal place could it hang, since it is too large for the private house and clearly unsuitable for a church? It seems to claim a place only in the museum, the space of other burial artifacts. Figuratively, its place in art history is equally problematic: it appears to de-dramatize prior grave painting, to deconstruct any tradition to which it might be said to belong—largely a Christian tradition. Once again, Flaubert appears the relevant literary counterpart.

The *Burial* has elicited extensive commentary in our own time, as critics try to come to terms with its revolutionary place in nineteenth-century painting: the work of Fried, of Clark, of Linda Nochlin has been especially important. From my perspective—that of "realist vision"—the painting is as crucial in its medium as *Madame Bovary* in the literary. It achieves the same arrest of our attention, in subject and manner—indeed because subject and manner have been made consubstantial in a very new way. Like Flaubert's use of *style indirect libre* to render the sociolects and the mental world of the citizens of Yonville l'Abbaye without espousing them, and without giving us any firm place to stand in understanding and judging them, Courbet's challenging and somewhat indecipherable composition and painterly style make us pay attention without providing a firm orientation to our attitudes and evaluations. And that surely is part of what Courbet is up to. The commentary his painting has elicited—often contradictory and contentious—points most obviously to a disorientation that is again comparable to Flaubert's. Reading, and viewing, have now become more uncomfortable.

Another conscious provocation on Courbet's part comes with the subsequent monstrously large painting *The Painter's Studio* (*L'Atelier du peintre*), subtitled "real allegory," *allégorie réelle*. To the listing of this painting in the catalogue of the Pavillon du Réalisme exhibit, Courbet defiantly appends a note to the effect that catalogues of previous exhibits that assigned him a master with whom he had trained were in error. "I have never had any other masters in painting than nature and tradition, than the public and work." While he accepts the notion of "tradition"—and clearly knows the tradition in painting well—his rejection of the very idea that he should have studied in the workshop of a master—as many of even the most innovative nineteenth-century French painters did—typifies Courbet's attitude, his public and polemic determination to be seen as new and nontraditional, to represent a moment of revolutionary potential in art as in politics. The oxymoronic subtitle to *The Painter's Studio* made Champfleury hesitant: "*real allegory* . . . here are two words that swear together and trouble me somewhat. . . . confusion about that famous term *realism* is already bad enough without its being necessary to fog things up more" ["*allégorie réelle*. . . voilà deux mots qui jurent ensemble, et qui me troublent un peu. . . . la confusion est déjà assez grande à propos de ce fameux mot *réalisme*, sans qu'il soit nécessaire de l'embrouiller encore davantage"]. The "real allegory" has been over the years an invitation to critical commentary from the sober to the delirious. For my purposes, it suffices to note Courbet's apparent claim that the painter's real—what has come into his studio—is subject to allegorization, and perhaps ultimately flows from and through that paintbrush Courbet brandishes in the middle of the vast canvas.

Somewhat smaller in size but also of revolutionary force was another painting from that Salon of 1850–51, *The Stonebreakers* (*Les Casseurs de pierre*), a work we now know only through its reproductions, since it was destroyed by the firebombing of Dresden during World War II (fig. 6). Again, it presents the humble of the earth on a scale considered inappropriate for such subject matter. These rustic workers engaged in unskilled and exhausting manual labor are notably unsentimentalized. What we feel most of all are the gestures of their work, the downward swing of the hammer, the strain of lifting the stone-filled basket. And we see these movements through the folds and creases and strains of their ragged clothing, not in the naked musculature of Greek statuary. The man is old, we almost feel too old for such labor, and the boy with his torn shirt and single suspender no doubt (as Courbet himself commented) will end up resembling his older partner. As Michael Fried has effectively shown, Courbet holds a major place in the antitheatrical tradition of painting: that tradition which reacts against overt theatricality and display in painting, and does so in part by turning its figures away from the gaze of the spectator, showing them absorbed in their own activities, unaware that they are on display. Not only are the two figures looking away, their faces are completely unknowable to the spectator—another way of refusing sentiment, and directing our attention to the bodily gestures of the painting. Again, as with Flaubert one senses a de-dramatization of representation, a refusal to allow the world recorded to take on a more than literal meaning.

This literalness of *The Stonebreakers* is perhaps most striking and significant because of its subject, that is: work. The representation of work is an interesting topic in its own right, and clearly related to the realist claim to embrace new areas of life never before considered representable, as in the Goncourt brothers' notion of a "right to the novel" for all social strata, and in Zola's systematic conquest of new areas of social life for representation. The "painting of modern life" brought by Edouard Manet and his followers would include some of the gestures and postures of work, perhaps most particularly by Gustave Caillebotte and Edgar Degas. Earlier, one can (in too sweeping a generalization) say that most images of work are romanticized and, especially, seen as part of a pastoral convention of happy and picturesque peasants. This is still true in the work of Millet, who clearly attempts to present a more particularized image of the peasant at work, and to capture the bodily movement and gravity of work, but who nonetheless seems to us to romanticize, sentimentalize, and in the process depersonalize his peasant characters. His *Sower* (*Le Semeur*, fig. 7) hung in the same Salon of 1850 with Courbet's *Burial* and *Stonebreakers*. Its claim on our attention is quite dif-

Fig. 6. Gustave Courbet, *Les Casseurs de pierre*, 1849, oil on canvas. Formerly Gemäldegalerie, Dresden, destroyed 1945. Photo: Yale Visual Resources

Fig. 7. Jean-François Millet, *Le Semeur*, 1850, oil on canvas. Museum of Fine Arts, Boston. Gift of Quincy Adams Shaw through Quincy Adams Shaw, Jr., and Mrs. Marian Shaw Haughton. Photo: © 2004 Museum of Fine Arts, Boston

ferent from that of Courbet's paintings, and the contrast may further demonstrate how Courbet was intent to demythologize and deromanticize his images of work. It is tempting to introduce here, as another kind of contrast, Ford Madox Brown's painting *Work*, started in 1852 though completed only in 1865, commissioned for Manchester City Hall (fig. 8). As a mural in the municipal building of the chief site of the Industrial Revolution in England, Brown's painting is not surprisingly an allegory. Even so, its view of work may be excessively Ruskinian (and comparable to what Dickens appears to value in *Hard Times*) rather than an attempt to come to terms with the reality of work in Manchester. The conception of work in the mural is suggested by the sonnet written to accompany it, which begins: "Work, which beads the brow and tans the flesh / Of lusty manhood, casting out its devils."

It is worth considering Champfleury's third "scandal," *The Bathers (Les Baigneuses)* of 1853—which did indeed cause a scandal when exhibited at the Salon of 1853 (fig. 9). "A Hottentot Venus," Théophile Gautier huffed; and most contemporary reactions insisted on the incomprehensible ugliness of this fleshy woman emerging from a sylvan pool. The painting remains enigmatic today: What to make of the bather's seemingly sublime gesture—recalling that of Christ in traditional paintings of the *noli mi tangere*—and the responsive ecstatic gaze and posture of the clothed acolyte? Like a later painting that will play off this one, and also create a scandal, Manet's *Le Déjeuner sur l'herbe*, Courbet evidently wants to use the iconography of the pastoral, even Arcadian setting—the rich, verdant foliage, the clear forest pool—to make a statement that demythologizes the tradition. His woman is fleshy, the folds of her body emphasized, because the Arcadian nude is airbrushed, smoothed, her body elegantly unrelated to muscle and fat. Courbet's bather has hung her clothing on a tree branch, as anyone would before going in the water; whereas Arcadian nudes have drapery—if any covering at all—not clothing. In a distinction applied by some critics contemporaneous with Courbet, his nude is naked more than she is nude in the traditional sense. One thinks, in contrast, of François Boucher's numerous Venuses and Dianas coyly undressed with a foot about to enter the water, or drying themselves after the bath. But of course this tradition of the nude continued in Courbet's time, absent the playfulness of Boucher: most of the mid-nineteenth-century salon nudes are humorless, a diligent exercise in pin-up art.

Fig. 8. Ford Madox Brown, *Work*, 1852–65, oil on canvas. Manchester City Art Galleries. Photo: © Manchester Art Gallery

Fig. 9. Gustave Courbet, *Les Baigneuses*, 1853, oil on canvas. Musée Fabre, Montpellier. Photo: © Frédéric Jaulmes

To take only the greatest of the mythologizing nudes with which Courbet had to contend, consider Jean-Auguste-Dominique Ingres's *The Spring* (*La Source*) of 1856 (fig. 10). Ingres may make good on a claim to revive and modernize for contemporary taste a classicizing tradition of the nude, though one in which the support of the classical reference has become purely conventional, almost camp. Ingres's imitators—such salon artists as Alexandre Cabanel, Eugène-Emmanuel Amaury-Duval, William Bouguereau—would do far worse. The Ingres type of nude is perhaps the best context in which to understand the deconstructive enterprise of Courbet's *Bathers*: his desire to say no to an idealizing and impersonalizing, while simultaneously an eroticizing, treatment of the nude. Courbet will later—in the 1860s—produce some overtly erotic nudes himself, though always with an effort to pry them away from the salon tradition. But in the painting of 1853, he seems most of all to want to denounce the very tradition of the nude itself, to make the claim of massive flesh as what demands the attention of the realist.

The nude, as a number of critics have noted, was increasingly a problem to nineteenth-century painters who wanted to break with the academic tradition and to do something closer to real life. The human body was surely a central phenomenon of the real, needing representation. Yet the nude was preeminently a product of culture rather than nature, a generalization and idealization from nature, wholly conventional and therefore very difficult to rethink in realist terms, or in terms of the "painting of modern life" pioneered by Manet. If in Greek art the male nude had offered the baseline of the heroic body—in a tradition one finds successfully revived and illustrated as late as Jacques-Louis David—in the nineteenth century the female nude comes to predominate almost exclusively, no doubt because the ideal became largely one of erotic beauty not heroic activity, and also because in the neoclassicizing canon the female body was more susceptible to idealization, to a kind of representation that doesn't so much observe as perpetuate a myth. Courbet in his *Bathers*—like Manet ten years later in his *Olympia*—takes on the nude precisely as a way to denounce that tradition. As a result, it is easier to say what *The Bathers* is not doing than what it is: its rejections are clearer than its affirmations.

At this point, we need an excursus on photography. One can date the invention of photography from 1839, when Louis Daguerre's procedure was

Fig. 10. Jean-Auguste Dominique Ingres, *La Source*, 1856, oil on canvas. Musée d'Orsay, Paris. Photo: Herve Lewandowski, Réunion des Musées Nationaux / Art Resource, NY

presented to the French Assembly by François Arago—though experiments by Daguerre and others, including the Englishman Henry Fox Talbot, start even earlier. Thus the coming of photography largely coincides with the coming of realism in the visual and literary arts. Is this to say that photography creates realism, by offering the first true reproduction of the real? One could I think with equal plausibility say the opposite: that realism, as an aesthetic, a project, a stance toward the world, invents photography. At least, the invention of photography almost seems inevitable in the context of realism; and when it is invented, it appears at once as the ally and tool of realism. The camera obscura had been around for centuries: the box with a pinhole to admit light, which threw an image against the wall opposite. Artists used the camera obscura as an aid to drawing: they could trace or copy the image produced in the box. The nineteenth century saw an accelerating search for a substance that would fix the image projected in the box—so that it would be light itself doing the drawing (the meaning of *photography* or the other early name, *heliography*). Thus would the hand of the artist be eliminated. You would realize the effort, most evident from Flaubert to Zola, to eliminate the subjectivity of the author or artist, creating that sort of "transparent screen" on the real world that Zola hoped to achieve. Of course the hand of the artist is not gone, it has rather been displaced: to the manipulation of the lens. Nonetheless, with nature as apparent artist, photography seems to promise the truest record yet of the exterior world, a medium in which the term *representation* might be replaced by "presentation," since there is no apparent translation into another code, another system of conventions of representation. If we know this to be false, and can talk about the aesthetic composition and choices of a photograph, nonetheless there does also seem to be a sense in which the photograph, unlike any other medium, records a moment of the real. It confers a special importance on the actual referent of the image: something that was once there, for a moment, and now has no doubt changed, perhaps even disappeared. As Roland Barthes and other critics have suggested, photographs seem particularly allied to death, in the absoluteness of the photographic image, its message of: this was once here, and no longer is. This may in turn suggest how photography is complicit with an emotion that comes to the fore with new intensity in the nineteenth century: nostalgia, the wistful love for that which is passing away.

Shortly after its invention, photography was enlisted in the recording of an urban landscape that was about to disappear. Charles Marville, in particular, was employed by the Second Empire to record the old, insalubrious quarters of Paris—dating back in some cases to medieval times—that would be replaced in Baron Georges-Eugène Haussmann's radical rebuilding of Paris in the 1850s and 1860s. Like so many of Marville's photos, this one leads the eye into a deep recess, in a fascination with perspective and depth-of-field that almost teaches optical nostalgia (fig. 11). That Marville's remarkable photos of old Paris suggest that he fell in love with what was condemned to the wrecker's ball underlines the fascination of the referent viewed through the lens.

It is striking that within only a few years of its invention, photography seems to discover all the uses to which it can be put: not only landscape, very much including cityscape, but also tourism, recording monuments seen (and leading quickly to the picture postcard). And then portraiture, including the deathbed portrait—taken shortly after death—and the photographic calling card. It was quickly enlisted also in the quest to record and classify the malefactors of society, the criminal populations that were more and more perceived as a threat in contemporary cities. The systematic descriptions and measurements invented by Alphonse Bertillon—known as *Bertillonage*—especially as a method for identifying recidivists included photographs as well. Somewhat later, Francis Galton would experiment with superimposed photographic negatives in an effort to define the physical "type" of the criminal. Bertillonage was the dominant European system for recording those who ran afoul of the law until its gradual replacement by fingerprinting, in the early years of the twentieth century. Photography also immediately was put to erotic and pornographic uses—uses that again seem almost predetermined, given the affinities of pinhole and peephole. It was immediately apparent that the photograph permits a spying into situations of privacy and intimacy. Many of the early erotic images imitate the poses of the academic painted nude. Others quickly learn to mime the invasion of privacy that they claim to perform. Photographs of the nude offer a prime example—portraiture is another—of how photography and painting will begin a continuing interchange, photographers learning composition from painters, painters using photos as studies for their projects (fig. 12). A number of the early photographers had trained as painters. Daguerre himself was originally a set designer for the popular theater—melodrama, for instance—

Fig. 11. Charles Marville, *Rue Chartière (Impasse Chartière)*, 1865–69, albumin print.
Photo courtesy Howard Greenberg Gallery, NYC

Fig. 12. Bruno Braquehais, *Reclining Female Nude Seen from the Back*, 1855–56, stereoscopic photograph. © Paris, Roger Thérond Collection. Photo: Patrice Schmidt

and the inventor of the diorama: someone interested in techniques of lighting and the creation of illusions.

When the invention of photography was announced in France—with some fanfare, since the state voted itself a monopoly of the new procedure—the history painter Paul Delaroche is said to have exclaimed: "This is the death of painting!" The attribution may be apocryphal, since Delaroche is also recorded as saying that the "accuracy of the lines" and the "nicety of form" in photography could be useful tools in the training of painters. Nonetheless, there may be an important sense in which the coming of photography did doom Delaroche's kind of highly theatrical, indeed stagy painting. Although there were plenty of attempts at staged photographic scenes, the use of the camera became essentially a record of the phenomenal world (especially, outdoor phenomena, given the limitations of artificial light at the time). Photography on the whole has a kind of sobriety (this may be especially true before the coming of color) and tends to beckon us with the implied statement "here is the real, look on it," that must have helped make Delaroche's hyperdramatic paintings soon appear dated (fig. 13). (For our own time, we have the highly ironized and sophisticated drama of Cindy Sherman's Film Stills, for instance.) More generally, it can be argued that the coming of photography proved a liberation for painting: the photo lens's view of the world now is present; it offers a possibly definitive image, but also a challenge. It is something to be gone beyond, toward a possibly more expressionistic image. One can see many painters, including Manet and Degas, using photos (including photos of prior art) as their starting point, precisely in order to be able to go beyond them.

Photography lent itself to the creation of a record—not only criminals but the illustrious dead. If it could not at this point in its history deal with fast motion, since it demanded a long exposure time, it early recorded warfare particularly through its dead and its devastation. The Crimean War was one of the first to leave a considerable photographic archive. And in the United States, the Civil War produced the remarkable photos of Mathew Brady and others. The insurgency of the Paris Commune in 1871, near the end of the Franco-Prussian War (the Communards were among other things opposed to a peace treaty with the Prussians), left a surprisingly large photographic record, especially of the destruction of Paris monuments caused by the fires set during the Commune's death agonies, but also of some notable events

Fig. 13. Paul Delaroche, *The Execution of Lady Jane Grey*, 1833, oil on canvas. © The National Gallery, London

before then. One event carefully recorded was the destruction of the column of the place Vendôme, a largely political act—the column was surmounted by a statute of the first Napoléon, and France had just gotten rid of Napoléon III—though there was the excuse that the hard-pressed Communards needed to melt the brass bas-reliefs with which the column was decorated to make musket balls. After the bloody suppression of the Commune by government troops, responsibility for the felling of the Vendôme column was laid squarely and personally on Courbet, who had served as chief of the Federation of Artists during the Commune (fig. 14). He was arrested, imprisoned, tried, and convicted to a six-month prison term. He entered Sainte-Pélagie prison in September 1871, and painted his self-portrait as prisoner, following his liberation. The conservative government of national reconstruction that ushered in the Third Republic decided that Courbet must personally bear the entire expense of reconstructing the Vendôme column—a sum of 323,000 francs. Under this judgment, Courbet, by then in exile in Switzerland, lost all hope of returning to France.

He offered another kind of self-portrait from exile in Switzerland in a painting of 1872, The Trout (La Truite, fig. 15). This hooked and doomed trout, bleeding already from the gills, is painted with the meticulous realism that Courbet brought to his numerous other paintings of animals, particularly in hunting scenes. Here the painting is, unusually, from the point of view of the quarry. And the painting could, like The Painter's Studio, carry the oxymoronic subtitle allégorie réelle: it is both a piece of the real and a representation of a state of being, as Courbet appears to stress in the Latin inscription he has written into the lower left-hand corner: "in vinculis faciebat" ("it was made in chains"). As such, it offers not only a painful image of the artist brought to bay by political reversal and the downfall of the camp he had remained faithful to since the Revolution of 1848. It also gives an image of the kinds of contradiction that may inhabit Courbet's realism—and perhaps all realism. If there is much of Flaubertian deconstruction in Courbet, the refusal of traditional systems of meaning-making, there also is a streak far closer to Balzac: a kind of expressionism, a use of the things of the real to write allegories of existence.

Baudelaire, who thought photography a degraded art inimical to the pursuit of the ideal, refers acidly, in his review of the Salon of 1859, to his compatriots' immediate enchantment with Daguerre's invention, their conclu-

Fig. 14. *Toppled Column on the Place Vendôme*, 1871, photograph. McCormick Library of Special Collections, Northwestern University Library

Fig. 15. Gustave Courbet, *La Truite*, 1872, oil on canvas. © 2004 Kunsthaus Zürich. All rights reserved

sion that "an industry that would give us a result identical to nature would be the absolute art." With the coming of photography, "this unspeakable society rushed, like a collective Narcissus, to contemplate its trivial image on the metal plate." He adds that photography should return to its real duty as humble servant of arts and sciences, comparable to printing and stenography. Baudelaire's dissent was clearly enlisted in a lost cause, as society since Daguerre has progressed from one visual self-representation to another and, indeed, become largely preoccupied with vision and spectacle. Baudelaire saw very well the links of visuality and realism, both of which represented to him certain spiritual impoverishment. He evokes the "thousands of avid eyes" that peered into the stereoscope when it was invented, "as if looking though the windows of the infinite." Baudelaire's scorn may not be merited, though: the realist vision can modulate to visionary forms, all the while affirming the primacy of the visual and the real.

CHAPTER 6

George Eliot's Delicate Vessels

SINCE SELF-CONSCIOUS "REALISM" IN THE NINETEENTH-CENTURY NOVEL IS SO much a French invention, it is never clear that any English novelist quite fits the rubric. But if any Victorian novelist does, it would seem to be George Eliot. At least: the George Eliot of *Adam Bede, Felix Holt,* and, especially, *Middlemarch.* My choice instead of Eliot's remarkable last novel, *Daniel Deronda,* may be a bit perverse. Yet it seems to me a novel that first sums up a certain Victorian tradition of the novel, then leaps beyond it, or explodes it. In this sense, its relation to its precursor texts is not unlike Proust's relation to Balzac and Flaubert, though of course its writing, its manner, remains within the conventions of Victorian fiction, which may make Eliot's accomplishment here all the more remarkable. It is a novel that at once exemplifies and explodes the tradition to which it belongs. Consider in this regard what it does with the traditional marriage plot, of Jane Austen and others: how it contains one of the fullest, most detailed examples of that plot, yet uses it finally as a springboard to something very different, radically heterogeneous.

Daniel Deronda from its very first sentence seems to want to confront the question of its relation to the tradition, in its evocation of all the scenes of visual inspection—especially, the looking-over of women by men—so characteristic of realist fiction.

> Was she beautiful or not beautiful? and what was the secret of form or expression which gave the dynamic quality to her glance? Was the good or the evil genius dominant in those beams? Probably the evil; else why was the effect that of unrest rather than of undisturbed charm? Why was the wish to look again felt as coercion and not as a longing in which the whole being consents? (7)

A wholly remarkable first paragraph, which turns into a series of interroga-
tions the usual presentation of woman as object of the gaze. You can often
find the Balzacian narrator interrogating the appearances before him (as in
his presentation of the denizens of the Pension Vauquer, at the start of *Le Père
Goriot*), but here the questioning vision turned on the world doubles back on
the observer himself, who will not be named until the first sentence of the
next paragraph: "She who raised these questions in Daniel Deronda's mind
was occupied in gambling." This delay in naming the observer raises in the
reader's mind a momentary doubt about his or her own position in regard
to this act of looking, our apparent implication in the looking game. If, as
Laura Mulvey famously taught us, women are coded for "looked-at-ness,"
here there is already trouble in that coding, in the looker's sense of "coer-
cion" in the act.

"Looking" is pursued throughout the early parts of the novel, and is indeed an integral part of Gwendolen Harleth's story. A few paragraphs from
the start, her eyes will meet Deronda's—and now his gaze at her will seem
to act as an evil eye, causing a reversal of fortunes at the gambling table. She
becomes conscious of his observation of her, and looks at him in turn. By
the end of the chapter, she searches for another opportunity to see him, to
observe his "measuring gaze"; then, after receiving her mother's letter announcing the family's sudden impoverishment, she decides not to return to
the gambling table because of the "exasperating irony" of Deronda's gaze.
Note that this is juxtaposed to her act of kissing her own image in the mirror
of her hotel room. And throughout this first section of the novel, titled "The
Spoiled Child," we see Gwendolen over and over again looking at herself
in mirrors—upon arrival at Offendene, for instance, and just before Grandcourt comes to propose marriage—and seeing herself as mirrored in the
gazes of others. At Brackenshaw Park, for example, where she will first meet
Grandcourt: "She was the central object of that pretty picture, and every one
present must gaze at her. That was enough: she herself was determined to
see nobody in particular" (107). Yet the narrator warns us in passing of the
limitations of the visual, noting that "Sir Joshua [Reynolds] would have been
glad to take her portrait"—and would have had an easier time of it than the
"historian," obliged not only to record "one beautiful moment" but as well
"to represent the truth of change" (117).

Of the "truth of change," of temporality as constitutive of the novel, there will be more to say. But I want to stay for another moment with the opening scene of the novel. Gwendolen is gambling, and incurring Deronda's disapproval, as well as fascination, for doing so. As the result of her losses at the table—which she blames on Deronda—and her summons home to a bankrupted family, Gwendolen pawns the necklace of turquoises she has inherited from her father, whom she has never known—whose place was early taken by the hapless Davilow—then redeemed by Deronda and returned in a small packet (the first of a number of packets in this novel) with a note expressing the hope "that she will not again risk the loss of it" (20). We will discover that jewels are to be the most important representation of Gwendolen, and of the feminine, in the novel, and particularly of the feminine as defined and regulated by patriarchy. And there is something in the pawning of the necklace, precisely a token of inheritance from the father, and about gambling that displeases as well as fascinates the gazing and rather priggish Deronda. It's not wholly implausible to recall Dora's *Schmuckkästchen*, in Freud's case history: the jewel box of Dora's dream that Freud wishes to interpret as a genital representation. Nothing in this novel better represents the patriarchal attempt to control and barter female sexuality than the drama of the jewels. And in this context, as in *Dora*, Gwendolen's gambling reads as a kind of illicit play, a kind of public masturbation, which both coerces Deronda's glance and triggers his moral censorship.

Eliot proleptically rewrites Freud's case history by making Gwendolen, too, subject to hysteria, hysteria that is precisely linked to self-display, most fully represented in the scene of the charades at Offendene. The episode of course recalls Austen's *Mansfield Park*, and the reprobation of amateur theatricals that there, too, are closely linked to the Crawfords' ill-governed sexuality. Gwendolen instigates the charades in order to strike a "statuesque pose" in Greek dress under the eyes of the enamored Rex Gascoigne, who selects the scene from act 5 of *The Winter's Tale*. But at the moment Hermione is to be redeemed from death—"Music, awake her, strike!"—Herr Klesmer's chord on the piano causes the mysterious wall panel to open, to reveal the picture of the dead face and fleeing figure, and to turn Gwendolen into "a statue into which a soul of Fear had entered" (61). Shakespeare's scene is about redemption from a "death" caused by Leontes' insane jealousy, and his subsequent long-suffering penitence—redemption through a kind of miracle of passionate love. "O! she's warm," exclaims Leontes. "If this be magic, let it be

an art / Lawful as eating" (5.3.107–9). The effect in *Daniel Deronda* is the opposite: Gwendolen goes from life to death, a Medusa-like freezing in fear, what
the narrator will call a fit of "spiritual dread" (63). Here, as in Shakespeare,
the effect is related to love, again with opposite results. The scene of charades is followed by Rex Gascoigne's declaration of love for her, which produces not only rejection but disgust, an excessive reaction against the possibility of sexual passion. As the narrator comments, "now the life of passion
had begun negatively in her" (81)—a curious and interesting characteriza-
tion, which stands on the threshold of her courtship by Grandcourt and her
glorying in the power to reject him. That she does not reject him seems indeed to derive from his elaborate repression of sexual aggressivity during the
courtship, his choice to speak of how he will provide for her impoverished
mother. "She had a momentary phantasmal love for this man who chose his
words so well, and who was a mere incarnation of delicate homage" (302),
and "She had no alarm lest he meant to kiss her" (304). Grandcourt's virility
at this moment in the novel is transferred onto the horses he parades before
Gwendolen's window: "the beautiful creatures, in their fine grooming, sent
a thrill of exultation through Gwendolen. They were the symbols of command and luxury" (304).

Gwendolen's decision to marry Grandcourt is largely the subject of the
first three hundred pages of this novel—the length and matter of many an
ordinary novel—which in *Daniel Deronda* seem to offer (and this is not unlike
Balzac's practice) a very long and explicit, and in this case very subtle, motivation for its central plot. Here is a prime instance of Eliot's claim to realism: the scrupulously detailed account of the socioeconomic constraints that
create the impasse from which Gwendolen sees an exit only in a marriage
she does not want. Her marriage to Grandcourt will of course be not only a
mistaken choice, like so many such choices in the nineteenth-century novel,
but also a moral fault; and it is important, Eliot believes, that the reader
understand all the extenuating circumstances pleading for Gwendolen: the
family's plunge into poverty, the impending loss of the house at Offendene,
her mother's prostration under calamity, her own destiny as governess at
Mrs. Mompert's, her aspiration to a professional singing career thoroughly
deflated by Klesmer. In her rewriting of the traditional marriage plot, Eliot
gives the most detailed possible circumstantial justification for Gwendolen's
act and allows us to see how she becomes Grandcourt's wife almost despite

her will, certainly despite her better judgment—and does so, one might almost say, because of his horses, those symbols of command and freedom.

The moral fault—what makes marriage to Grandcourt far worse than the deluded choice of an Emma Bovary, for instance—is the knowledge of Grandcourt's ex-mistress and illegitimate children, and their claim to happiness. It is part of Eliot's genius here to have Lydia Glasher and her claim appear *before* Gwendolen consents to Grandcourt. Lydia Glasher's first appearance in the novel, at the Whispering Stones, is, like her name, a moment of high melodrama. But I think conventional melodrama would have had this figure from Grandcourt's past appear only after Gwendolen's marriage. Eliot wants the effect to be, not merely melodramatic, but charged with moral dilemma: Gwendolen indeed promises Lydia that she will refuse Grandcourt's marriage proposal—and she will in fact flee to the Continent to avoid it, until she is constrained by poverty to return. The import of Lydia's appearance is stated in the mode of moral terror: "it was as if some ghastly vision had come to her in a dream and said, 'I am a woman's life'" (152). I am a woman's life: and when she comes on Lydia again, while riding in Rotten Row, Lydia appears as a "Medusa-apparition" (605, 606). Eliot asks throughout Gwendolen's story: How, as a woman, can one live life? What are the possibilities of life in such a system of patriarchically imposed constraints?

In one of those ruminative passages we associate with Eliot's narration, the narrator at the end of chapter 11 memorably evokes the American Civil War in contrast to the trivial domesticities of the marriage plot: "Could there be a slenderer, more insignificant thread in human history than this consciousness of a girl, busy with her small inferences of the way in which she could make her life pleasant?"—at a time when "women on the other side of the world would not mourn for the husbands and sons who died bravely in a common cause, and men stinted of bread on our side of the world heard of that willing loss and were patient: a time when the soul of man was waking to pulses which had for centuries been beating in him unfelt, until their full sum made a new life of terror or of joy." At this moment of contrast between the usual matter of the Victorian novel—"this consciousness of a girl"—and the epic struggle and its consequences, the narrator turns the tables, to ask: "What in the midst of that mighty drama are girls and their blind visions? They are the Yea or Nay of that good for which men are enduring and fighting. In these delicate vessels is borne onward through the ages the treasure of human affections" (124). We could read this as an apologia for what one might call the Richardsonian novel: the novel focused on domesticity, woman's private life and moral choices, and on, ultimately, the womb, as that delicate vessel of transmission—which is certainly a central subject of this novel. And yet, if it is within the delicate vessels of woman's moral consciousness that the great issues of history must be tested, the delicate vessels mainly appear in the novel as subjected to a sociosexual marketplace, to a system of barter. The marriage market to which Gwendolen is submitted—and her uncle the Reverend Gascoigne is forever commenting on what kind of a marriage she may or may not expect to make—and the off-market represented by Lydia Glasher suggest ironic readings of the narrator's eloquent apologia for the novel's marriage plot. And in Gwendolen's marriage to Grandcourt, the delicate vessel will appear to be struck with a curse—from which Gwendolen can never recover in a reproductive sense; it strikes her with sterility.

I am referring to the moment when, at the threshold of her wedding night with Grandcourt, Gwendolen receives from Lydia Glasher the packet containing the ancestral diamonds—Grandcourt's mother's diamonds—he earlier gave Lydia and has demanded back for his legitimate wife. This has been preceded by still another packet, containing the engagement ring, which would also merit discussion—why does Grandcourt send the ring and force Gwendolen to place it on her finger herself?—and will be followed by much more business with jewelry. It is in her new mirror-paneled boudoir at Ryelands that Gwendolen sinks into a "creeping luxurious languour" as she awaits Grandcourt, dinner, and bed. The arrival of the packet of diamonds changes all that. It is worth quoting here from Gwendolen's opening of the packet all the way to the end of the chapter:

> Within all the sealed paper coverings was a box, but within the box there was a jewel-case; and now she felt no doubt that she had the diamonds. But on opening the case, in the same instant that she saw their gleam she saw a letter lying above them. She knew the handwriting of the address. It was as if an adder had lain on them. Her heart gave a leap which seemed to have spent all her strength; and as she opened the bit of thin paper, it shook with the trembling of her hands. But it was legible as print, and thrust its words upon her.
> "These diamonds, which were once given with ardent love to Lydia Glasher, she passes on to you. You have broken your word to her, that you might possess what was hers. Perhaps you think of being happy, as she once

was, and of having beautiful children such as hers, who will thrust hers aside. God is too just for that. The man you have married has a withered heart. His best young love was mine; you could not take that from me when you took the rest. It is dead; but I am the grave in which your chance of happiness is buried as well as mine. You had your warning. You have chosen to injure me and my children. He had meant to marry me. He would have married me at last, if you had not broken your word. You will have your punishment. I desire it with all my soul.

"Will you give him this letter to set him against me and ruin us more — me and my children? Shall you like to stand before your husband with these diamonds on you, and these words of mine in his thoughts and yours? Will he think you have any right to complain when he has made you miserable? You took him with your eyes open. The willing wrong you have done me will be your curse."

It seemed at first as if Gwendolen's eyes were spell-bound in reading the horrible words of the letter over and over again as a doom of penance; but suddenly a new spasm of terror made her lean forward and stretch out the paper towards the fire, lest accusation and proof at once should meet all eyes. It flew like a feather from her trembling fingers and was caught up in the great draught of flame. In her movement the casket fell on the floor and the diamonds rolled out. She took no notice, but fell back in her chair again helpless. She could not see the reflections of herself then: they were like so many women petrified white; but coming near herself you might have seen the tremor in her lips and hands. She sat so for a long while, knowing little more than that she was feeling ill, and that those written words kept repeating themselves in her.

Truly here were poisoned gems, and the poison had entered into this poor young creature.

After that long while, there was a tap at the door and Grandcourt entered, dressed for dinner. The sight of him brought a new nervous shock, and Gwendolen screamed again and again with hysterical violence. He had expected to see her dressed and smiling, ready to be led down. He saw her pallid, shrieking as it seemed with terror, the jewels scattered around her on the floor. Was it a fit of madness?

In some form or other the Furies had crossed his threshold. (358–59)

This is a passage of extraordinary audacity and effectiveness, one that demonstrates how Eliot can work with, and against, the constraints and conventions of the Victorian novel to create a psychosexual drama that is "legible as print," and indeed thrusts its words upon us. The "adder"-like letter from Lydia that she cannot fail to read dooms her marriage from the start. "I am the grave in which your chance of happiness is buried. . . . The willing wrong you have done me will be your curse." The delicate vessel is now the grave, a cursed vessel that can never produce happiness as it can never produce children. Gwendolen enters into a spasm of terror, a fully hystericized reaction, and she is petrified by the Medusa. "She could not see the reflections of herself then: they were like so many women petrified white; but coming near herself you might have seen the tremor in her lips and hands." A curious sentence, in its implication of the observer-reader, in the "coming near herself." We are summoned as witnesses to a truly primal scene. "Truly here were poisoned gems, and the poison had entered into this poor young creature." From this moment, Gwendolen's life is altered utterly, and the chapter ends with an abrupt shift to Grandcourt's perspective, and the entry of a madwoman into his life: "He saw her pallid, shrieking as it seemed with terror, the jewels scattered around her on the floor. Was it a fit of madness? In some form or other, the Furies had crossed his threshold."

We are again reminded of Dora's Schmuckkästchen, jewelry and jewel-cases as symbolic enactment of the control of woman's sexuality by patriarchy. Here it is the exploited Lydia who understands perfectly the functioning of the symbolic system, and uses the diamonds to strike at her rival, cursing her in her womb, ensuring that the patrilineal inheritance will pass to her own son by Grandcourt. The Furies are unleashed into the novel by way of the punished and hystericized womb. We are given no more details on Gwendolen's wedding night; we only know that when we later see Grandcourt and Gwendolen married, she is broken to his will, and he seems to take a sadistic pleasure in having obtained mastery rather than love.

But the jewels. If in Balzac jewelry was part of the array of accessories people used to represent themselves and their social significance, and in Flaubert contributed to the fetishization of the elusive object of desire, to Eliot jewelry seems to be particularly important, not only as a marker of social class and wealth but more pertinently as a kind of currency in socio-sexual exchanges and kinship systems, ways to both display and control women's sexes. Daniel himself wears a diamond ring that is comparable to the croix de ma mère of melodrama: token of his mysterious parentage, which he must wear when he goes to his meeting with the mother who has finally revealed herself and which at the last will be stolen by the awful Lapidoth, Mirah and Mordecai's father—the bad father who tried to prostitute his daughter. Grandcourt asserts his full control over Gwendolen by forcing her to wear the poisoned diamonds at the festive gathering at Topping Abbey.

As if in response, she winds the turquoise necklace—strung of the jewels left her by her father, the necklace Daniel redeemed from the pawnshop—around her wrist in order to signal to Daniel that she needs private talk with him—talk that is then all about gambling, and what it would mean to lose the necklace again. There is here a quasi-anthropological observation of a strange mating dance between Gwendolen and Daniel, where she is proposing sex to him without knowing it, and he is not quite accepting the offer, also without knowing it. The one who best understands is of course Grandcourt, who denounces her signaling with the necklace: "Only fools go into that deaf and dumb talk, and think they're secret" (447). Then, when she later summons Daniel to the house in Grosvenor Square for an interview that will be ended—in a Boulevard melodrama effect—by Grandcourt's entry, we learn that "she was hurting herself with the jewels that glittered on her tightly clasped fingers pressed against her heart" (610). Note that here language has broken down: "Words seemed to have no more rescue in them than if he had been beholding a vessel in peril of wreck . . . . He was afraid of his own voice" (610). Georges Bataille claimed that we best seize the meaning of a social group by way of its waste, its useless expenditure and display, of which jewelry is a prime example. Jewelry here becomes the vehicle of meanings that cannot be spoken, the best language of a system of exchange—of meanings as of persons—in which Gwendolen is absolutely imprisoned.

This long middle of the novel establishes a remarkable and unusual relation between Gwendolen and Daniel, where she turns the object of her increasingly erotic attention into a "priest." "Those who trust us educate us," the narrator claims (430), and through Gwendolen's appeal to him something close to a transferential bond is established between them. Like the psychoanalytic transference, it enables the person in the position of the analyst to construct Gwendolen's story, to understand her anguished relation to Lydia and Grandcourt's past. It is because Daniel sees himself as structurally in the position of Lydia's son—through the surmise of his own illegitimacy—that he can imaginatively construct the whole story. Yet of course his dispossession will turn out to be quite different from that of the traditional bastard or orphan of fiction, concerning not property but another kind of inheritance.

I have so far fallen into the trap this novel sets for readers, into which most critics have promptly enough fallen — that is, speaking almost uniquely of Gwendolen's novel, as if it stood alone. To many, perhaps most readers, from the novel's publication onward, this has been a common reaction, one indeed that Eliot has coded into the novel, by her long initial attention to Gwendolen's marriage plot. Yet the novel is after all titled for its hero, and his plot opens up dimensions that Eliot wants us to see both as complementary to the marriage plot, and as wholly other — as shattering of Gwendolen's world. The complementation is apparent in Daniel's first meeting with Mirah Lapidoth on the bank of the Thames, where she is ready for suicide. "His own face in the glass had during many years been associated for him with thoughts of some one whom he must be like" (186). Since he believes Sir Hugo to be his father, the someone has to be his mother. And when a few pages later he encounters Mirah, his first thought is: "perhaps my mother was like this one" (191). Indeed she was, though Leonora Halm-Eberstein did everything she could to deny it. She denied her Jewishness, made sure that her son would be brought up in ignorance of it, and became a singer on the stage.

Singing, voice: as a young boy gifted with a beautiful singing voice, Daniel is asked by Sir Hugo if he would like to become an opera singer. "I should hate it!" he replies, from a sense that singing or otherwise performing in public is incompatible with being an English gentleman — as Gwendolen in her interview with Klesmer will discover that she cannot be an English lady and a performer at the same time. Mirah sings exquisitely, but her voice is too weak for stage performance — she can sing only in private assemblies — unlike Daniel's as yet unrevealed mother. Singing is of great importance in the novel, and is positively valorized; whereas performance — from Gwendolen's public gambling through Lapidoth's stage antics to Madame Halm-Eberstein's career — is censured as discreditable, indecent, something verging on prostitution. Singing is associated with the Jewish cast of characters in the novel, and the singing voice is related to the character who is almost pure voice, Mordecai: the prophetic voice who will in the course of the novel run out of breath, literally, while passing his messianic prophecies on to Daniel for realization.

On one hand, then, Gwendolen's novel is resolutely, insistently visual, a conspiracy of looking, spying, mirroring, exploring fully the visual logic of the realist tradition, most especially where the focus of looking is the young woman up for barter on the marriage market—the woman whose price, you might say, is stated in jewels, here a kind of euphemism for the cash nexus, or perhaps a version of the cash nexus that still insists on hereditary currency, "old money." On the other hand, Daniel's novel as he pursues Mirah's identity, and his own, enters a world where the visual is discounted in favor of voice—in a religious tradition that rejects the graven image, that disfavors representation and favors revelation. It is not surprising that Daniel's diamond ring will eventually be stolen and pawned: it's of no importance compared to the chest he receives from Joseph Kalonymos, which contains no jewelry, adderlike or not, but writings attesting to his inheritance. If in Gwendolen's story Eliot sums up a certain English novelistic tradition, in Daniel's she leaps into something else—indeed into the unrepresentable. It is a question in my mind, and probably in any reader's, whether Mordecai is quite tolerable as a character. Nonetheless, I admire the attempt Eliot has made to place a kind of biblical prophet into a realist fiction, and to suggest precisely the limits of representation as a mode of understanding the world within a work that depends for its existence on representation. Mordecai reaches beyond the confines not only of this novel but of the very novelistic project. He bursts its seams, he dismantles its systems. The problem may simply be that he does so too literally, that Eliot is guilty of a kind of imitative fallacy with Mordecai: the iconoclast whose image-breaking includes the novel itself.

Yet the Jewish plot is not only Mordecai, and not prophetic voice alone: Eliot has the good sense to anchor it more firmly in Mirah, set in contrast, of course, to Gwendolen. Remember that when Daniel first sees her he is "reminded" of the mother he has never known. He is at the time singing an aria from Gioacchino Rossini's *Otello* that cites Dante's Francesca da Rimini: "Nessun maggior dolore / Che ricordarsi del tempo felice / Nella miseria" (187)—a complex allusion, crowding together not only Rossini and Dante but also Shakespeare and the pilgrim Dante's guide, Virgil, and a striking antithesis to Mirah, who is no adulteress. On the contrary, Mirah's presentation is all about her virginity, despite the threats to it enacted by her father, and the worthiness of her womb. When Daniel at last reveals Mirah to her brother Mordecai, he identifies her as "one who is closely related to your departed mother" (570). And since Mordecai is terrified Mirah may not have been able to maintain a pure life, Daniel at once adds: "Your sister is worthy of the mother you honoured." We are of course summoned by this kind of language to remember that Jewishness is passed through the womb, and that it is the matrilineal definition that counts for Mirah, for Mordecai, and for Daniel. And I should note in passing that this insistence on the matrilineal is in and of itself a radical dissent from the main tradition of the nineteenth-century novel, which is all about fathers and sons.

Not only is Mirah chaste, she is, we are given to believe, fertile: the descriptions of her tend to favor images of ripeness and flowering, and we are given every expectation that her marriage to Daniel will be productive, a place of transmission forward through the ages of an ancient culture. Whereas Gwendolen is "reduced to dread lest she should become a mother" (672–73), compounding her wrong against Lydia Glasher; and late in the novel she appears with a black veil, like a nun. With Grandcourt drowned and Daniel married off to Mirah, it appears that Gwendolen will be cast in the role of a beneficent widow. Lydia's curse on her womb has been effective. We must see in contrast the fate of these two "delicate vessels," Gwendolen's and Mirah's, the one cursed and the other blessed, yet both destined, I think, to a certain role in transmission "onward through the ages."

The novel has two climaxes coming fast upon each other before reaching its resolution. One is Daniel's summons to meet his mother, the other Grandcourt's drowning. Daniel's trip to Genoa to meet his mother is preceded by what is called "a sacramental moment" between himself and Sir Hugo, over the question of his paternity, finally disposing of the supposition that he might be Sir Hugo's bastard son. This question disposed of, we can move on to the more important one: his mother. "I have thought of you more than of any other being in the world," Daniel at once tells her (625). And yet, he wants only one thing from her. When she proudly declares, "I relieved you from the bondage of having been born a Jew," Daniel immediately replies: "Then I am a Jew? . . . My father was a Jew, and you are a Jewess?" All his mother's self-justifications of her need to escape from bondage have little effect on him. Her emotional enactments, what the narrator calls "sincere acting," at once authentic and dramatized, appear to belong to a world with which he has little sympathy, and he cannot forgive his mother for having hidden his birthright. And his choice of Mirah he presents to his mother as a repudiation of theatricality: "I think that the artist's life has been made repugnant to her" (665). Daniel's mother at last matters only as the vessel who has, despite herself, transmitted Jewishness from Daniel's grand-father, Daniel Charisi. (It is curious to note that in a novel so much about inheritance and transmission, there appear to be no good parents.)

Gwendolen's crisis replays her hysterical reaction to the painted dead face revealed during the charades at Offendene. She emerges from the sail-boat "pale as one of the sheeted dead, shivering, with wet hair streaming, a wild amazed consciousness in her eyes, as if she had waked up in a world where some judgment was impending, and the beings she saw around were coming to seize her" (686). In her subsequent conversations with Daniel, she reveals that if she did not kill Grandcourt directly, "I did kill him in my thoughts" (695). This echoes the narrator's comment on the "iridescence" of Gwendolen's character back at the close of chapter 4: "For Macbeth's rhetoric about the impossibility of being many opposite things in the same moment, referred to the clumsy necessities of action and not to the subtler possibili-ties of feeling. We cannot speak a loyal word and be meanly silent, we can-not kill and not kill in the same moment; but a moment is room enough for the loyal and mean desire, for the outlash of a murderous thought and the sharp backward stroke of repentance" (42). Like the children and "primitive peoples" Freud refers to in his essay "On Narcissism," Gwendolen comes to believe in the "omnipotence of thoughts," the making effective in the world of her wishes for Grandcourt's death. "I know only that I saw my wish outside me," she says (696). And Daniel is forced into the role of trying to silence her confession. "He was not a priest. He dreaded the weight of this woman's soul flung upon his own with imploring dependence" (689). He is forced into the role of the analyst in the transference, turning aside the affect proffered to him and attempting to put it to the work of cure. These scenes in the Genoa hotel, remarkable for their charge of melodrama held back, repressed—on its way to becoming Henry James's melodrama of con-sciousness—tend to come out on silence: "speech was too momentous to be ventured on rashly. There were no words of comfort that did not carry some sacrilege" (697). Gwendolen's love for Daniel, which in another kind of novel would have wrought an overt melodrama, here is repressed as if to signal, once again, that this novel has redefined the tradition.

When, back in England, Daniel tells Gwendolen of his discovery that he is a Jew, she asks: "What difference need that have made?" (801). A perfectly sensible question, it seems. "You are just the same as if you were not a Jew," she continues, with a fine dosage of liberality and blindness. The question whether Daniel's Jewishness need have made a difference is not answered, since it has made all the difference, not only in his choice of the womanly vessel he considers worthy for his own reproductive project, but also because he is launched into a new world-historical mission, "that of restoring a political existence to my people, making them a nation again" (803).

With this grandiose project, "the world seemed to be getting larger around poor Gwendolen." And now the narrator once again calls upon the American Civil War as a momentous world-historical and moral struggle that trumps individual lives:

> There comes a terrible moment to many souls when the great movements of the world, the larger destinies of mankind, which have lain aloof in newspapers and other neglected reading, enter like an earthquake into their own lives—when the slow urgency of growing generations turns into the tread of an invading army or the dire clash of civil war, and grey fathers know nothing to seek for but the corpses of their blooming sons, and girls forget all vanity to make lint and bandages which may serve for the shattered limbs of their betrothed husbands. (803)

Eliot's prose is superheated here, conjuring up something that now seems to consign the slender "consciousness of a girl" to irrelevance. Gwendolen feels herself "for the first time being dislodged from her supremacy in her own world" (804). Not only Gwendolen, but the novel in which she figures, and the kind of novel she represents. We are launched into something new with Daniel's departure eastward. It is not clear that Eliot could at this point turn back from the dire clash of armies to claim that girls are the yea and the nay for which they are fighting, that their delicate vessels of human affection are the enduring vehicles of transmission.

And yet, I don't think Daniel's future mission trumps in this manner the social novel in which Gwendolen and he have up until now figured. Daniel's future mission is beyond the frame of this, or any, novel: it is in the mode of Mordecai's prophecies, in the wild blue yonder. He goes as called to, to a realm beyond representation. Gwendolen is left with: "I will try—try to live" (806). And then she sends Daniel a letter on his wedding day, announcing her resolution to try to be "one of the best of women, who make others glad they were born" (810). This is tentative rather than triumphant, but it very much belongs to the realm of "the novelistic": I mean, it is the kind of project that novels are about. This novel asks, in several registers, how can a woman lead her life? It explores that question with great complexity and tentativeness. And it is a question that from Samuel Richardson onward has been crucial to the novel—especially the English novel, but I think also the novel as genre. To the extent that novels exist to inquire into the history of private life, and the subjective consciousness of life, women's experience has rarely been far from the center of attention, though often inadequately filtered through a male observer. That "slender" consciousness of a girl is first and last the stuff of novelness; whereas Daniel's entry into his future messianic world cannot be contained within the novelistic.

Gwendolen appears to assume, in her final letter to Daniel, the role of the benevolent spinster aunt of fiction, who has renounced personal pleasures "to make others glad that they were born." This is not unlike the role Dickens assigns to Louisa Grandgrind at the end of Hard Times, acting as benevolent educator of Sissy Jupe's children. It is appropriately an image of transmission in a novel all about transmission. "In these delicate vessels is borne onward through the ages the treasure of human affections." Gwendolen, and perhaps Eliot also, at the end remain faithful to this quite traditional image of women as bearers of culture and civilization by way of emotional education, affectivity. And surely Mirah furthers this sense of transmission by way of her predicted motherhood and the passing on of a Jewish heritage. Daniel's mission is also a passing on, a working to complete, in some unimaginable future mode, the history of his people. But I don't want to suggest that the two modes of transmission coexist in easy harmony at the end. I don't think they do. Gwendolen quite correctly feels that Daniel's story "dislodges" her from supremacy in her own world, and Daniel's story also dislodges us from our complacencies about the novel and what it is for.

Henry James wrote: "The universe forcing itself with a slow, inexorable pressure into a narrow, complacent, and yet after all extremely sensitive mind, and making it ache with the pain of the process—that is Gwendolen's story." James, like so many readers since, privileges Gwendolen's story to the detriment of Daniel's, but his sentence is nonetheless finely accurate, in its emphasis on the *process* of Gwendolen's recognitions, her consciousness expanding painfully through time: the "truth of change" that means the novelist, unlike the painter, cannot fix a portrait at one moment, but must rather make it accumulate through temporal process. James is accurate also in his

choice of the word "universe." It is indeed the universe that is brought to
bear, on Gwendolen and on the Victorian novel, in *Daniel Deronda*—as in recognition that the very capaciousness of the novel may lead it to absorb more
than it can represent—or perhaps better, in acknowledgment of the need to
represent worlds elsewhere that are beyond its systems of representation. In
Daniel Deronda, the Victorian novel both achieves and explodes itself.

And criticism—including my own—has since the publication of the
novel simply rehearsed this achievement and this explosion. To complain
with so many critics (including James, including F. R. Leavis) that the novel
splits into its two parts is I think merely to reiterate Eliot's intention. If the
traditional Victorian double-plot novel works toward a kind of harmonic
resolution of the plots—which, as William Empson long ago pointed out,
may offer two possible outcomes to the same story, or two versions that
comment on one another—the "point" of *Daniel Deronda* may be to contest
the possibility of such resolution—to leave the chord unfinished, to show a
final irresolution of form.

Yet a question still arises—has arisen, for me, in teaching this novel. If
Daniel's novel is about its difference from Gwendolen's novel, if it finally
contests her version of experience and the ways in which experience is normally represented, why is it that his great adventure should come, not only
as a product of his free choice and decision, his making of himself, but as
the discovery of his predetermination to this story—that is, his Jewish birth?
Isn't that something of a concession to an old tradition of the novel, where
the foundling at the end discovers he is a prince, lost at birth, brought up
under false pretenses, revealed as what he is, and delivered to his true destiny, through a recognition that identifies his birthright? Daniel chooses to
be a Jew, but that choice seems to be predetermined because he is a Jew. As
Cynthia Chase has argued, Daniel's discovery of his origin is the "effect of its
effects"—Daniel must discover he is a Jew because that is the only thing that
will justify his narrative of interest in Jewishness. In this sense, the events of
his discovery are the product of a narrative need for meaning, rather than
vice-versa: his novel is predetermined by the end that lies in wait for it. This
is to recapitulate Jean-Paul Sartre's objection to narrative fiction as a whole:
that it is end-determined, that beginnings are only apparently random, in
fact "promises and annunciations" of an end to come, an end that is there
from the beginning, transforming everything. When the end turns out to be

the discovery of one's origins, we catch the novel at work in its plotting of its story from finish to start.

True enough. But to have it otherwise—to have Daniel's choice of Jewishness unmotivated, a kind of free ethical choice—would be unfaithful to the premises of realism as Eliot understands them. No more than Gwendolen reduced to poverty is free to refuse Mrs. Mompert's offer to employ her as governess, Daniel is not free to choose his cultural heritage. His quest is indeed for the discovery of what was there all along—as in the fateful case of Oedipus the King, for instance. Eliot's sense of the constraints on action in the world—those imposed by being a woman, or being illegitimate, or discovering one is Jewish—are very much part of her claim to be considered the greatest English realist. If in *Adam Bede* Eliot famously compares her novel to Dutch genre painting, in *Daniel Deronda* she appears to go beyond that model. If we wanted to look for a pictorial analogy, it might—despite the vast cultural and temperamental differences between them—be precisely in Courbet, in his sense of the gravity of those gestures that we are required to accomplish by who we are and where we are situated. Even the extraordinary adventure, the one that splits apart the traditional novel, is somehow obligatory, part of the lot assigned to us. Eliot's fiction is so often about discovering what that lot is, and what that discovery entails.

CHAPTER 7

Zola's Combustion Chamber

I HAVE NOTICED OVER MY YEARS AS A TEACHER A REAL REVIVAL IN ZOLA'S fortunes. I can remember my own teacher, Harry Levin, asking his seminar to read some Zola novels with a certain embarrassment and condescension, a suggestion that they were no longer quite readable. Whereas now Zola seems indispensable. This revival may derive partly from our fascination with Second Empire Paris as the capital of the nineteenth century and the center of European culture in the age of high capitalism, to use Walter Benjamin's terms. Zola's novel cycle, *Les Rougon-Macquart*, calls itself a "natural and social history of a family during the Second Empire"—the period from 1852 to 1870 when Napoléon III ruled in a Paris more and more known as the place of European culture and pleasure; and this Paris has become a key "site of memory" to us postmoderns. The phenomenology of the urban landscape is crucial to Zola's project, and it has been renewed at various moments by the Surrealists, by Benjamin and other critical thinkers, and by modern urbanists concerned with the quality of social life. And what may have seemed to an earlier generation unacceptable in Zola's narrative and descriptive style— in its range from the didactic detail to the mythic or allegorical image—may now seem consonant with our appreciation of a kind of stylistic eclecticism. Even where Zola is kitsch, he is part of our sensibility.

Many of Zola's novels are organized around a machine or an institution seen to function as a machine: the locomotive of *La Bête humaine*, the coal mine of *Germinal*, the central market, Les Halles, in *Le Ventre de Paris*, the department store of *Au Bonheur des Dames*, the stock exchange of *L'Argent*, the alcohol still of *L'Assommoir*, which the novel both explicates, as a determining context of modern life, and takes as its dynamic principle, that force which motors the plot. The still of *L'Assommoir* is the simplest of the machines, but it contains all the principles: heat, combustion, pressure, creating an energetic source for the novel. That still returns inexorably in the novel, constantly heating, making a purring noise, producing a constant drip of distilled alcohol from its copper tubing, and it powers the lives of the characters toward catastrophe and destruction. The locomotive in *La Bête humaine* gives the most evident example: heat, pressure, steam, speed, leading to the runaway locomotive, to accident and explosion. And Jacques Lantier the engineer, like most of Zola's central figures, is himself a steam engine, characterized by the hereditary *fêlure* of his family, that fault or crack, that will allow explosive interior energies to escape in murderous fashion. Michel Serres in his masterful book *Feux et signaux de brume: Zola* offers a full thermodynamic reading of Zola; and you find that is nearly always possible. In *Nana* (1880), the machine is going to be Nana herself, and particularly Nana's sexuality, which will power the novel forward and produce all its effects.

A word about the prostitute as central figure. Nana stands in a long tradition, reaching back to a Romantic image of the fallen woman, in Victor Hugo for instance, and a woman with a special social destiny, as in Balzac, and including Eugène Sue's best-seller prostitute with a heart of gold, Fleur-de-Marie, Flaubert's Rosanette, and a host of other figures in the Goncourts, in Huysmans, in Proust. Nineteenth-century France was obsessed with prostitution, as a semihidden, semitolerated world that enabled discussion of sexuality in a way still subject to self-censorship where "proper" women were concerned. Curiosity about prostitution had been fed a great deal of information in the survey published in 1836 by Dr. Parent-Duchatelet, *De la prostitution dans la ville de Paris*, one of the first in a series of remarkable medical and sociological investigations of the underworlds of Paris in the nineteenth century. Parent-Duchatelet provided an impressive anatomy of the lives of prostitution, from the streetwalker to the bordello dweller to the high-flying courtesan, with great detail on the causes and conditions of life in this shadow world. Novelists immediately put his work to use. Zola, as with all his novels, undertook his own investigations, largely with acquaintances familiar with the world of prostitutes, and left pages of notes in his *cahiers*. One senses his desire to get it right, to find those details—what Stendhal called the "petits faits vrais"—that would make his novel decisively more

accurate than its predecessors. He also, of course, brings to bear the over-
arching determinist scheme of the *Rougon-Macquart*: the hereditary flaw of
the family, Nana's parentage in Gervaise Lantier and Jacques Coupeau, prolos and alcoholics. We in fact see Nana as a young girl toward the end of
L'Assommoir, working as a milliner's assistant and making her debut in petty
prostitution. What Nana becomes seems largely inevitable, a choice determined before her birth. And this is I think one of Zola's strengths: his scrupulous, nonjudgmental explanation of Nana's choice of "profession" and way
of being in the world. Yet, I want to argue, he can't quite maintain his im-
passive neutrality. Zola may create Nana from sociological and "scientific"
conditions and drives, but then what he creates provokes a strange reaction
in her creator. Zola takes fright at his own creation.

I'll come back to that. I want to return to the thermodynamics of the
novel for a moment. The first chapter opens in the year of the great Exposition Universelle of 1867—the Second Empire is now at its height of wealth,
power, and corruption—with the play set in the Théâtre des Variétés, which
its director insists on calling a bordello. *La Blonde Vénus* offers a "pasteboard
Olympus" where a "carnival" unfolds: "legend was trampled on, antique
images smashed." The carnival, the world turned upside down, is a principal metaphor and also technique of *Nana*. The upside down opens the way
to sex: Nana's appearance by the third act naked—though not quite naked:
slightly veiled by her shift—brings a kind of sexual madness, "le coup de
folie de son sexe," opening onto the abyss of desire, "l'inconnu du désir"
(38) [25]. (*Sexe* in French means both "the genitals" and "sexuality," and both
are relevant here.) Desire now fills the theater, and the novel. It is installed
as a force. By the end of the chapter, the theater is overheated. "People were
gasping, their hair was sticky with sweat . . . their breath had warmed the air
with a human odor. In the flare of the gaslights, a thick haze hovered under
the chandelier. The house reeled, slipped into a tired and excited vertigo,
gripped by those tired midnight desires that murmur deep in alcoves" (39)
[27]. The engine is heated. A dynamic has been created from Nana's sexual
presence that will drive the novel forward.

The chapters that follow are what you might call demonstrative: Zola's
careful representation of the life of the prostitute. In chapter 2, we see its
disorder, the arrival of a pack of men, without any means to perform a triage

on them, and meanwhile an accumulation of debt that dictates a quick rendezvous with an anonymous male arranged by the mysterious and omnipresent procuress with the lovely name of La Tricon. Then, in chapter 3, the aristocratic world of the Muffat, but a world already infected by talk of the *partie de filles* that the men are arranging at Nana's, and by Fauchery's speculations on the Countess Muffat's susceptibility to seduction—establishing the parallelism whereby the House of Muffat will be destroyed by the pervasive power of Nana's sexuality. Then, in chapter 5, that party at Nana's, an evocation of the *demi-monde*, that mirror-world where the men are all the same as at the Muffat soirée—but the woman all different, replaced by *filles*. Again, it is the world of carnival, the respectable and publicly visible world turned upside down in a gesture that Zola makes one of degradation. The night ends with breakage and ruin—pouring bottles of champagne into the piano, for instance; and the breaking and ruining of pretty objects will indeed be part of Nana's career.

I want to dwell a moment on chapter 5, which takes us backstage in the theater-bordello—recall the importance of the backstage in Balzac's *Illusions perdues*: the place of the machinery that creates the illusions of life, at once disillusioning and more deeply fascinating and erotic. Here, the visit backstage is accomplished through the visit of the foreign Prince (rather transparently modeled on the Prince of Wales), accompanied by Muffat. For Muffat, it is a journey into a place of disorientation, fearful and intoxicating. He is now close to the central furnace of the novel: "what especially bothered him was the stuffy air, thickened, overheated, with the trace of a strong smell, stinking of gas, the glue of the scenery, the dirt of dark corners, the dubious underwear of the extras" (143) [121]. Nana in her loge is half-naked, and presides over a "solemn farce" as the real Prince Royal drinks champagne with the actor Bosc done up as the Roi Dagobert—and since Zola's fictive Prince so closely represents the historical Prince of Wales, there is a double farce or parody at work, a carnivalesque moment in which desire for Nana exercises a kind of Circean effect of transformation. Muffat has here entered into the zone created by Nana's sex; he begins to feel himself invaded by her; by the end of the chapter he will be irrevocably possessed by her. But perhaps the most remarkable moment of this remarkable chapter comes when Muffat looks through a peephole in the backdrop out onto the stage and the house as Nana makes her naked entrance:

Now Muffat had to see; he put his eye to the peep-hole. Beyond the daz-
zling arc of the footlights, the house looked dark, as if filled with a reddish
smoke; and against this neutral background, Nana stood out white, magnified, blotting out the boxes from the balcony to the ceiling. He saw her from
the rear, her back stretched, her arms opened wide, while down below, at
the level of her feet, the head of the prompter—with the face of a poor and
honest old man—looked as if it had been severed from his body. At certain
moments in her opening number, undulating movements seemed to start
from her neck, run down to her waist, to die out in the trailing edge of her
tunic. When she had sung her last note in the midst of a tempest of bravos,
she bowed, her flimsy shift floating around her, her long hair reaching
below her waist as she bent forward. And seeing her in this way, bent over
with her buttocks magnified, backing toward the peep-hole from which he
was staring, the Count straightened up, his face gone pale. (159–60) [136–7]

The passage, I think, alludes to Lucien's discoveries backstage. But here it is
specifically the naked Nana seen from the backside that becomes the image
of disorientation and possession, a life revolutionized by the discovery of
sex—from the rear—and the start of a world well lost for sex. Nana's sexuality makes the world go round, and turns it upside down, and wrong side
around. The underside, like the extras' underwear—Zola's word is "les des-
sous"—takes over, forces itself on our attention.

We have after this a pastoral interlude, when Nana rents a house in the
country, which brings all the respectable men of the neighborhood to her
door. She takes young Georges Hugon, disguised as a girl, to bed, but then
gives him up for more serious business: Muffat. The reason would seem to
be her vision, in the nearby village of Chamont, of Irma d'Anglars, former
whore become respectable old churchgoer and landed gentry. Irma d'Anglars is to Nana a lesson in where prostitution can get you if you play things
right—as, later, we will be given the lesson of la Reine Pomaré, the tooth-
less old hag searching for food in dustbins—the more obvious fate if you
don't invest your earnings properly.

Chapter 7—at the precise midpoint of this novel that itself comes mid-
way in the *Rougon-Macquart* cycle—brings the moment that the dynamic created at the start of the novel seems to have been ineluctably driving toward:
the stripping of Nana bare, seeing her finally wholly naked, no longer with
the shift that veiled the kitsch stage Venus—so comparable to those nudes
painted by Cabanel or Bouguereau—of chapter 1. Nana strips before the mirror, in which she looks at herself, while Muffat looks at her looking, in this

intensely visual moment that is accompanied by his reading of an article in *Le Figaro* in which Fauchery has allegorized Nana as the "mouche d'or," a golden insect spawned from the garbage of gutter and come to infect the dwellers in palaces. She represents the revenge of the proletariat, "corrupting and disorganizing Paris between her white thighs." It is from the perspective of reading this tract that Muffat now looks up to watch Nana in her autoerotic self-regarding:

> Nana was standing still. With an arm behind her neck, one hand clasped in the other, her elbows wide apart, she bent back her head. He saw her foreshortened in the mirror, her eyes half-closed, her lips parted, her face bathed in loving laughter; while behind, her blond hair loosed from its chignon covered her back with the mane of a lioness. Bent back with her hips thrust out, she displayed the solid thighs and the hard bosom of a woman warrior, with strong muscles under the satiny finish of her skin. A fine line, bowed just a bit by her shoulders and her hips, ran from one of her elbows to her foot. Muffat followed this tender profile, these melting lines of blond flesh bathing in a gilded light, these round contours which the candlelight made shine like silk. He thought of his former horror of woman, of the monster of the Bible, lubricious, smelling of the beast. Nana was covered with down, the down of a redhead made her body velvety; while in her rear and her thighs like a wild mare's, in the swelling flesh carved with deep folds, which gave to her sex the troubling veil of their shadow, there was the beast. It was the golden beast, unconscious like a force, whose odor alone spoiled the world. Muffat looked and looked, obsessed, possessed, to the point where, having closed his eyes to see her no more, the animal reappeared in the depths of the shadows, magnified, terrible, exaggerating its pose. Now it would be there, before his eyes, in his flesh, forever. (218) [191–92]

Several things need to be said about this central moment. Most obviously, Nana naked provokes not only desire but, especially, fear. Fear and loathing, as well as frustration at her narcissism. Then, Nana naked is strangely veiled: when we reach the essential of her nudity: "dans les renflements charnus creusés de plis profonds, qui donnait au sexe le voile troublant de leur ombre, il y avait de la bête." The passage challenges translators: the most recent, Douglas Parmée, gives us: "behind which lurked the disturbing slit of her genitals"—which translates what precisely isn't there. The woman's sex is veiled, both a presence and an absence, as in the childish scenarios of Freud, the discovery of anatomical difference (always from the point of view of the male) as absence, as "castration," and simultaneously the denial of what has been seen — "Je sais bien mais quand même." At this moment of maximal seeing in the novel, there is an avoidance of seeing what is there. Nana's *sexe* is presented as hidden, an occult source of power, as of heat and energy, all the more powerful for not being seen, or seeable. And the descriptive prose veers into the mythic, toward the biblical beast, and a larger-than-life monster.

This is Muffat's vision, and I'm not certain how far we can tax Zola, or the Zolian narrator, with Muffat's failure to see here, and his swerve into myth and allegory. But it is worth noting that this novel that promises to strip Nana bare, to inspect her thoroughly — as she inspects herself — never quite does so. Compared to the anatomized machines, engines, motors of many other novels — the locomotive, the coal mine, the department store, the markets — the anatomization of Nana is strangely incomplete. On one hand, we can say this is part of Zola's thematics: that woman, in her sexuality, and precisely in her *sexe*, remains a mystery to the men whose lives are driven by the desire she creates. It is one more example of men turning the feminine into enigma. On the other hand, I sense that Zola is truly panicked by what he has created: that he, too, finds Nana ultimately unknowable, and all the more powerful for that. The scene of Nana before the mirror will end with Muffat grabbing Nana and throwing her on the carpet, to possess her in an act that he knows represents his "defeat" — not possession at all, but dispossession. And that seems to be the Nana-effect in the novel: disorientation, troubled vision, imperfect knowledge, dispossession.

Most Zola novels include a number of passages explicating their central machines and engines, moments where we are led through the mine or the department store in order to understand how it functions, to calculate its expansion, to demonstrate how it provides a context that wholly governs the lives of those who work and live with it. These are moments of "naming of parts," which among other things show us how much the novel as genre thrives off exploiting our curiosity about how things work, and the drama that can be found in the inner lives of complex mechanical and social organisms and the way they intersect with human existences: the kind of curiosity that will give us novels about airports and police precincts and even universities. *Nana* is no different in Zola's scrupulous undertaking to inventory the types of prostitution in Paris, and the elements of the prostitute's life. But when it comes to the naming of parts of his central dynamic engine here, he is somewhat at a loss.

This novel exaggerates what I think is a tendency in all Zola's novels: a bifurcation of descriptive realism into detailed sociological presentation on one hand and mythic and allegorical evocation on the other. Perhaps bifurcation is not the right term: the descriptive can veer into myth and allegory. The prose warms up, takes off—not, as in Balzac, through the narrator's attempt to penetrate surfaces and appearances in order to wrest from behind a hidden drama (there are no hidden dramas in Zola) but rather through the narratorial effort to make the visible comprehensible, to understand its determinative force in life. And here understanding Nana is, not surprisingly, more difficult than understanding coal mine or locomotive. As motor force of the narrative, she elicits and promotes a more excessive movement from description to evocation.

It's notable, in this context, that following the chapter where Muffat observes Nana before the mirror, Zola has Nana run off with the actor Fontan, abandoning the world of high prostitution to which she is becoming accustomed to sink into the lower depths of the streetwalker. Chapter 8, one of the starkest in the novel, gives us the life of the streetwalker, the pimps, abused women, police raids. This chapter is written from Parent-Duchatelet and other sources, and has a ring of authenticity. The moment when, beaten by Fontan and chased from her apartment, Nana goes to bed with Satin in a cheap hotel—the idea that lesbianism is common among prostitutes also comes from Parent-Duchatelet—which then is raided by the police gives a powerful picture of the arbitrary and brutal force exercised on an activity that is tolerated, considered a necessary part of urban social existence, indeed encouraged by a system that permits no return from prostitution, yet also seen as shameful, an object of contempt and repression. "During close to an hour, there was the sound of heavy boots on the stairs, doors hammered with fists, shrill quarrels ending in sobs, whispers of skirts along the walls, all the sudden awakening and terrified departure of a herd of women, brutally rounded up by three officers" (275–76) [245–46]. The police raiding the hotel ask to see the girls' hands, on the theory that the honest *couturière* will have the marks of needle pricks on her hands, whereas the whore's will be unmarked—an interesting class demarcation, where the lack of signs of the most menial (and low-paid) labor on a woman's body indicates to the police her desire to rise to a higher status by sexual use of her body. In fact, the whole system of policing of prostitution devised by the Paris police in the nineteenth century seems to be motivated by an obsession with distinguishing the prostitute from the "honest" woman, making sure that there is no confusion between the two, that the one doesn't illegitimately usurp the appearance of the other. The deep male fear here seems to be that one might be duped into taking a prostitute for an honest woman—marrying her perhaps. Eugène Sue's *Les Mystères de Paris* evokes the issue. Rodolphe wants to have Fleur-de-Marie—prostitute with heart of gold who after all is of good birth and sold into prostitution against her will, and long since reformed—struck from the police registers and made his bride; but she explains that this will never do—that she could never offer her soiled body in bourgeois marriage—and then decorously dies to solve the dilemma. Where Zola is dealing with the social conditions of prostitution and its subjection to a brutal disciplinary regime, he is capable of great sympathy and understanding, and of spare and effective descriptive prose.

As for Nana herself, she will bounce back from the pavement and move to a yet higher stage as chic *courtisane*, set up by Muffat in a *hôtel particulier* in the avenue de Villiers—in the new quarters of Haussmann's Paris, developed amid the speculation and corruption detailed in another novel of the *Rougon-Macquart*, *La Curée*—where she reigns as "marquise of the high pavement." She reaches an apogee of public chic at the running of the Grand Prix de Paris at Longchamp, where the horse from Vandeuvres's stable named after her wins the race and a crowd of thousands chants her name. The double naming here, of the horse and the woman, gives Zola an opportunity to move from the detailed visual presentation of the races, in all their color and movement —something Degas repeatedly tried to capture at around the same time— to something that is, once again, more ambiguous and allegorized, as the crowd chants in praise of the racehorse and/or the woman, both splendid physical specimens.

Simultaneously, it turns out that Vandeuvres, last specimen of the old aristocracy, has cheated, secretly betting against another horse from his stable, the favorite, who is held back to allow Nana to win. Vandeuvres ends, apparently, a suicide in his stable set on fire. And this announces the coming collapse of the House of Muffat as well, with the marriage of the daughter of the house to the disreputable Daguenet, and the party celebrating the marriage contract is contaminated by the waltz from *La Blonde Vénus*—Nana's first stage performance. The hereditary crack, the fêlure of the Rougon-Macquart family, becomes visible in the very walls of the Muffat house. This is one of Zola's moments of "ceci tuera cela," to use Victor Hugo's phrase on the book versus the cathedral: old society is doomed before the kind of force represented by Nana. By this point in the novel, Nana and the Comtesse, Sabine Muffat, have in fact undergone a sort of chiasmus (one of Zola's favorite figures), where Sabine has become a kind of sex addict, whereas Nana tries to play the respectable woman.

We are at the point of climax and catastrophe now. I want to dwell on chapter 13, the next-to-last, which packs in an extraordinary amount of event and demonstration. By this point, the engine of the novel is explicitly overheated, burning too much fuel, creating intolerable pressure. "In her hôtel, it was like a burst of the ironsmith's forge. Her continual desires flamed out, a tiny breath from her lips changed gold into a fine ash that the wind rapidly blew away. No one had ever seen such a rage for spending. The house seemed to be built over a pit, men with all their goods, their bodies, even their names, disappeared into it, without leaving even a trace of dust behind" (407) [367]. Appropriately, to complete and celebrate this life subject to higher and higher combustion, Nana orders a splendid bed, costing fifty thousand francs, decorated with the bas-relief of a naked woman for which she serves as the model. All of her lovers and admirers bring her precious gifts. When Philippe Hugon brings her a rare porcelain dish (to buy which he's stolen fifteen thousand francs from his regimental treasury), Nana clumsily breaks the lid, then goes into a paroxysm of destruction, smashing the rest of the dish, then breaking everything in sight. It is in the energetic logic of the novel, one might say, to lead to the smashing of things, as in demonstration of both Nana's destructive force and her power to renew continually the tribute of objects furnished by men. Philippe goes to prison for his theft, and his younger brother, Georges, who like Philippe proposes marriage to Nana, at her refusal stabs himself with a pair of scissors, and dies.

The *gâchis* of objects quickly becomes a wasting of persons as well, of men. In two weeks, she destroys Foucarmont, wiping out the thirty thousand francs he has saved for his retirement, sending him back to a far outpost in the navy. Then she turns to the investment banker Steiner, whose last great speculation is an ironworks in Alsace: "out there, in a corner of the provinces, there were workers black from coal, soaked with sweat, who night and day taxed their muscles and heard their bones crack, in order to satisfy Nana's pleasures. She devoured everything, like a great fire" (432) [392]. Steiner finished, she turns to La Faloise, whose fortune is in land. "He had to sell rapidly, one after another. With each mouthful, Nana devoured an acre. Foliage shivering under the sun, ripe stands of wheat, vineyards gilded by autumn, pastures with grass reaching to the cows' bellies, everything went, in a sinking into the depths; there was even a waterway, a plaster quarry, and three mills that disappeared. Nana passed, like an invasion, like a cloud of locusts whose flight is like a wildfire laying waste a province. She scorched the earth where she set her little foot" (433) [393]. If the novel began with the degraded myths, the carnival, of *La Blonde Vénus*, by now Nana has become her own myth, the man-eater who incidentally, along the way, reduces things into nothingness.

Georges Bataille, in the visionary political economy of *The Accursed Share*, suggests that one best understands a society through its waste, its by-products, its unproductive accessories, such as jewelry, and activities, such as gambling. Nana as myth evokes an entire social economy in the wastage she causes and represents, and in an unreproductive but all-motivating sexuality. The explicit commentary here is provided by Mignon, when he pays a visit to the hotel, and finds himself filled with admiration at its luxury, "ce luxe écrasant," the gilded furniture, the silks and velvets, and then the bedroom with its throne of a bed. Mignon is reminded of vast public works he has seen:

> Near Marseille he had been shown an aqueduct whose stone arches straddled an abyss, a cyclopean work that had cost millions and ten years of struggle. At Cherbourg, he had seen the new port, an immense construction project, hundreds of men sweating in the sun, machines filling the sea with great blocks of stone, erecting a wall where sometimes the workers were crushed into a bloody pulp. But that seemed to him small stuff, Nana elated him more. He experienced once more the respect he had felt one festive evening in a château that a sugar-refiner had built for himself, a royal palace paid for by just one thing, sugar. But she, she had done it with something else, with this dumb little thing that everyone laughed at, this bit of

her delicate nudity—it was with this nothing, shameful and so powerful, whose force moved the world, that all alone, without workers, without machines invented by engineers, she had shaken Paris and built this fortune under which dead men slept.

"God! what a tool!" exclaimed Mignon in his ravishment, with a new surge of gratitude. (445–46) [404–5]

Here Nana's *sexe*, her genitals, are specifically set in contrast to male workers and phallic tools, in a reversal of the usual analogy. Her sexe is "nothing"— as in the earlier passage, before the mirror, where it turned out to be indescribable—yet also a powerful tool, the most powerful tool, the tool that motivates the invention of all the others. Nana the devourer is at once the force of destruction and of production, a one-woman economic motor of consumption as waste.

By the end of the chapter, Nana is allowed to speak in self-excuse, following Georges Hugon's death from his self-inflicted wound. It's not her fault, she says. "Society is all wrong. They blame women, when it's the men who come after those things. Look, I can tell this to you, now: when I went with them, you know, well, it didn't give me any pleasure, no pleasure at all. It just annoyed me, I swear to you! . . . It's their fault. I didn't do anything" (448–49) [407]. Her plea seems entirely justified. Note, though, that the excuse for her sexual conduct comes in the form of her claim that she took no pleasure in it—as if to say that taking pleasure in sex would void her claim of innocence. The *métier* of prostitution is excusable, and everything in the novel tends toward demonstrating that it is the creation of men, with women merely its victims. And it is perfectly plausible to believe that Nana finds no pleasure with her venal lovers. But I think it may be a characteristic concession, or compromise, on Zola's part to use lack of pleasure in sex as part of Nana's excuse. She would be even more terrifying, even more out of control, if she liked it.

The end of the chapter offers a mythic apotheosis of Nana. Like a "monster from antiquity whose feared domain was covered with bones, she set her feet on skulls" (449) [409]. There is a reprise of the "mouche d'or" bringing germs from the slums to infect bourgeois men. Then the last paragraph of the chapter concludes:

And while her sex rose as in glory and blazed over her supine victims, like a rising sun lighting up a field of carnage, she was no more aware of the havoc she caused than a splendid animal, still the good-natured girl. She still was big and plump, bursting with good health and gaiety. All that really didn't count for much, her hôtel struck her as stupid, too small, full of furniture that got in her way. Nothing much, just a beginning. She was dreaming of something better. And she left, all done up in her finery, to give Satin a last kiss, looking clear, solid, brand-new, as if she had never been used. (449) [409]

Parmée's translation really breaks down here: he gives "the fiery red of her pubic hair glowed triumphantly over its victims stretched out at her feet," which represents a misguided attempt to naturalize a passage which is unabashedly allegorical and visionary, where Nana's sexe becomes a sun rising to shine on a the carnage of a battlefield. This source of heat, energy, and movement in the novel finally becomes the ultimate heat source, the sun, and the center of a kind of symboliste tableau—one might think of Gustave Moreau—that elevates her to entirely mythic proportions.

There are similar moments of mythic apotheosis in other Zola novels: the collapse of the mine, le Voreux, in Germinal, the final frenetic white sale in Au Bonheur des Dames, the spectacular end of the runaway locomotive, la Lison, in La Bête humaine. Nana's may be more over the top precisely because she is the least describable, the least explainable of his machines and motors of narrative. As in the classic Freudian scenarios I mentioned earlier, the visual inspection of Nana leads to a certain denial of what is seen, a turning away from the truth, a slippage into the mythological evocation. But I do think Nana represents only a more extreme case of a general tendency of Zola's descriptive prose. One may ask how this tendency toward mythologization and allegory squares with Zola's declared principles as a Naturalist, and particularly his claim, in his famous "Letter to Antony Valabrègue," that whereas Romanticism viewed the world through a colored lens, Naturalism views it through a clear glass screen. One could, I think, show that in allowing for lenses or screens in that manifesto—in allowing that there is some optical apparatus between the observer's eye and the real—and in equating that screen with the artist's "temperament," Zola gives himself room to allegorize. He is, I think, less naive than he may appear in some of his polemical pieces. After all, the choice to center a novel on a powerful machine that appears to propel its characters' lives is already an allegorizing gesture. That machine typically is anatomized and explained—subjected to inspection and a naming of parts—but also enlarged, heightened, made less specific and more grandiose in order to give it an organizing and dynamic force in the novel. Thermodynamics itself becomes myth in Zola. In fact, you could say that science in general is given the status of myth—never more so than in the hereditary determinism of the *Rougon-Macquart*. When in the last volume of the series Dr. Pascal goes to work on the family genealogy, the result may be an explanation of how Tante Dide passed on the fatal fêlure that afflicts the family, but it is equally the creation of a kind of mystical Tree of Life.

Beware, then, of Zola's advertisements for himself, which usually convey only part of what he is doing, and knows he is doing; though he was an astute enough publicist (his first profession, after all, at the publishing house of Hachette) to know that science, in the wake of Darwin and Claude Bernard, was a good battle flag. Born in 1840—thus a generation beyond Flaubert, two beyond Balzac—Zola writes in the age of the triumph of science as an ideology. Returning to *Nana*: look for a moment at its very end. Nana lies dying of smallpox, contracted from her illegitimate and abandoned son, seen to be the low point in hereditary degeneration, though also an agent of an older poetic justice. Does Nana die because her way of living makes her a designated victim of infection—or because she must be struck down by a medical deus ex machina? One in fact has the impression that nothing could stop her, short of the novelist's intervention. It's as if he had to kill Nana off, to make an end to her depredations. And the narrator seems to take pleasure in detailing the destruction of her beauty under the action of smallpox. At the very end, for instance: "Venus lay decomposing. It seemed that the virus she had caught in the gutters, from the carrion society left there, this germ with which she had poisoned a people, now had risen to her face and rotted it." Note that Zola doesn't have Nana brought down by venereal disease: the sins of the genitals are displaced upward, to her face, in another allegorizing move. One may recall Madame de Merteuil at the end of Choderlos de Laclos's *Les Liaisons dangereuses*, also struck with smallpox, which is said to have turned her inside out, so now "she wore her soul on her face."

But this is not the very end of Zola's novel. The last line brings through the open window the chant of the crowd out on the boulevard: "To Berlin! to Berlin! to Berlin!" The crowd is calling for war against Bismarck's Prussia, and war it will get, and with it defeat, the capture of the emperor by the Prussians, the fall of the Second Empire, the siege of Paris, the insurrection of the Paris Commune, and then its bloody suppression. The last line of the novel points directly to the closure of the period frame of the *Rougon-Macquart*. Beyond Nana's own end, a larger end is in sight. And I think Zola here saves his novel from mere horror, and possibly a moralizing bathos, at the last, by returning us to the collectivity—the crowd—and to historical event. It is one of Zola's prime contributions to the novel (as Henry James noted in some distress) to deal in crowds, collectivities of people, and to make their collective life and will felt in the novel. In this sense, he delivers on the Goncourt brothers' "droit au roman" in a way that no earlier novelist does. So at the end of *Nana* we have the reassertion of historical reality, which tracks perfectly onto the private lives of the novel insofar as the decadence, corruption, waste, and destruction represented in the novel seem to call for social cataclysm and change. (Though cataclysm would bring a change of regime, it didn't bring all that much of a change in life.) And with it, we have a reassertion of the primary social reality of the crowd, the mass of people—who here are calling for a war in which they will be cannon fodder, in a useless and senseless slaughter that Zola grimly details in the novel devoted to the Franco-Prussian War, *La Débâcle*. Public history, History capital H, and private history coincide and interlock perfectly at the end of this novel, and offer the reader a privileged glimpse into a dark future.

Back in chapter 10, Nana reads a novel—about a whore. She finds it false, but especially she is indignant about this kind of literature, with its claim to represent nature: "as if one could show everything! As if a novel shouldn't be written for entertainment! On the subject of novels and plays, Nana had fixed opinions: she wanted works that were tender and noble, things to dream upon, to enhance the soul" (332) [298]. Zola's *mise en abyme* here of the novel we are reading is amusing, and also suggestive, especially on the question of "showing everything." *Nana* claims to "show everything." I have tried to suggest that it doesn't quite make good on that claim, perhaps for reasons that are overdetermined. Zola can't quite show everything, I think, because the everything in this case is everything-and-nothing, the "petit rien" that motivates everything. He can't show quite everything, also, because he does want to entertain—he wants his book to be readable (in England it was judged unreadable, and banned). Finally, he can't quite show everything because you never can—saying everything is after all the mad ideal of the Marquis de Sade. You encounter the limits of representation, the limits imposed pre-

128   cisely by the detail, by the process of metonymy. This allows you to speak
details, to produce an accumulation of details that evoke a whole. But it
doesn't quite, ever perhaps, allow you to speak of their organizing principle
or prime mover, except metaphorically, or as allegory. Zola's prime motors
and machines in his novels are elaborately detailed, patiently described, but
in their essence unsayable. The principle of their pressure and motion is de-
tectable, but not quite visible or sayable. And in this sense, again, Nana and
her not quite visible sexe are only the extreme version of all Zola's machines
and motors.

There are, then, forces that are beyond representation in Zola's understanding of representation—forces that can be detected only in their effects.
Not for Zola Balzac's ambition to write œuvres philosophiques that would reveal
the causes behind social effects. The causes are there, and sexuality in Zola
is certainly one of the most powerful, not only in Nana but throughout the
Rougon-Macquart (most flamboyantly in La Faute de l'abbé Mouret). But sexuality is
all in its effects, in Zola's showing: Nana is finally more than anything else
the "Nana-effect," already established in the first chapter, at the Théâtre des
Variétés. As she says, it's not her fault; it's the way men react to her. In this
sense, Zola is wholly faithful to his naturalist premises: Nana is a biodynamic
force. It is, I think, when he takes fright at his own creation and begins to
moralize the force she represents that his project becomes more ambiguous.

Let me end, in a gesture toward a coming chapter, by noting that Zola
played an important role as art critic, as journalist militating for the new art
of the 1860s and 1870s. He championed Courbet (already an established artist) and Manet, whose first "scandals" correspond with Zola's youthful journalism. And he was a schoolmate and boyhood friend of Paul Cézanne, like
himself a native of Aix-en-Provence who moved on to Paris. But at a certain
point Cézanne went beyond him, into a kind of radical redefinition of representation where Zola was unable to follow. In 1896, after a long break in
his art journalism—and two years before his life was wholly changed by his
heroism in the Dreyfus Affair—Zola went back to the Salon, to do a piece
for Le Figaro. This Salon—the moment of Postimpressionism, if you will, of
Pierre Puvis de Chavannes, of Paul Gauguin, of Cézanne—leaves Zola per-
plexed and even outraged. He recalls with nostalgia the effect of paintings by
Manet and Camille Pissarro in earlier salons: "It was the window open onto
nature, the famous plein air wafting in." It becomes clear here (as in his novel

about a painter, L'Œuvre), that to Zola Impressionism was especially this: a renewal with the natural world, in an attempt to paint its effects, of light and shadow and movement, directly, without the inherited conventions of academic art. The next step, into the more radical work of late Monet or Gauguin or Cézanne, did not seem to him a logical development from Impressionism but a betrayal. He complains in 1896: "Here are truly disconcerting works, multicolored women, violet landscapes and orange horses . . . . [Is he responding to Gauguin here? He doesn't name names.] Oh, the women who have one blue cheek, in the moonlight, the other vermillion, in the shaded light of a lamp! Oh, the horizons where the trees are blue, water red and skies green! It is frightful, frightful, frightful! [C'est affreux, affreux, affreux !]" (374). And finally: "The seeds that I saw sown in the earth have germinated in monstrous fashion. I shrink back in terror" (376). Here I think we can hold in some sort of balance Zola's audacities and his limitations. To the extent that representation opens that window to let in the outside air, to the extent that it allows you to see better—to make use of optics better to render natural effects—he is for bold experimentation, he is himself a bold experimenter. But when the limits of the natural world are breached, when you go beyond into something that makes other kinds of claims on the symbolizing imagination (as in Gauguin and Cézanne), then you risk creating the monstrous, something that he shrinks from in fright: "Je recule d'effroi." It is interesting to think that in Nana he does himself create the monstrous—and shrink from her in fright. But his system of representation stops short of trying to understand the monstrous in its inner workings. It's the effects that count.

CHAPTER 8

Unreal City
Paris and London in Balzac, Zola, and Gissing

> Unreal City,
> Under the brown fog of a winter dawn,
> A crowd flowed over London Bridge, so many,
> I had not thought death had undone so many.
> (T. S. Eliot, *The Wasteland*, lines 60–63)

T. S. ELIOT TELLS US IN HIS FOOTNOTES TO *THE WASTELAND* (THESE LINES COME from part 1 of the poem, "The Burial of the Dead") that he is alluding first of all to Charles Baudelaire, to one of the French poet's "Tableaux parisiens" (part of *Les Fleurs du mal*), the poem "Les Sept Vieillards":

> Fourmillante cité, cité pleine de rêves,
> Où le spectre en plein jour raccroche le passant!
>
> [Crawling hive of a city, city full of dreams,
> Where the ghost in daylight solicits the passerby!]

Then he slides to Dante in *Inferno* 3, overwhelmed by the long line of the dead, "ch'io non avrei mai creduto / che morte tanta n'avesse disfatta" [I would never have believed / That death had undone so many] (3.55–57). Eliot manages to combine in this manner the dense, crowded, anthill-like character of the city—"fourmillante" derives from *fourmi*, meaning ant—and its dreamlike, spectral quality—the night-by-day of a thick London fog— as well as the city's mortuary quality, the sense of its inhabitants as ghostly, as the walking dead. What Eliot doesn't say in his footnotes is that behind Baudelaire's murky and disquieting cityscape stands Balzac's (as Baudelaire himself would have been the first to acknowledge). In fact, the lines from "Les Sept Vieillards"—a poem about a queue of spectral old men in a Paris fog—could derive from a famous description of the people of Paris at the start of Balzac's novella *La Fille aux yeux d'or* (*The Girl with the Golden Eyes*): Here, Parisians are "a people exhumed from the grave," "a people horrible to behold, haggard, yellow, weathered." Paris, asserts the Balzacian narrator, is like a vast windswept field where the earth cuts the human harvest more often than elsewhere, only to have it reborn in ranks as crowded as before. What do they want, these cadaverous Parisians? Gold, and pleasure, replies the narrator, in what will become the leitmotiv of this tale of gold, forbidden pleasure, and violent death.

Realism is nothing if not urban: it is most characteristically about the city in some important way, as the new total context of modern life. It's significant that Balzac's criminal mastermind Jacques Collin, alias Vautrin, among other names, carries in his head a kind of pastoral, anti-urban dream: if his first protégé, Eugène de Rastignac, would only agree to marry Victorine Taillefer, whom Collin has made an heiress by killing off her brother in a stage-managed duel, he, Collin, would take as commission enough money to buy a plantation in Virginia, to spend the rest of his days as rural squire. It's as if these urban dwellers of the first generation of realist novels carried with them a pastoral dream derived from Rousseau, in England from William Wordsworth: the longing for a purer life in the country, an ideal of a better humanity elsewhere. But of course Collin never will realize his dream; he is a wholly urban creature, dependent for his very being on the conditions of urban life. There are no worlds elsewhere anymore. The dream of a retreat to the country (still today very much a dream of city dwellers, who settle for the weekend house in the Hamptons or the *maison de week-end* in Normandy) haunts many of those Balzac characters who most powerfully master the urban. They have a nostalgia for an impossible, prelapsarian existence.

It is impossible to think of realism without the city, and vice-versa. The city is the condition of the kind of novel Sainte-Beuve in the 1840s referred to as "industrial literature," and the kind of struggle for survival as a writer dramatized by Balzac in *Illusions perdues* and then, half a century later, reprised by George Gissing in his *New Grub Street*. It is in particular the movement from country to city that might be said to trigger the realist impulse: the impulse, and the need, to describe, to account for, to perform a kind of immediate phenomenology of one's new surroundings. In Stendhal, Balzac, Dickens, Flaubert, and a host of other writers, youth arrives from the provinces and must make sense of the overwhelming sensations of the metropolis. The "London" episode of Wordsworth's *Prelude* gives a sense of how the poetic imagination overwhelmed never quite can recover from the shock of the urban:

> How often in the overflowing Streets,
> Have I gone forward with the Crowd, and said
> Unto myself, the face of every one
> That passes by me is a mystery.
> (*The Prelude* [1805], 7.595–98)

The experience of the urban stroller becomes more and more phantasmagoric, until it is interrupted, and summarized, in the famous encounter with the blind beggar:

>   lost
> Amid the moving pageant, 'twas my chance
> Abruptly to be smitten with the view
> Of a blind Beggar, who, with upright face,
> Stood propp'd against a Wall, upon his Chest
> Wearing a written paper, to explain
> The story of the Man, and who he was.
> My mind did at this spectacle turn round
> As with the might of waters . . . (7.609–12)

Whereas that shock would be precisely what some other writers—particularly the French ones, most especially Baudelaire—made their subject: as, for instance, in Lucien de Rubempré's first stroll in the Tuileries Garden after he has just reached Paris, in *Illusions perdues*, where he encounters the signs of everything he will have to understand and master. Encounter with the city is perhaps first of all a semiotic crisis: the discovery that there is a whole new sign-system that needs to be deciphered, and that it points to a social code yet to be learned.

 Another Balzac novella, *Ferragus* (it stands alongside *La Fille aux yeux d'or* as part of *Histoire des Treize*), opens with the narrator reading the social and moral meanings of the streets of Paris:

> There are in Paris certain streets dishonored as much as a man convicted of infamy; then there are streets that are noble, others that are simply honest, then young streets on whose morality the public hasn't yet formed an opinion; then murderous streets, streets older than old dowagers are old, es-

timable streets, streets always clean, streets always dirty, laboring, working, mercantile streets. That's to say: the streets of Paris have human qualities, and each by its physiognomy forces certain ideas on us. There are streets of bad company where you wouldn't want to live, others where you would willingly set up house. Some streets, such as the rue Montmartre, have a fine head but end in a fish tail.

The passage goes on, detailing for nearly a page other examples of streets and their social and moral qualifications. Then the narrator steps forward to say:

These observations, incomprehensible outside of Paris, will doubtless be grasped by those men of mind and spirit, of poetry and pleasure who know how to cull in strolling though Paris the mass of delights that float, at any hour, between her walls; by those for whom Paris is the most delicious of monsters: here, a seductive woman, over there old and impoverished; here brand new like the coin of a new régime; in this corner, elegant like a fashionable woman. A full-fledged monster, moreover! Its attics, a kind of head full of knowledge and genius; its second storeys, replete stomachs; its ground-floor shops veritable feet: from there set out all the runners and the commercial travelers.

And he goes on to describe the movements of the monster: how the last carriages return from society balls, in the center of Paris, as on the outskirts laboring arms set off to work. The image of a vast lobster with its articulated carapace—each part seeming to move separately but also in unison—comes to the narrator's mind.

This start of *Ferragus* provides a fairly simple act of reading Paris: assignment of moral epithets to its streets and quarters, then its anatomization as monster, as a living, breathing ensemble, each part of it a "fragment of cellular tissue." It is the starting point for a multitude of acts of reading Paris in Balzac's work, either by the narrator or by one of those young protagonists newly arrived from the provinces who must learn the signs of Paris in order to survive. Numerous are the scenes where we find one of those protagonists, sometimes in the company of an older mentor, initiator into the Paris labyrinth, standing on one of the places of high ground in Paris— such as Père-Lachaise cemetery—looking out and down at the city he must understand in order to conquer it. Paris must be made legible if one is to possess it—and the classic expression of that comes in a famous moment at the end of *Le Père Goriot*, when Eugène de Rastignac stands at the heights of Père-Lachaise, buries his "last tear of youth" in the tomb of Old Goriot, then looks down at the *beaux quartiers* of Paris lying along the two banks of the Seine where the lights are beginning to go on for the evening, and issues his famous dueler's challenge: "A nous deux maintenant!"

In the passage from *Ferragus*, the narrator designates himself as someone who strolls and loafs through Paris: "en flânant dans Paris." The person of the urban stroller, the pedestrian who wanders through the city without any fixed itinerary or goal, will become a famous figure, from Balzac to the Surrealists and beyond. The *flâneur* gets its full early development in that poet who was a devoted admirer of Balzac, Baudelaire. The point of the flâneur is that he is disengaged from the primary business of the city—the city as the space of commercial transactions—an apparently aimless wanderer, a figure of the philosopher and poet who observes and understands the city. One of Balzac's early occasional texts was an essay on the shop signs of Paris—at that time still the medieval type of hanging sign, usually with a visual emblem of the kind of goods or services offered within: a boot, say, or a cow's head— that is, a kind of elementary course on how to read the nature and use and meaning of the street you are in. Baudelaire's flâneur tends toward greater ironic disengagement, a sense of alienation from the bourgeois crowd—as well as a fascination with it—and an acute alertness, surely derived from Balzac, to the allegorical potential of daily incident (see, notably, the long poem "Le Cygne," explicitly about the allegorization of the cityscape). The city throws up in chaotic and kaleidoscopic fashion unforeseeable experience, brusque encounters with the random and the disturbing—the experience that Walter Benjamin, whose vision of nineteenth-century Paris derives from Baudelaire, describes as "shock." In one of Baudelaire's greatest poems of Paris, the sonnet "A une passante," this shock is explicitly erotic, about the potential of the encounter on a Paris street corner that does not quite become a meeting:

> La rue assourdissante autour de moi hurlait.
> Longue, mince, en grand deuil, douleur majestueuse,
> Une femme passa, d'une main fastueuse
> Soulevant, balançant le feston et l'ourlet;
>
> Agile et noble, avec sa jambe de statue.
> Moi, je buvais, crispé comme un extravagant,
> Dans son oeil, ciel livide où germe l'ouragan,
> La douceur qui fascine et le plaisir qui tue.

Un éclair . . . puis la nuit!—Fugitive beauté
Dont le regard m'a fait soudainement renaître,
Ne te verrai-je plus que dans l'éternité?

Ailleurs, bien loin d'ici! trop tard! *jamais* peut-etre!
Car j'ignore où tu fuis, tu ne sais où je vais,
O toi que j'eusse aimé, ô toi qui le savais!

The traffic roared around me, deafening!
Tall, slender; in mourning—noble grief—
A woman passed, and with a jeweled hand
Gathered up her black embroidered hem;

Stately yet lithe, as if a statue walked.
And trembling like a fool, I drank from eyes
As ashen as the clouds before a gale
The grace that beckons and the joy that kills.

Lightning . . . then darkness! Lovely fugitive
Whose glance has brought me back to life! But where
Is life—not this side of eternity?

Elsewhere! Too far, too late, or never at all!
Of me you know nothing, I nothing of you—you
Whom I might have loved and who knew that too!
("In Passing," trans. Richard Howard)

It is the nature of urban eros to be "fugitive," momentary, something that strikes like lightning. In the midst of the deafening noise of the street, this woman in mourning emerges from the crowd, to create in the observer a re-action of intoxication, excess, an instant certainty of erotic potential and re-birth canceled at the moment of its dawning by the interrupted quality of the encounter. Urban "love" is by nature *interruptus*. Its frustration and its pleasure derive from its momentary nature. "Un éclair . . . puis la nuit!"—the experi-ence is over before it has really begun. And yet the speaker carries away from the experience a certitude of erotic fulfillment had they only managed to turn encounter into rendezvous: "O toi que j'eusse aimé, ô toi qui le savais!"

This sonnet is exemplary in its presentation of the experience of urban life. It is emblematic of experience described, in prose and at far greater length, in numerous novels that evoke the urban context—or, more pre-cisely, that have to come to terms with the urban context. That, it seems to me, is the essential point: nineteenth-century novelists who want to deal with the real conditions of life, who want to be realists, are forced almost ineluctably to face up to the conditions of life in the modernizing city. The emergence of realism corresponds to the emergence of the modern city. As I mentioned earlier, the first half of the century sees a great increase in population, and population density, in both Paris and London. The city draws artists and writers to it, they become a critical mass of the national intelligentsia and in turn know and describe, sometimes celebrate, the "vie de bohème" of the aspiring writer and artist. The English novel—despite the example of Dickens, despite the industrial novels of Elizabeth Gaskell—remains more resolutely wedded to country and small-town life: George Eliot's *Middlemarch*, usually considered the triumph of realism in English fiction, eschews London in favor of small town and county. The real urbanization of the English novel comes a bit later: its exemplary figure is the self-conscious realist, even naturalist, George Gissing.

I am working my way toward Gissing and his London. But I wish to stay with Paris for a moment more. There would be much to reflect on in Flaubert's presentation of Paris, mainly in *L'Education sentimentale*, where he so often is rewriting Balzac's Paris, choosing the same places and kinds of experience, now focused through a protagonist whose relation to the metropolis is both affectionate and anxious. When Frédéric Moreau returns to his native Nogent and tries to become part of the local legal profession, he is seized by a "nostalgie du boulevard"—a sense that life other than on the Parisian street is amputated, mournful. There is nothing in particular Frédéric wants from Paris. Rather, he wants and needs it as the only possible context of life for a young man of taste and sensibility. No world elsewhere is possible. The account of his trip back to Paris (after inheriting from an uncle the money that will enable him to live there) takes us through the ugliness, the lumpy deformity of the suburbs and then develops as a kind of hymn to Paris as we enter into the heart of the city, where Frédéric breathes "that good Paris air that seems to contain all amorous odors and all intellectual emanations." Flaubert's Paris is a place of sadness and loneliness and aspirations disappointed and time wasted, but it is always susceptible of displaying a majestic beauty.

But the novelist of Paris who demands the most attention is Zola, for the breadth and systematicity of his inspection of and report on the city, and for the detail of his descriptions. Zola's novel cycle, *Les Rougon-Macquart*, begins and ends in the south of France, and reaches into far corners of the country —the coal mines of the north, the farms of the Beauce, the eastern provinces devastated by the Franco-Prussian War. But it keeps coming back to Paris as the center of the productive forces that are reshaping France, and especially the capital itself, under the Second Empire: the Paris of the central markets, Les Halles, in *Le Ventre de Paris*, of the stock market in *L'Argent*, and the apartment house of *Pot-Bouille*, and the packed proletarian slums of *L'Assommoir*, and so on. Then there is *La Curée*, which records the frenetic and largely criminal speculation that accompanied the rebuilding of Paris by Baron Haussmann—Napoléon III's master planner and administrator—under the Second Empire. It is the novel of insider trading, if you will: knowing where a new avenue would be pierced through the old Paris, where a new hotel could be built, gave the possibility of buying up properties you knew were targeted for destruction, jacking up their value through fictitious leases and tenants, then having yourself expropriated at a handsome profit. There is all of this, and more, in *La Curée*, combined with incestuous and perverse sexuality, which points to the essential unhealth of the new Paris. Yet there are also the hymns to piles of fruit and vegetables in *Le Ventre de Paris*, the most painterly of Zola's novels (even more than the novel about a painter, *L'Œuvre*): visits to Les Halles in the first chapter of the novel take us through the full cycle of a day, from a tableau that might be called *Légumes soleil levant* to the *Plein soleil* of noon to the dusky views of evening.

There would be much, much more to say about these two novels, and others. But even more notable, perhaps, is the novel about a department store, *Au Bonheur des Dames*, which seizes upon an essential product and dynamic of the transformation of the city in the age of high capitalism. The department store is a creation of (and for) the new city: it depends for its existence on the cutting through of the new wide avenues and boulevards that link the old impacted districts of the city in a new dynamic whole: a city where one can travel from one part to another with ease, by omnibus and later by Métro, and stroll with pleasure on wide, tree-fringed sidewalks. The nostalgia for the old Paris you find in Baudelaire (and many others), and represented here by the old textile commerce of the Baudu family, inexorably doomed by the cheaper pricing and monopolistic industry control of the department stores, appears to be trumped by a kind of triumphalist social Darwinism. If there is distress and melancholy in the decline of the old commerce, including the literal wasting away of its practitioners, it is overridden by a joyful necessity: that the ruins of old Paris will be the manure to fertilize a new and healthier city. Denise Baudu, the protagonist of the novel, comes to see herself as a chosen figure of destiny: someone who comes out of the old commerce but understands the necessity of the new, espouses its laying waste of the old toward a new form of more rational social organization. The department store itself grows over the course of the novel in spectacular fashion, coming to occupy an entire city block (following some skillful insider maneuvering on the location of a new avenue) and to include a world within itself, from the packing and shipping department and the employees' cafeteria in the basement to the shopgirls' dormitory in the attic, and in between not only every conceivable article of commerce but also a restaurant and a reading room.

Where store meets street we have the new phenomenon of the *vitrine*, the plate-glass window, and in the *vitrine* the *étalage*, the display of goods for sale. In the narrow shops of the old textile trade, you went inside and asked the clerk to show you a sample of merchandise, which he would then take down from a high shelf and unroll on the counter before you. Denise and her brothers, just arrived in Paris from Normandy, discover Au Bonheur des Dames, and in particular that attenuation of the wall between store and street, inside and outside, produced by the plate-glass windows with their artful displays and bright lighting, luring the shopper inside. It is a particular relation of commerce to street that we are today losing in the suburban mall, which abolishes the street in favor of a continuous inside, the outside become nothing but parking lot. But you can of course still experience it in New York and Chicago and a few other cities, in the kind of glamour and excitement created by the display that greets you at street level, the seductive invitation to enter into what Zola sees as the successor to the church, the place of a new materialist and erotic cult of woman. "Now there's a store!" exclaims Denise, as she and her brothers follow the windows down the street, marveling at each new display. Finally they reach the ready-to-wear clothing, in a window that is "a chapel raised to the religion of female beauty."

The display of clothing for women along the city street represents for Zola the promiscuous urban meeting place of sex and commerce, which in this first chapter of *Au Bonheur des Dames* is embodied in the mannequin, the display dummy: "The rounded bosoms of the dummies swelled the fabric, their wide buttocks exaggerated the narrowness of the waist; the missing head was replaced by a large label stuck with a pin into the red velvet of the neck; while the mirrors on both sides of the display case in a clever play reflected them, multiplied them endlessly, peopled the street with these gorgeous women for sale, wearing their prices in bold numbers in the place of their heads" (15). By the end of chapter 1, as rainy night is falling, a dummy from this window is imagined as "a headless woman rushing through the downpour to some party, in the unknown shadows of Paris." The department store display window in this manner transforms the city into a machine for erotic reverie and for the seduction of women through the alienation and commodification of their own bodies. It's no wonder that Zola's novel ends with a spectacular sale of undergarments, where men—the captains of commerce—propose to women shoppers the purchase of articles of clothing that the men have fetishized—and then convinced the women that they must have, at any price. In this novel, Zola invents for literature that most modern of comportments: shopping, including its pathologies, from binge buying to shoplifting.

The department store, and particularly its counters upon counters of clothing and accessories for women, marks a commodification of women's bodies almost more striking than that in Nana, and a representation of commodity fetishism that conjoins Marx and Freud. Not only are articles proposed for sale invested with a kind of prestige, given an aura that makes them desirable even if not necessary, they are also erotic tokens, stand-ins for desire. And of course the new commerce of the department stores, based on a much quicker turnover of inventory, and therefore the quicker turnaround of invested capital, represents an acceleration of the Balzacian dynamic of things and money. If things are spectacular and desirable, they nonetheless are at the mercy of money. If money is supposed to be a system of symbolic values that allows you to acquire those things you need and want, the speedup of capitalist production and marketing seems almost to produce the opposite: things come to stand for the money that went into their sale or acquisition, or would be necessary to acquire them. Recall Marx: "Everything that is solid melts into air." Despite all the heavy machinery in Zola's novelistic universe, there is a certain liquidity to things, even a liquefaction. Octave Mouret, the owner of Au Bonheur des Dames, the genius of display

140   and salesmanship, stands at the top of the grand staircase in the store and breathes in the odor, the gaseous emanation created by the frenetic buying and selling going on below him.

The city as place of commercial transaction—of money, essentially—is perhaps more and more characteristic of realism of the later nineteenth century—the realism that often called itself naturalism. It's as if the prestige of the unique, individuated object that you find still in Balzac and even in Flaubert has melted under the alchemy of capitalism. In Flaubert's *L'Education sentimentale*, there is the prophetic figure of Jacques Arnoux, who founds a company called "L'Art industriel" and who devotes his career to producing "le sublime à bon marché": the sublime at discount prices, the cut-rate sublime. Writers seem to be particularly sensitive to the commodification of everything, including the beautiful, the loss of aura associated with modernity. That is probably inevitable in that writing, however commercial its means of publication and dissemination, remains a handcraft, a *Handwerk*, as Benjamin says. In an age of industrialization and commercialization that includes literature, the writing of literature generally remains a solitary and artisanal kind of work.

That is one of the profound themes of George Gissing's best-known novel, *New Grub Street*, which, like Balzac's *Illusions perdues* a half-century earlier, explores what literature is becoming in the new and transitory regime of publishing in the 1880s and 1890s. The successful character in that novel is the supple journalist without much of a conscience; the most abject of many failures is the novelist Edwin Reardon who, after a modest success with his first productions, falls further and further into debt as he cudgels his brains to produce yet another triple-decker novel—the novel in three volumes, soon to give way to shorter fare. The more he writes the more he loses money. He mercifully is killed off by pneumonia. *New Grub Street* also fields an explicitly realist novelist, Harold Biffen, who works steadily at a book with the enticing title of *Mr. Bailey, Grocer*. "What I aim at," says Biffen, "is an absolute realism in the sphere of the ignobly decent. The field, as I understand it, is a new one; I don't know any writer who has treated ordinary vulgar life with fidelity and seriousness" (144). Biffen criticizes Dickens for his melodrama, and his humor; and Zola for writing heroic tragedies. Whereas Biffen aims at the tedious. "That is the stamp of the ignobly decent life. If it were anything but tedious it would be untrue. I speak, of course, of its effect upon the ordinary reader." When *Mr. Bailey, Grocer* finally breaks into print, the extra-ordinary readers who recognize its merit—perhaps something like Flaubert's in *Bouvard et Pécuchet?*—are predictably scarce, and Biffen, facing imminent starvation, commits suicide.

Reardon at one point tells Biffen he's invented a riddle: "Why is a London lodging-house like the human body?" The answer turns out to be: "Because the brains are always at the top" (341). Reardon's claim to originality here must be disputed, since the riddle is a version of the metaphor Balzac uses in *Ferragus*: there, houses are human bodies with feet (the active shops of the street floor) and bellies (the well-nourished bourgeois of the main floors) and brains in the artists' garrets. Gissing may well have been aware of his borrowing: he was keenly conscious of his predecessors in the realist tradition—he wrote a book on Dickens, for instance—and was perhaps the most self-conscious English realist, or even naturalist, since he clearly is indebted to Zola's example, at a time when Zola had been banned in England and his publisher jailed (on the occasion of the publication of the English translation of Zola's novel about peasants, *La Terre*), and his kind of deterministic and biological fiction considered offensive to English morals.

What I think is absolutely distinctive and important in Gissing was suggested by Henry James, who found this younger contemporary an interesting case: the fact that he had made himself "the authority" on the lower, indeed the lowest middle class, a "region vast and unexplored." James goes on:

> The English novel has as a general thing kept so desperately, so nervously clear of it, whisking back compromised skirts and bumping frantically against obstacles to retreat, that we welcome as the boldest of adventurers a painter who has faced it and survived. We have had low life in plenty, for, with its sores and vices, its crimes and penalties, misery has colour enough to open the door to any quantity of artistic patronage. We have shuddered in the dens of thieves and the cells of murderers, and have dropped the inevitable tear over tortured childhood and purified sin. We have popped in at the damp cottage with my lady and heard the quaint rustic, bless his simple heart, commit himself for our amusement. We have fraternized on the other hand with the peerage and the county families, staying at fine old houses till exhausted nature has, for this source of intoxication, not a wink of sociability left.

This is an eloquent definition and defense of Gissing's realism, which James contrasts to the Dickensian lower depths and the Anthony Trollope–type high society. Gissing is to some extent a more successful Flaubert—not in aesthetic terms, since James deplores Gissing's lack of a sense of composition, but in the attempt to render "middling" experience, the life of most city dwellers.

More accurately, London dwellers. Gissing knows his London, including that particular London phenomenon of the suburb, the kind of imitation of the town within the city. His working title for In the Year of Jubilee (1894) was in fact Miss Lord of Camberwell, referring to the suburb in which Nancy Lord grows up and which indeed very much defines both her aspirations and her limitations. One of the first things we learn about Nancy, when she is introduced in chapter 3, is: "She was haunted by an uneasy sense of doubtfulness about her social position" (16). Her father, a dealer in pianos, while earning a decent living from his warehouse in Camberwell Road, has failed to accumulate the fortune that would make his commercial roots irrelevant. Nearly every page of the novel makes reference to issues of class distinction—not so much between well-marked upper and lower classes but rather fine gradations traced out within the lower-middle to middle-middle classes. Stephen Lord married slightly above his station—but badly, since his wife deserted him. His children, Nancy and Horace, have been better educated than he— yet again the results are not certainly good. "She thinks herself too good for the life she leads here, and yet I don't believe she'll ever find a place among people of a higher class. . . . I have made her neither one thing nor another," Stephen Lord says of his daughter (69). Her suitor despite himself, Lionel Tarrant, regards her as "in every respect his inferior. She belonged to the social rank only just above that of wage-earners; her father had a small business in Camberwell; she dressed and talked rather above her station, but so, now-a-days, did every daughter of petty tradesfolk" (123). He considers her "a sample of the pretentious half-educated class . . . turned out in thousands every year, from so-called High Schools." Lionel has an Oxford education; but he is only two generations from the ancestor who made a fortune in "Tarrant's Black Lead": his snobbery thus is riven by a certain anxiety. He would not have chosen Nancy as a wife. It's more that she chooses him, and gives herself to him in a moment that is both sexually passionate and possibly calculated. Then Lionel must marry her because she is not lower-class enough simply to be abandoned to the sidewalk or kept as an invisible mistress.

The full incarnation of Camberwell is the man Stephen Lord brought into partnership in the piano business, Samuel Barmby, who lives in a "new and respectable house" in Dagmar Road, a name "which looks well at the head of note-paper." The Barmby sisters live a kind of life that Nancy will revolt against: "In the strictest sense their life was provincial; nominally denizens of London, they dwelt as remote from everything metropolitan as though Camberwell were a village of the Midlands" (177)—that possibility of escape from the city within the city which was, and still is, a peculiarity of London's urbanism, and dictated the growth of the city at Gissing's time, with the creation of endless rows of "villas" and semidetached brick cottages with miniscule front "areas" and back gardens. Jessica Morgan, the young woman who seeks success through examinations—and ends up in the Salvation Army—lives in a sinister product of London's rapid expansion: "It was one of a row of new houses in a new quarter. A year or two ago the site had been an enclosed meadow, portion of the land attached to what was once a country mansion; London, devourer of rural limits, of a sudden made hideous encroachment upon the old estate, now held by a speculative builder; of many streets to be constructed, three or four had already come into being, and others were mapped out, in mud and inchoate masonry, athwart the ravaged field" (183–84). And the passage goes on to detail the destruction and ugliness brought by this cheap new construction, which starts to fall apart even before completion.

Barmby speaks with the voice of Camberwell, just as his father repeatedly writes letters to the newspapers in its style: "'No, sir'—this sentence frequently occurred, —'it was not thus that our fathers achieved national and civic greatness.' And again: 'All the feelings of an English parent revolt,' &c. Or: 'And now, sir, where is this to end?'—a phrase applied at one moment to the prospects of religion and morality, at another to the multiplication of muffin-bells" (179). Spoken Samuel Barmby is almost as good as something from Flaubert. In his pretentiousness, Barmby appears even more loathsome than the slovenly Peacheys and Frenches, who speak "a peculiar tongue, the product of sham education grafted upon a stock of robust vulgarity." (10) Yet Barmby will turn out to be capable of a certain Camberwell nobility.

But it is Luckworth Crewe who really takes Nancy to London, to real London, the place of crowd, spectacle, danger, and excitement. Crewe is from the north of England, rough, unpolished, but full of energy and good spirits, and sexual presence. He will become a successful advertising agent, and associate in Beatrice French's South London Fashion Club, designed for the "servant-keeping females in Brixton, Camberwell, and Peckham" who have no inkling how to dress. Advertising in this novel very much represents the latest vulgarity — Tarrant deplores it, for instance — and a vision of the future. As Nancy rides the tram to London, and the Jubilee, she avoids conversation with Samuel Barmby by scanning the advertisements above his head:

> Somebody's 'Blue;' somebody's 'Soap;' somebody's 'High-class jams;' and behold, inserted between the Soap and the Jam — 'God so loved the world, that He gave His only-begotten Son, that whoso believeth in Him should not perish, but have everlasting life.' Nancy perused the passage without perception of incongruity, without emotion of any kind. Her religion had long since fallen to pieces, and universal defilement of Scriptural phrase by the association of the market-place had in this respect blunted her sensibilities. (52–53)

The narratorial comment closing this paragraph is heavy-handed (one regrets there is so much of it in Gissing), but the passage is also prophetic of Joyce, of Leopold Bloom's wandering consciousness passing over Dublin advertisements; and the evangelical message inserted between soap and jam heralds a distinctly modern world.

The Jubilee itself — celebrating the fiftieth year of Queen Victoria's reign, in 1887 — allows Nancy to shake off Barmby's chaperonage, to make an assignation with Crewe, and then to plunge into the crowd alone:

> No one observed her solitary state; she was one of millions walking about the streets because it was Jubilee Day, and every moment packed her more tightly among the tramping populace. . . . But for an occasional bellow of hilarious blackguardism, or for a song uplifted by strident voices, or a cheer at some flaring symbol that pleased the passers, there was little noise; only a thud, thud of footfalls numberless, and the low, unvarying sound that suggested some huge beast purring to itself in stupid contentment.
>
> Nancy forgot her identity, lost sight of herself as an individual. Her blood was heated by close air and physical contact. She did not think, and her emotions differed little from those of any shop-girl let loose. The "culture," to which she laid claim, evanesced in this atmosphere of exhalations. Could she have seen her face, its look of vulgar abandonment would have horrified her. (58)

That a clerk will in a moment pay her compliments, and a drunk put his arm about her waist, draws the lesson of this abandonment, this melting of individuality and social distinction into the urban crowd. But for all the strictures on how Nancy would have judged her own behavior with a cooler head, there is a sense of real enjoyment in the crowd, and when the evening generates thwacking encounters with the police, that's the kind of thing Crewe quite enjoys, as he makes clear later when describing his delight in the Lillie Bridge Riot. The city is a place of menace and animality, sexually as well as commercially arousing.

It's also with Luckworth Crewe that Nancy climbs the winding stairs to the top of the Monument:

> On issuing into daylight, he became silent, and they stood side by side, mute before the vision of London's immensity. Nancy began to move round the platform. The strong west wind lashed her cheeks to a glowing colour; excitement added brilliancy to her eyes. As soon as she had recovered from the first impression, this spectacle of a world's wonder served only to exhilarate her; she was not awed by what she looked upon. . . . Here her senses seemed to make literal the assumption by which her mind had always been directed: that she—Nancy Lord—was the mid point of the universe. No humility awoke in her; she felt the stirring of envies, avidities, unavowable passions, and let them flourish unrebuked. (87–88)

Crewe tells her that she is at this moment "the most beautiful girl to be found anywhere in this London!" To which she suggests that if he wants to have her, he needs to earn twenty thousand pounds a year. That's a large order, says Crewe, to which Nancy replies: "Of course it is. But what was it you said? The most beautiful girl in all London? That's a large order, too, isn't it? How much is she worth?" (88–89). This kind of language disturbs Crewe, and of course Nancy must eventually be chastened for a certain willingness to trade her body for money and social ascension.

The scene from the Monument has illustrious precedents, reaching back at least to the Temptation of Christ, and very much including Rastignac's view of Paris from Père-Lachaise at the end of *Le Père Goriot* and perhaps also Wordsworth's view of London from Westminster Bridge, where beneath the sleeping houses "All that mighty heart is lying still." The city is vitality, including erotic arousal, even lust, and lust conjoined with money. Beauty is power, but only if relayed through money. And it is Baudelaire's "fugitive beauty," brought into momentary encounter with the desiring glance but bound to escape if not seized immediately. The city, curiously, resurges in the country, in Teignmouth, where Nancy and Tarrant will become lovers. It's when she hears that Tarrant has arrived in Teignmouth: "A debilitating climate and absolute indolence favoured that impulse of lawless imagination which had first possessed her on the evening of Jubilee Day. With luxurious heedlessness she cast aside every thought that might have sobered her; even as she at length cast off all her garments, and lay in the warm midnight naked upon her bed" (94). There are not many moments when Victorian, even late Victorian heroines are stripped naked—strip themselves naked— and the passage is intentionally daring, an evocation of that "impulse of lawless imagination" that will soon lead to unwed sex with Lionel Tarrant. And it is an impulse she first discovered in the London crowd.

Nancy Lord is a rich character because of the contradictory impulses and dictates that compose her character: she is at once sexual and repressed, with aspirations to originality but hampered by middle-class conventionality. She learns—when apparently abandoned by Tarrant—to be an independent woman with something of a feminist ideology, though she later seems to renounce that in favor of what the narrator calls "rational acquiescence" to her husband (343). She goes to work for Beatrice French's South London Fashion Club—and is accused by Tarrant of becoming a "shop-girl" for the effort. She writes a novel—but consigns it to a drawer when Tarrant criticizes the effort. Her limitations are in part Gissing's, since he appears to be somewhat alarmed as well as fascinated by the "modern woman." But they are also no doubt an accurate reflection of her definition by the milieux that determine her, Camberwell and London, and the uneasy middle-class transit between the provincial and the urbane.

At the low point of her relations with Tarrant—when she thinks herself a single mother who will receive no support from him—Nancy mails him a letter, then continues walking simply "to combat mental anguish by bodily exercise" (271). She walks toward Newington (a district qualified as "repulsive") through the streets of outer London:

> It was one of those cold, dry, clouded evenings of autumn, when London streets affect the imagination with a peculiar suggestiveness. New-lit lamps, sickly yellow under the dying day, stretch in immense vistas, unobscured by fog, but exhibit no detail of the track they will presently illumine; one by one the shop-fronts grow radiant on deepening gloom, and show in silhouette the figures numberless that are hurrying past. By accentuating a

pause between the life of daytime and that which will begin after dark, this grey hour excites to an unwonted perception of the city's vastness and of its multifarious labour; melancholy, yet not dismal, the brooding twilight seems to betoken Nature's compassion for myriad mortals exiled from her beauty and her solace. Noises far and near blend into a muffled murmur, sound's equivalent of the impression received by the eye; it seems to utter the weariness of unending ineffectual toil. (272)

This is a poetry of the urban in a new key, not quite like the tonalities one finds in Balzac or Dickens or even Baudelaire. In its evocation of exile from the beauty and solace of nature, though in a mode of melancholy that is not dismal, it conjures up the contradictions inherent to city life, though perhaps most marked in London as a city that often seems to resist becoming one, to prefer the suburban. And in its evocation of the muffled murmur of "unending ineffectual toil," the passage finally draws our attention to the city as, not spectacle, not animation or amusement, but rather the place of repetitive and unrewarding middle-class work.

Unreal city? The city of the realists is detailed and mapped, named and described, made a replica, a *modèle réduit* of London or Paris. It is determinative of the lives lived within its confines. It is an object, a space, a map. Yet when you plunge into it, it appears as a kind of primal jungle as well, a psychic space of dangerous drives and erotic temptations—as well as of exploitation and oppression. Once again, realism in the quest to know and to detail the environment in which ordinary experience unfolds discovers that vision alone is inadequate, that sight triggers the visionary. The phenomenology of the city discovers that urban space produces a particularly concentrated and dramatic form of existence, an exacerbation, and exhilaration, of human forces. In responding to the new conditions of urban existence, the realist novel finds not only a site needing description, detailing, explanation, but as well the primary stuff of the novelistic. From prostitution to middle-class sexual seduction, the city offers the dream of an intenser experience realized. It is not surprising that where the fascination of the city is concerned, it is the Surrealists who pick up the project of the realists.

CHAPTER 9

Manet, Caillebotte, and Modern Life

PARIS IN THE NINETEENTH CENTURY HAS BECOME ALMOST TOO MUCH OF A cliché to be talked about—something for Flaubert's *Dictionnaire des idées reçues.* I'm not entirely sure why we are so much enamored of nineteenth-century Paris; it's as if we had permanently succumbed to a Jacques Offenbach version of *la vie parisienne:* Paris as the site of pleasures, corruptions and venalities, of wealth and display. But Paris was in fact the cultural capital of Europe in the age of high capitalist expansion and optimism, and that culture included the city itself as artifact. The Second Empire was repressive, corrupt, brutal, ultimately self-destructive; but it created the myths, and to some extent the realities, of *la ville lumière,* the city lit up first by gaslight, then by electricity, as in representation of its advanced civilization. The realities created had much to do with the transformation of the city—a process itself brutal and corrupt, but effective—by Napoléon III's prefect of the Seine, the Baron Haussmann. It has been fashionable among left historians to censure Haussmann, to wax nostalgic over the old city that he ripped apart with his broad avenues and wide *places*—the better, of course, to use cavalry and cannon in the case of yet another insurrection by the Parisian prolos. The Marville photograph reproduced in chapter 5 (see fig. 11) suggests the picturesqueness— though also the suffocating density—of the old city. Haussmannization was not a pretty process, as Zola demonstrated dramatically in *La Curée.* And the taste of the age, most elaborately incarnated in the Garnier opera house, is in many ways the apotheosis of nineteenth-century kitsch, the gilded luxury of an overnourished high bourgeoisie.

But there is this: Haussmann's opening up of Paris made it visible in a new way. If there is a loss of the old picturesque, there is the creation of new vistas and perspectives. Paris becomes the *figurable* city par excellence. If you think back to some of Balzac's meditations on how to see and to understand the city—in *Ferragus*, for instance—you find always an initial difficulty in seeing and reading, which leads to interrogation of the meaning of streets and facades, which then often issues into an allegorical vision. Whereas the new Paris is highly legible, immediately so. It is the place of appearance and impression. And the painters of modern life will understand and exploit the city's light and color and visibility. It is spectacle, it is even pretty, especially when seen in a plunging perspective, from a balcony, as in Claude Monet's view of the boulevard des Capucines in 1873–74 (fig. 16).

Near this site, the Garnier opera house, like a number of other vast Parisian public works of the Second Empire, was just reaching completion. It would open in 1875, under a new regime: the Third Republic, born in the defeat of the French by the Prussians in 1870, a republic that took root only slowly and tentatively—threatened in its early years by a monarchist revival—and then became part of the context of the new painting, what from the first Independents' Exhibit in 1874 became known as "Impressionism." Republicanism is rarely the overt subject of these artists, yet its spirit can be felt in some of their claims to liberation.

But my subject—in Baudelaire's phrase, the "painting of modern life"—begins a bit earlier, in the 1860s, chiefly in the painting of Edouard Manet, then develops in the 1870s, in his work and that of Gustave Caillebotte, neither of whose vision quite fits with Impressionism as it came to be known. Manet and Caillebotte remain more doggedly attached to the urban than most of the Impressionists. We don't necessarily think of Impressionism, or even of Manet, in the context of realism—the connotations of the label Impressionist mainly suggest to us a concern with light, color, and a new kind of brushwork, and avoidance of the "finish" of academic painting. But to contemporaries, such as Zola, the new painters of the 1860s and 1870s were first of all "naturalists" and "actualistes," painters of the real and passing moment. The painting of modern life is done "on location" (as you say in filmmaking), on the spot and at the moment. Manet and his followers had the great merit of moving art outside, leaving the studio for the *plein air*. Manet, unlike Monet and some other Impressionists, didn't usually paint his final canvases outdoors; rather, he did his sketches there, then moved into the studio for the finished version. *Pleinairiste* becomes a defining term in the

Fig. 16. Claude Monet, *Le Boulevard des Capucines*, 1873–74, oil on canvas. The Nelson-Atkins Museum of Art, Kansas City, Missouri. Purchase: The Kenneth A. and Helen F. Spencer Foundation Acquisition Fund, F72-35

abandonment of academic painting for something fresher, more immediate, nature seized at the moment. And "nature" here means not just the forest and the rural landscape (as it mainly was for the Barbizon painters) but also the cityscape: the city as landscape, as entire context of existence.

Baudelaire in his essay *Le Peintre de la vie moderne* (which concerns the minor artist Constantin Guys) defines the beauty of modern life: it consists of two parts, one eternal — beauty as classically defined — and the other transitory, fleeting, contingent, fugitive, the beauty of fashion. It is the beauty brought by the urban crowd observed by the urban stroller, the flâneur whom he made famous. Recall Baudelaire's sonnet "A une passante," discussed in chapter 8. The sonnet records a moment of urban encounter — not a meeting, since the speaker never truly meets the majestic woman in mourning. It commemorates an experience of "shock," Walter Benjamin will say, which belongs exclusively to urban life: visual encounter, the instant creation of a sense of erotic possibility, followed by instant nostalgia. The painting of modern life seems to be largely about the moment, an instant observed in the flux of city life, transitory in its nature, yet by that very fact characteristic. It is clear that Manet and Caillebotte carry on from Courbet in breaking away from history painting — still the genre of greatest official prestige — to record scenes of everyday life. They continue Courbet's project of de-theatricalizing painting, de-dramatizing scenes and poses. They eschew narrative — very much a part of traditional history painting — in favor of what you might call mere incident. They seek the nonchalant, the "candid" moment, the observed that is not conscious of observation.

Manet of course begins his public notoriety with two paintings that create scandal, *Le Déjeuner sur l'herbe* (1863) and *Olympia* (1863; shown in 1865). These paintings, and especially the latter, may in our context be taken to indicate Manet's desire to break with a tradition — indeed to take on, as challenge, that genre of painting that had accrued the heaviest weight of tradition and convention, the nude. For him, as for the Impressionists, the nude was a problem. He worried about finding plausible settings for the nude, in the countryside in summer time. He noted that the nude had become "the first and last word in art"; yet he is reported to have suggested that the models in Thomas Couture's studio, where he trained, put their clothes back on, to provide more realistic subjects. This confirms the impression that we will gain from the large majority of Manet's paintings: that the clothed interests him more than the naked. In this he is in step with his admirer Baudelaire, for whom modern beauty is allied to fashion, to cosmetics, to the accessory: a product of culture and artifice more than nature.

One of Baudelaire's famous nudes—from the poem "Les Bijoux," one of those censored from the first edition of *Les Fleurs du mal*—is fully naked except for her jewelry. This contrast of the artifice of fashion with the naked body creates the eroticism, "candor joined to lubricity," that the speaker of the poem particularly appreciates. There is some of this quality in *Olympia*: the woman's body is presented as the meeting place of nature and artifice, and her bold gaze suggests both candor and lubricity in her self-awareness. Zola understands that *Olympia's* beauty and eros are peculiarly modern: "When our artists give us Venuses, they correct nature, they lie. Edouard Manet asked himself: why lie, why not tell the truth; and he introduced us to Olympia, this *fille* of our own time, whom you will meet on our pavements." Much of Zola's defense of Manet—in the brochure he published in 1867, to accompany Manet's private exhibit of his work—is couched in formalist terms, as the best strategy to turn aside cries of scandal and moral outrage. But in this sentence on *Olympia*, he touches on an essential element of Manet's painting: like that of Constantin Guys praised by Baudelaire in *Le Peintre de la vie moderne*, it responds to the types, the characteristic expressions and decorations and accessories of contemporary life.

Take for instance Manet's *Masked Ball at the Opera* (*Le Bal masqué de l'Opéra*, 1873), which captures a famous contemporary amusement, a form of pleasure-seeking familiar from many novels, notably Zola's *Nana*, where upper-class men go slumming with women who are actresses, *rats d'opéra*—bit players and dancers—and simply prostitutes (fig. 17). (Henry James, reporting on Paris life for the *New York Tribune* in 1876, duly goes to the Bal de l'Opéra, though one suspects without any after-prom.) The men are in evening dress, and masked, the women in a variety of costumes that are erotic in their mockery of formal wear and their transvestism. The girl nearest the center of the canvas wears the costume of the *débardeuse*—a female stevedore—made famous in the sketches of Paul Gavarni, reprised by Flaubert in *L'Education sentimentale*, and a clear sign of erotic availability. This is that famous *demi-monde*, where the men are the same as at the respectable dinner parties—but the women an entirely new cast. There is excitement and confusion in the mixture of social classes, and a certain erotic defilement of the

Fig. 17. Edouard Manet, *Le Bal masqué de l'Opéra*, 1873, oil on canvas. National Gallery of Art, Washington, D.C., Gift of Mrs. Horace Havemeyer in memory of her mother-in-law, Louisine W. Havemeyer. Photo: © 2004 Board of Trustees, National Gallery of Art

respectable precincts of the opera house (Manet paints the old house; the Palais Garnier has not yet opened): see, in particular, the pair of a woman's feet hanging from the balcony into the space of the painting. It is a motif Manet will use again later, in his *Bar at the Folies-Bergère*, and there, too, it seems the sign of a certain troubling and arousing disorder, a transgression full of fun and mockery and the promise of a carnivalesque end to the evening.

It is not only the boisterous pleasures of Paris that interest Manet. The simple subject of *The Railroad* (*Le Chemin de fer*, 1873) is an outing on a pleasant day in the city, where a mother?—or a nanny?—has taken a young girl to the parapet over the railway tracks where they emerge from the Gare Saint-Lazare (fig. 18). It is the most "modern" of settings: the railway line, here casually integrated into everyday life, and the simplest of urban pleasures: reading a book outdoors on a sunny day while a child amuses herself looking down at the trains below. The scene and the poses are notably nonchalant, antitheatrical. They suggest no drama, scarcely even a narrative, or an anecdote. Like the young girl in the painting, Manet turns his back on theatricality and artificiality, refuses to look at the camera, as it were. The woman looks up from her book as if interrupted in her reading by the passerby or the painter—though she doesn't really focus on him, or on the spectator looking at the painting. Her concerns lie within the world of the painting, not in anything she is trying to project outward. Here is the fleeting, contingent beauty of everyday life, unremarkable except that painter-observer has chosen to capture it, has had his gaze arrested by it. It is the kind of beauty commended by Baudelaire in *Le Peintre de la vie moderne*, and one might claim that Manet's work here offers the perfect figuration of the painting of modern life: its subjects, its settings, its attitudes. It may add some piquancy to the ordinariness to realize that the model for the reading woman is Victorine Meurant, ten years earlier the challenging nude of *Olympia*.

Just around the corner from the setting chosen by Manet is the subject of a painting done three years later by Gustave Caillebotte, *Le Pont de l'Europe* (1876; fig. 19). Only within the past couple of decades has Caillebotte emerged from the shadow cast by his Impressionist friends, whom he collected and supported, but from whose work his own subtly differs. It is closer to Manet's, and perhaps all the more resolutely engaged with the contemporary cityscape. Even more than the better-known *Paris Street, Rainy Day* (1877; Art Institute of Chicago), Caillebotte's painting of the bridge that

Fig. 18. Edouard Manet, *Le Chemin de fer*, 1873, oil on canvas. National Gallery of Art, Washington, D.C., Gift of Horace Havemeyer in memory of his mother, Louisine W. Havemeyer. Photo: © 2004 Board of Trustees, National Gallery of Art

Fig. 19. Gustave Caillebotte, *Le Pont de l'Europe*, 1876, oil on canvas. Petit Palais, Musée d'Art Moderne, Geneva. Photo: Erich Lessing / Art Resource, NY

crosses the railway tracks that emerge from the Gare Saint-Lazare engages the materials and shapes of the contemporary. The bridge, completed in 1868, is of cast iron, structured by the triangles that we have become used to from the great bridges of the twentieth century, but then relatively new in a Paris landscape characterized by the stone bridges across the Seine. Here is the material of the new, which interested Zola, too, who praises the architect of his fictional department store in *Au Bonheur des Dames* for working in cast iron and glass; and the Parisian landscape would be completed toward the end of the century by Gustave Eiffel's audacious tower. The pont de l'Europe is very much part of Haussmann's Paris of new broad perspectives, leading the eye to distant vanishing points (remarkable also in *Paris Street, Rainy Day*). If the ironwork of the bridge itself dominates the painting, there are nonetheless figures on it—figures who challenge our viewing and our interpretative efforts. The worker in his smock who is staring down from the bridge at the railway lines below is, like the young girl in Manet's painting, a sign of what Michael Fried would call absorption, a statement of the painting's refusal to engage in a direct or stagy appeal to the viewer. There is, however, a couple walking toward us. Yet on inspection the couple is almost wholly illegible. It's not even certain that we can rightly call it a couple: the man appears to be a few paces ahead of the woman and appears to be turning back toward her—but is it the voyeuristic inspection of the stranger, someone who has just passed her and now looks back at her, or rather the more familiar address of the spouse? The man's face, his eyes shaded by the brim of his hat, is not entirely decipherable, but on close viewing appears more annoyed than pleased. The woman's face, in a gesture used more than once by Caillebotte, is veiled. If the woman's veil is a mark of bourgeois distinction, and a kind of protection against the city's promiscuity, it also confers a certain opacity on her, almost as a sign of the limits to our viewing.

Our surrogate for entry into the viewing space of the painting is that dog trotting into the picture plane and over the bridge, resolutely turned away from us, brandishing its tail more or less in our faces. Though "brandishing" may too much imply motion: while there is plenty of movement in the scene—the dog, and the man advancing toward us, and a soldier with red trousers in the background, are all very much taking steps—the painting nonetheless gives an impression of immobility, of fixity. Like *Paris Street, Rainy Day* and a number of other Caillebotte paintings of Paris, the effect is slightly eerie, almost surrealist—on the way to being one of Giorgio de Chirico's mysterious landscapes. Its combination of eeriness and punctilious attention to the detail of the cityscape provokes an ungoverned play of interpretation. It is tempting to see some representation of urban anomie, of the affectless relations of citizens of the city, strangers despite themselves. Though the number of persons in the painting doesn't make up what we would call a crowd—there is too strong an impression of empty space—there are still suggestions of the impersonality of urban life, almost its effect of alienation. But to spin allegories off this painting, as off *Paris Street, Rainy Day*, may be a temptation that should be resisted. Before, and beyond, the interpretative enigmas it may pose, the painting is remarkable by the thereness of the objects and the cityscape that it presents. As an up-to-date phenomenology of the city, it is notable.

Caillebotte eventually moved into an apartment on the boulevard Haussmann—a gesture we may want to see as symbolically appropriate for someone who paints over and over the sights opened by the renovation of Paris. Again and again, he gives us scenes taken from balconies, where the gaze is led vertiginously downward from on high, in a technique favored by much photography of Paris as well. He painted what must be his own balcony on the boulevard Haussmann in 1880 (fig. 20). We are outside one of those fifth- or sixth-story apartments typical of the new construction of Haussmann's Paris, with two well-dressed bourgeois men enjoying the view and the elevation, the luxury of belonging to the city but with a certain separation from it. The elevated view of Paris returns often in the painting of Manet, Degas, Monet, Pissaro, more often from the privileged, panoramic perspective provided by the second or third story than from the vertiginous height you find in Caillebotte (see fig. 16). Caillebotte was himself a wealthy bourgeois—this enabled him to build the first great collection of the work of his contemporaries, which he left as a bequest to the Louvre, where it formed the nucleus of holdings of the new painting of the 1860s, 1870s, and 1880s.

It is hence probable that the floor of the paneled and gilded apartment being scraped for refinishing in the very large painting *The Floorscrapers* (*Les Raboteurs de parquet*, 1875) is Caillebotte's own (fig. 21). The biographical detail is without importance, except that it may add to our sense of the remarkably dispassionate attitude of the painting, its cool, distanced observation of manual labor. The workers are stripped to the waist, yet their torsos and arms

Fig. 20. Gustave Caillebotte, *Un Balcon, Boulevard Haussmann*, 1880, oil on canvas.
Private collection, Paris. Photo: Comité Gustave Caillebotte, Paris

Fig. 21. Gustave Caillebotte, *Les Raboteurs de parquet*, 1875, oil on canvas. Musée d'Orsay, Paris. Photo: Herve Lewandowski, Réunion des Musées Nationaux / Art Resource, NY

don't at all give the heroic effect of classical male bodies. Here the bodies are sinewy, tough, but not what one would call beautiful. They are bodies strained by work of a strenuous and repetitive kind. Their task is not glamorized, it is rather strictly observed, with a fine attention to the details of the tools used, the scrapings produced, the postures and gestures of the task. The workers are absorbed in their labor; they do not look up at the proprietor — if that is the way to identify him — in whose pay they are working, though one of them turns an apparently quizzical glance toward the man working next to him, as if to compare progress. A wine bottle and half-filled glass stand on a table. This detail seems to me, again, dispassionately observed and registered. There is no overt moralization of the wine drinking that enables the workers to carry on: there seems to be far less commentary than in Zola's L'Assommoir, for instance. The dark wine bottle to our right stands in visual contrast to the window, a rooftop visible though the typically Parisian luminous gray of the air, beyond the gilded iron tracery of the balcony railing. The visual contrast is also a class contrast, but again Caillebotte does not insist, does not dramatize.

Much more could be said about the whole question of work as a subject for painting — continuing a discussion begun with Courbet's Stonebreakers (see fig. 6). Those we have come to know as the Impressionists tended on the whole to avoid pictures of hard work — the leisure of the garden, the dinner table, boating on the river, or the life of passers-by in the city street were more appealing subjects. When Claude Monet paints men unloading coal from barges in the Seine, his Déchargeurs de charbon, the result looks something like a Japanese print, with a delicate notation of the steep angles of the gangplanks the men cross from barge to shore carrying a great sack of coal that must weigh heavy, but does not look so in Monet's representation. Edgar Degas will do a number of paintings (and pastels) of laundresses and other women at work behind the scenes of the bourgeois household. Many of them are notable in their capture of the motions and gestures of work. His Woman Ironing (Repasseuse, 1873), for instance, seizes the weight of the body shifted into the arm that presses down with the iron. Compared to the Caillebotte, the work of the repasseuse is graceful, even pretty — to the observing artist, at least. Yet as in the Caillebotte, one senses a commitment to making representation of the working body accurate — making of the painting as it were an embodiment of the work action (fig. 22).

Fig. 22. Edgar Degas, *Repasseuse*, oil on canvas, 1873. The Metropolitan Museum of Art, New York, H. O. Havemeyer Collection, Bequest of Mrs. H. O. Havemeyer, 1929 (29.100.46). All rights reserved

Caillebotte's painting in the 1880s includes a number of still lifes, among them some scenes from the butcher's display that have a raw and troubling quality (fig. 23). It is hard to know how to react to such brutally anatomical representations. The choice of the calf's severed head, hanging from its nose, its eye closed but somehow gentle and appealing nonetheless, shocks, and turns us as spectators and eaters into something almost cannibalistic. The tongue, with its attached matter, is more bloody and aggressive still. I don't think it is merely the squeamishness of the twenty-first-century American used to packaged meat that makes the painting disturbing. While traditional still life could often include dead game birds and dead fish, for instance, these tended to be graceful signs of abundance rather than shocking challenges to the eye, as I think we have in Caillebotte's painting. *Tête de veau et langue de bœuf* is quite unlike the tradition of the still life, indeed a bit of a scandal in the terms of that tradition. It is in any event of an uncompromising realism. The nearest literary analogue I can think of is Zola's scene of viewing bodies in the Paris morgue, in *Thérèse Raquin*.

But what you get most of all, especially in Manet, is the life of the more or less well-clad body of everyday Parisian activities, especially leisure activities, the experience of the café and the public park and the sidewalk. Take among a number of possible examples Manet's *Au Café* of 1878, which captures a quintessential urban place and moment (fig. 24). It is at the same time very much about vision of this place and moment. The marble countertop sweeps through the picture plane at an angle, defining the crowded space of the persons represented, and insisting that we notice its reflective surface, its optical brilliance. The casualness and unimportance of the moment captured—its resolutely undramatic quality—seem to be noted in the definition of space, in the foregrounding of the glasses and glass canister on the shiny countertop, and by the nonchalant poses of the figures. Two of the figures don't look at us at all; they look forward over the bar, toward the invisible bartender. The woman in the foreground glances toward us, as if distracted by the painter-spectator who has joined the group at the bar, much in the manner of the reader of *Le Chemin de fer*. Like that figure, too, she doesn't look at us quite directly: her gaze takes account of our presence, but it does not recognize us. We are simply part of the urban crowd that comes and goes in the café, a space of what you might call public intimacy, impersonal encounter with strangers.

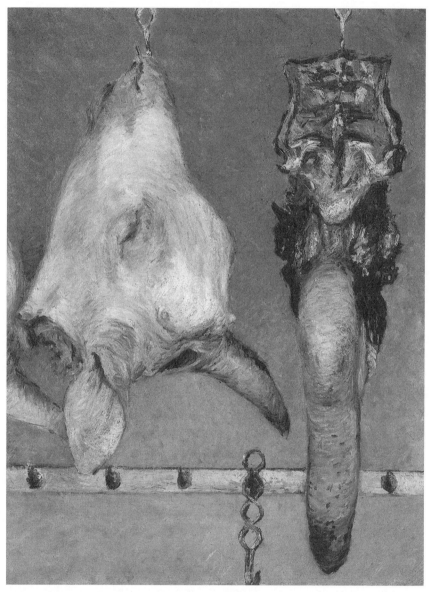

Fig. 23. Gustave Caillebotte, *Tête de veau et langue de bœuf*, 1882. Private collection, Paris. Photo: Comité Gustave Caillebotte, Paris

Fig. 24. Edouard Manet, *Au Café*, 1878, oil on canvas. Collection Oskar Reinhart "Am Römerholz," Winterthur, Switzerland

Behind the heads of the three figures seated at the bar are other heads, not surely but probably the same heads reflected in a mirror on the wall. As with the marble countertop, the reflective glass is a repeated motif in Manet's painting of Parisian life, and no doubt an appeal to the pleasures, as well as the ambiguities and disorientations, of vision itself. There is a certain shine and glitter to modern life as Manet views it: it is notable for its surfaces. And since surface is what painting does best—in some sense what it is about: its own surface—the representation of surface is full of vitality, fun, celebration. This is Baudelaire's modern beauty, of fashion, the contingent, the fleeting, something to be enjoyed without seeking to pose it, to immobilize it, or to give it theatrical significance. It is resolutely a painting of the insignificant.

Take another Manet café scene, this one in pastel, his *Café, place du Théâtre-Français*, known also as *Intérieur de café* (1881; fig. 25). The figure of the woman alone in the café is itself telling, suggesting a new urban freedom for women. Her identity is unclear. She could be a prostitute. On the other hand, she is fully clothed, dress and hat, in respectable bourgeois black. If she is not a respectable *bourgeoise*—there does seem to be something a bit frumpy about her—she can pass for one, thus troubling the official attempts throughout the century to impose clear distinctions between the respectable and the deviant. In any case, she appears to be making a claim to enjoyment of the space of the café, which in this case appears a luminous refuge from the world outside (perhaps from the domestic world as well). The bright illumination of marble tabletops, gilded chairs, the woman's face, the lighted side of the column or pilaster set before the mirror—these all suggest the presence of electric light in the café, a recent innovation that naturally fascinated a painter so concerned with shine and reflection from surfaces. Mirror and illumination together give the painting a frosted quality. Once again, there is a love of surface for itself. As Henry James once remarked, the true superficial aspect of Paris has great charm. Manet sees himself as the painter of that true superficiality, someone whose rendering of visual surface is key in understanding the life played out amid these surfaces.

One more Manet painting of the lives played out in the café seems indispensable, since it is to my mind one of the very greatest, *The Plum* (*La Prune*, c. 1877; fig. 26). The Manet café motifs are all here: the reflective marble tabletop in the foreground, the gilt frame of what is probably a mirror in the background, the subject's gaze off, as one might put it—looking forward

Fig. 25. Edouard Manet, *Café, place du Théâtre-Français*, 1881, pastel. Glasgow Museums: The Burrell Collection

Fig. 26. Edouard Manet, *La Prune*, c. 1877, oil on canvas. National Gallery of Art, Washington, D.C., Collection of Mr. and Mrs. Paul Mellon. Photo: © 2004 Board of Trustees, National Gallery of Art

but avoiding meeting the eye of painter or spectator. She has before her a glass cup with a plum in brandy, part dessert, part drink, and in her left hand she holds an unlighted cigarette. And she is apparently unaccompanied. She is then a figure of audacious modernity: a young woman alone in a café consuming a fruit in alcohol and about to smoke a cigarette. A number of commentators have jumped to the conclusion that she must be a prostitute. Maybe, yet that seems to me far from certain. She is more likely a *grisette*, a shopgirl or otherwise independent young woman. She is elegantly dressed in her pink dress with white lace ruffles at the neck, and black hat with pink chiffon. She has none of the flamboyance, and none of the fatigue, that one finds in Henri de Toulouse-Lautrec's prostitutes, for instance, nor does she seem to display the sad vulnerability of Degas's monotypes from the bordello. If her face may register a certain vacant quality, a lack of focus and concentration, it does not appear unhappy, or demanding, or needy. She seems to be in contented possession of her plum and her place in the café, enjoying the privileges of modern urban existence — including the privilege of being accountable to no one for her presence in the café, and in Manet's painting.

This, like many other Manet representations of everyday Paris life, was in fact posed in his studio, probably using the young actress Ellen Andrée as model, and the marble table that the painter kept on hand for his many café scenes. Knowing that Manet staged the scene of the painting to look like an observed moment in a Paris café may, curiously, enhance our sense of his realist illusionism: his desire not so much to paint the real as to create in the spectator a convincing sense of the real. Manet's understanding of the measure of illusion involved is part of his profundity, as one might say. It is an understanding that is part of the subject in his later work, nowhere more so than in his famous *Bar at the Folies-Bergère*.

It may help us to understand what Manet is doing, and not doing, by a sideways glance at James Tissot, a contemporary who was born and trained in France, compromised in the Paris Commune of 1871, then a refugee in England, where he stayed to pursue a commercially successful career. Such a painting as his *Ball on Shipboard* (c. 1874; fig. 27) presents the English equivalent of the middle and upper-middle classes who inhabit a number of Manet's paintings, and with a cognate feel for the cut of fashion. The painting has much of the color and light and gaiety that we associate with some Manet works, and with such of his followers as Monet and Auguste Renoir. (All,

Fig. 27. James Tissot, The Ball on Shipboard, c. 1874, oil on canvas. Tate, London. Photo: Tate Gallery, London / Art Resource, NY

for instance, used flags to decorative effect.) Tissot uses space with some of the flair and drama of Manet, though more conventionally: he doesn't create the impossible spaces that at times interest Manet. But his painting is in some other ways very different in effect. One senses a narrative in this as in most Tissot paintings, a story to be told, a social chronicle unfolded. It approaches the theatrical, even the stagy in its presentation. It doesn't give us that sense of the nonchalant and the unimportant that Manet achieves: for all the triviality of the event represented, its participants are posing for us.

A painting from ten years later, painted that it is to say shortly after Manet's death, makes yet more evident the difference in their ways of recording modern life. *The Bridesmaid* (c. 1883–85; fig. 28) presents the appurtenances of fashionable modern life—the hackney cab, the umbrellas, elegant dress for men and women—that are familiars of Manet's painting, but it is evident here that they are laid on for a special occasion, for the wedding in which the bridesmaid is about to participate. She is dressed up for the occasion, with all that term implies: this is not her daily existence, it is rather playing queen for a day. Thus the painting is anecdotal, it registers a class consciousness, a humorous or ironic distance between reality and fantasy. The very fact that we are forced to recognize that she is all dressed up for the wedding—and that the citizens of her populous commercial neighborhood have come to view her as she sets out in her finery—means that we cannot view the painting in the same spirit as a similar work by Manet. We are forced into its narrative action. We cannot see it as the pure play of vision on urban surface and spectacle. Tissot's painting comes dangerously close to moralizing; it has the effect of amusing us.

Tissot's *London Visitors* (1874; fig. 29) is one of his best-known works. Like a number of Parisian scenes by Caillebotte and Manet, it celebrates a specific London place, the portico of the National Gallery in Trafalgar Square, framing the Church of Saint Martin's-in-the-Fields—self-consciously celebrates it though the device of the tourist (evoking popular "views" of Roman ruins, for instance, sketched for tourists). The painting is remarkable in its technical virtuosity, its use of the perspective planes (as in a stage set?), its nearly trompe-l'oeil realism (note the cigar set facing us on the step, as a kind of challenge to and joke about our viewing of the painting). The tourists are consulting their guidebook, as if to find out where they are and what they are looking at, which gives the viewer of the painting the addi-

Fig. 28. James Tissot, *The Bridesmaid*, c. 1883–85, oil on canvas. Leeds Museums and Galleries, City Art Gallery. Photo: UK/Bridgeman Art Library

Fig. 29. James Tissot, *London Visitors*, 1874, oil on canvas. Toledo Museum of Art, Purchased with funds from the Libbey Endowment, Gift of Edward Drummond Libbey, 1951.409

tional amusement (again a kind of joke) of knowing (or being supposed to know) what they don't. While the boy in the foreground (like the other boy, in the uniform of Christ's Hospital) turns sideways in the absorptive pose, refusing our gaze, the woman tourist glances directly at the spectator. It's almost as if she is winking at the spectator, sharing a joke about the ponderous ineptitude of her husband with his encumbering guidebook. It is almost as if she were proposing a more interesting rendezvous with whomever she exchanges glances with. This may appear an unsupported reading of the painting. But the point is that it solicits narrative readings, the spinning out of possible stories from its representations, in a way that Manet's paintings refuse. Henry James, reviewing another of Tissot's paintings, *The Gallery of HMS Calcutta* (c. 1876, Tate Britain), asks: "What is it that makes such realism as M. Tissot's appear vulgar and *banal*, when an equal degree of realism, practised three hundred years ago, has an inexhaustible charm and entertainment? . . . His humour is trivial, his sentiment stale." An overly harsh judgment on a painter who renders modern life with fidelity, charm, and wit. Yet it is hard not to see James's point.

Returning to Manet, I want to talk about two more paintings, both from late in his career. First, *Reading the "Illustré"* (*Lecture de "L'Illustré,"* 1878–79; fig. 30). Once again, we have a representation of one of the pleasures of modern urban life: sitting at a café and reading the illustrated newspaper, provided by the establishment. But here it is not the nighttime café, and there would seem to be no question about the respectability of the woman—once again alone, so far as we can tell—who is reading. She is dressed, and accessorized, with full fashionability, including her elegant kid gloves and the chiffon around her neck. Manet's technique here, compared to his earlier work, is more notational, sketchy, impressionist. The sketchy, smudgy, illegible cover of the illustrated newspaper that confronts us perhaps offers something of a reading lesson. It suggests that we cannot penetrate too far into the putative message of the newspaper, or the painting: like the very notion of an illustrated newspaper, this is a moment of repose from strenuous interpretation, or the struggle for existence. Reading, or simply: looking at, the illustrated newspaper while taking your refreshment on the terrace of the café—or is she inside, in front of a large window?—in what appears to be fine spring weather is pleasure in itself. It does not demand strenuous effort, from the participant or the spectator.

Fig. 30. Edouard Manet, *Lecture de "L'Illustré,"* 1878–79, oil on canvas. The Art Institute of Chicago, Mr. and Mrs. Lewis Larned Coburn Memorial Collection, 1933.435. Photo: © The Art Institute of Chicago

The kind of absorption that that Manet creates in his newspaper reader's face might be called seductive. She is wholly absorbed in her perusal of the paper, yet also fully visible to us, her rouged lips and cute nose and bright eyes alluring in an indirect, unself-conscious way that sets up a nice contrast to Olympia's challenge to our spectatorship. Such a painting by Manet indeed lures one into unauthorized interpretation, even allegorization, of the scene, the temptation to embroider an anecdote of urban life around the woman, to want to make her acquaintance, as it were, and to learn more about her. She is a figure of a certain simple yet sophisticated enjoyment that we might wish to share. Manet of course refuses us such narrative and participatory pleasures. The very sketchiness of his brushwork seems a kind of defensive maneuver, saying: you can only go so far in your approach to what I have captured here, it won't yield a more detailed meaning. What it is, rather, is instantaneous, a piece of fugitive beauty, a momentary encounter in the restlessly moving urban crowd.

Finally, there is Manet's Bar at the Folies-Bergère (Un Bar aux Folies-Bergère, 1882; fig. 31), painted in the year before his death, a painting that has elicited unending commentary, quite understandably since I think it can make a claim to being the greatest painting of the nineteenth century. If realism is in part about creating the illusion of the real—and about the process of disillusioning that forces a Lucien de Rubempré or an Emma Bovary to understand that the real is not there where you thought it was—and about viewing that real, then Manet's painting speaks to, summarizes, and critiques the whole tradition. Its place in the history of its kind of painting strikes me as similar to the place of Daniel Deronda, if not Bouvard et Pécuchet, in the history of the realist novel. The face of the barmaid who, unusually for Manet, confronts us directly, and yet, more faithful to his practice, does not quite look at us, has provoked contradictory commentary on her mood, her profession, her social status, her desires. As a barmaid in the glittering but somewhat louche context of the Folies-Bergère, the assumption that she may, like the refreshments she sells, be available for a price, seems reasonable. And the discovery that the viewer of the painting soon makes—that her image from the back, reflected in the mirror behind her, shows her in converse with a gentleman—may reinforce this assumption. Yet the very contradiction between the two presentations of the barmaid, which appeared to some contemporary critics as a simple ineptitude on Manet's part, may signal, as in the café

Fig. 31. Edouard Manet, *Un Bar aux Folies-Bergère*, 1882, oil on canvas. The Samuel Courtauld Trust, Courtauld Institute of Art Gallery, London

pictures, a difficulty of interpretation, a warning against certitude. The back view of the barmaid suggests a certain animation, an engagement with the gentleman—she appears to bend a bit toward him. The frontal view, on the other hand, resolutely resists legibility. Her face may be a representation of urban anomie, of an alienation resulting in passivity, withdrawal, and lack of protest against her lot. Or it may on the contrary suggest autonomy, a re- fusal of the male gaze, an insistence on her professional status, as barmaid. One can't tell. The illegibility of her face—like the illegibility of the journal in *Reading the "Illustré"*—is surely part of the point in a painting that is, among other things, about the difficulty of interpretation from visual evidence.

That mirror, of course, poses problems. It clearly is a mirror (though some interpreters have denied it): you can see the gilt lower edge of the frame, and the reflection of the back edge of the marble bar top, with the bottles of ale and champagne standing on it, is clear enough. Then we reg- ister that the balcony and orchestra of the Folies-Bergère that we see behind the girl are also a reflection in the mirror: they are in fact in front of the bar; and between the spectators and the bar hangs the trapeze, noted by way of the pair of feet hanging down in the upper left-hand corner. The mirror is frosted, slightly hazy in the bright yet vapor-heavy atmosphere lit by the electric globes. But then, why doesn't the reflection of the barmaid from be- hind line up with her frontal representation, in an orderly process of mir- roring, such as Ingres used in many a portrait, in order to show his sitter from more than one side? Somehow the mirror must be tilted at a slight angle—or the bar angled in relation to the mirror—with the result that the rear image of the barmaid is detached from her, at the same time herself and another (there is a strong temptation to posit a second barmaid, at another countertop set behind the first one—but brief reflection, on the reflections precisely, shows this to be impossible). If the barmaid in rear view must be the same as the one facing us, then the gentleman who is gazing intently at her—is he simply choosing his drink, or does he have other designs?—is precisely in our place, and we in his. He has evicted us from the comfortable place of spectatorship or, perhaps more accurately, taken the comfort from that place, crowded us with his elbows, as it were, nudged us perhaps with the knob of the walking stick he holds, to make us ask: What are we doing here gazing at this young woman? What are our motives? Is spectatorship, is representation, an innocent activity?

Like other commentators on the painting, I risk slipping into the allegorical—a move hard to resist with a canvas that reworks all of Manet's tools and tropes of representation. This one may say with some certainty: that the painting is about the illusionism of reality (and the realism of illusions), about how the flat surface of a painting can only represent other surfaces, juxtaposed in ways—and here skewed in ways, to make the point—that create the illusion of depth, volume, and life. One is tempted to say, along with Shakespeare's Troilus discovering a deceptive version of his beloved, "This is, and is not, Cressid." This is and is not a barmaid—the one barmaid. This is and is not the real. If Roland Barthes wished to see the apparently superfluous descriptive detail as a sign of the real—a sign that says: "I am the real"—here Manet appears to say in his details: I am that system for viewing and representing the real that is all you will ever get, all that you will ever know. The painting may strike us as proto-Cubist, in its representation of the same persons and things from different perspectives. Yet it is so only within the classic tools and tropes of representation, very much including that heavily used tool and trope, the mirror.

The *Bar at the Folies-Bergère* may also suggest another version of Baudelaire's "fugitive beauty"—not that she is fleeing, but that in her very immobility she eludes us. The experience of shock in the modern urban landscape includes the moment of illegibility—as in Wordsworth's encounter with the blind beggar. Manet's painting elicits unending critical babble just because it is not quite legible, and its heroine is not quite available to our desire. The painting creates great sensuous pleasure, a true lust of the eye, but without quite providing satisfaction.

CHAPTER 10

Henry James's Turn of the Novel

HENRY JAMES'S RELATION TO THE REALIST TRADITION IS COMPLEX, NUANCED, evolving over time—yet ultimately, for all his modernist experimentalism, very solid in that James cannot conceive of the novel except as representation. His critical strictures on novelists he finds unsatisfactory turn again and again on their failure to represent, their failure to give us the sense of life. Though of course what kind of life, and how it is perceived—at what angle, through what peephole—he quite radically redefines. James, born in 1843, grew up in a tradition stamped by Dickens and George Eliot, and Eliot in particular represented for him the English novel in its highest reach. But he grew up reading Balzac, all Balzac, and other French novelists as well. Balzac became his instinctive measure of how effectively other writers produced a sense of the real, a representation not necessarily wholly documentary— Zola's trust in his documents and notes led him to "the most extraordinary *imitation* of observation that we possess"—but one that shows "that respect for the liberty of the subject which I should be willing to name as the great sign of the painter of the first order." As an adolescent in Paris—his family made frequent visits to Europe, especially France—he picked up the parental copy of *La Revue de Paris* containing the first serial installment of *Madame Bovary*, and Flaubert soon became an important point of reference.

James is that strangely American figure, the restless cosmopolitan, eventually the expatriate: when in 1875, he decided to settle in Paris, he proclaimed that only the French novelists did honest work—artistic, professional, instructive work—from which he could learn his *métier*. He carried a letter of introduction to Ivan Turgenev, through whom he soon met Flaubert, and the group of younger writers around him—Zola and Maupassant, especially. Yet he complains that the French novelists haven't read *Daniel Deronda*—just appearing in serial form when James is in Paris—and indeed never have heard of George Eliot. And he over and over again reaches back over the heads of Zola, Maupassant, even Flaubert, to proclaim his deepest allegiance to Balzac, as "the father of us all," as the writer who must be studied if the novel is to recover its "wasted heritage." Consider that when James met Flaubert, the French novelist was engaged upon writing *Bouvard et Pécuchet*, that strange deconstruction of the very meaning-making systems of the novel, or of writing itself; whereas James was starting work on *The American*, a novel deeply faithful to a certain Balzacian social melodrama and its opening up of dramatic ethical conflict. James never would come to appreciate *Bouvard et Pécuchet*, perhaps because he rightly sensed that it threatened the very kind of novel he had staked his life on. And he would never abandon his commitment to the kinds of large moral issues—the issues of how to live life as an ethical person—that so animate Eliot's fiction.

Yet he would learn, no doubt mainly from Flaubert and his followers, something about the radical uses of perspectivism in the presentation of narrative, and about the epistemological uncertainties that go with trying to know the lives of others. The lesson of Flaubert, and of the "the modern" in literature and art in general, seems to reach James with a certain delay—but then it hits hard, and especially in the 1890s his fiction turns on questions of how we know, what we can know, in the gaps and blanks out of which we never can—though also we must—construct our actions. Such texts as *The Turn of the Screw*, *The Figure in the Carpet*, *What Maisie Knew*, *The Sacred Fount*, and *The Beast in the Jungle* date from this period, and they all play out a nearly epistemological drama, where what we think we know is always open to contest and reversal, without any sure principle for finding a firm, immovable optic. Their relation to the traditional Victorian realist novel is uneasy: the elements of that traditional novel all are present, but seen in a kind of disoriented perspective, like Degas's sketches of women at their toilette. They are on the whole shorter novels and novellas, work in which James seems to be trying out his methods and materials before arriving at the relative— though still agonized—serenity of his final great novels, *The Ambassadors*, *The Wings of the Dove*, *The Golden Bowl*.

In the *Cage*, from 1898, belongs to this experimental period and this preoccupation. At the same time, it is firmly linked to a dominant realist concern with the conditions of labor, social class, and what you might call the economic constraints on the imagination. I find it one of the most brilliant of James's works, as well as one of the most troubling. It concerns a young woman who works in the telegraph office set in a corner of Cocker's grocery store, taking the telegrams written by clients, counting the words—since the telegrams are charged by the word—then sending them out on the "sounder," the telegraph key. We are at a moment in communications technology before the coming of the telephone, when telegraphy is the state of the art, the quickest way—though an expensive one—for transmitting messages. And since Cocker's and its telegraph office are located in a posh quarter of Mayfair, the messages she transmits are often about the amorous transactions of the wealthy and well born. (James himself, incidentally, became a master of the telegraphic message in the conduct of his social life; as a single example, this telegram to a weekend hostess: "Will alight precipitately at 5:38 from the deliberate 1:50.")

Since this is a novella (a particularly French form, by the way, that James gratefully took up and developed), it sets up its issues swiftly and efficiently. Look for a moment at the first paragraph, which introduces us to the telegraph girl in her wired cage in the corner of the grocery store:

> It had occurred to her early that in her position—that of a young person spending, in framed and wired confinement, the life of a guinea-pig or a magpie—she should know a great many persons without their recognising the acquaintance. That made it an emotion the more lively—though singularly rare and always, even then, with opportunity still very much smothered—to see any one come in whom she knew outside, as she called it, any one who could add anything to the meanness of her function. Her function was to sit there with two young men—the other telegraphist and the counter-clerk; to mind the "sounder," which was always going, to dole out stamps and postal-orders, weigh letters, answer stupid questions, give difficult change and, more than anything else, count words as numberless as the sands of the sea, the words of the telegrams thrust, from morning to night, through the gaps left in the high lattice, across the encumbered shelf that her forearm ached with rubbing. This transparent screen fenced out or fenced in, according to the side of the narrow counter on which the human lot was cast, the duskiest corner of a shop pervaded not a little, in winter, by the poison of perpetual gas, and at all times by the presence of hams, cheese, dried fish, soap, varnish, paraffin and other solids and fluids that she came to know perfectly by their smells without consenting to know them by their names. (314)

As in other great first paragraphs of fiction, the whole story is here in *potentia*: the girl's "position," confined in her wire cage, leading to the question of whether her "transparent screen" (Zola's image of the naturalist's view of the world, remember) "fenced out or fenced in"—whether she is in a vantage point or a blind spot (it will of course be both). And this position at once raises the question of knowledge, and of kinds of knowing: "she should know a great many persons without their recognising the acquaintance"— which implicates what will be a large issue of how knowledge gained from within the cage may or may not apply outside it. There is a snobbery to what the girl "consents" to know, we learn at the end of the paragraph— she comes, we will discover, from a family once genteel, now considerably declined on the social scale, but clinging to its distinction from the world of trade, though we'll learn in the next paragraph that she has "irredeemably" recognized the grocer, Mr. Mudge, as her future husband. That snobbery will be highly relevant to her kinds of knowing. Especially, we have the question of people whom she might know "outside" the cage in contrast to the "meanness of her function."

Her "function" indeed is crucial; it includes minding "the sounder" and counting "words as numberless as the sands of the sea." This function is a matter of transmitting messages: not her own but those she receives from clients and turns into telegraphic signals. There is a texture of mythological allusions in the story—Lady Bradeen is Juno, the telegraph girl herself is like Danae in the shower of gold, which implicitly makes Captain Everard into Jupiter—and we realize that functionally she is more than anything else Mercury, Hermes, the divinity who presides over the exchange of messages. She is neither the person who utters these communications nor their intended addressee. She rather presides over the channels of their communication—over what Roman Jakobson would call the "phatic" function, that which assures the proper functioning of the contact of addresser and addressee. But a peculiarity of these messages is how much they cost. "The pleasures they proposed were equalled only by those they declined, and they made their appointments often so expensively that she was left wondering at the nature of the delights to which the mere approaches were so paved with shillings" (325). We encounter here a certain seduction and illusion of signifiers themselves: if words are so expensive, if the Mayfair ladies and gentlemen are so willing to spend on them, they must point to referents even more splendid. Costly messages surely underwrite a life of extraordinary pleasures.

What makes this conclusion obvious is the girl's leisure-time reading: of "a book from the place where she borrowed novels, very greasy, in fine print and all about fine folks, at a ha'penny a day" (316). Like Emma Bovary, the telegraph girl is a reader of romance, which will have a determinative role in her understanding of reality. As I argued was the case with Emma, here, too, the effects of viewing the world through the screen of romance fiction are troubling, creative of false illusions, of course, but also of creativity itself, of the imaginative reformation of reality. "She was perfectly aware that her imaginative life was the life in which she spent most of her time" (317). If her friend Mrs. Jordan claims to approach the higher orders and their romances through her arrangements of flowers for Lord Rye, what the telegraph girl "could handle freely, she said to herself, was combinations of men and women" (317). And her understanding of the romance genre does allow her, up to a point, to participate vicariously in the construction of a breathtaking romance in which she comes to participate—up to a point— nonvicariously: as if to step out of the silver screen on which the cinema is projected, as in Woody Allen's *Purple Rose of Cairo*, or, to use the terms of the novella, out of the cage and into the world.

It's the correspondence between Lady Bradeen—alias Cissy, alias Mary, alias Juno—and Captain Everard that allows our nameless girl (and her namelessness is of course important) to move from her purely hermeneutic function, her role as passer-on of messages, to a more participatory role in the novel-within-the-novel that is being created between Everard and Lady Bradeen. Her greater participation arises from her thorough mastery of the contact-function of message sending. This Jakobsonian language seems to me so pertinent that it is worth a moment's explication. Jakobson sees all verbal communications as activating six language functions, diagrammed as follows:

$$\begin{array}{ccc} & \text{CONTEXT} & \\ & \text{MESSAGE} & \\ \text{ADDRESSER} & \cdots\cdots\cdots\cdots\cdots\cdots\cdots\cdots\cdots & \text{ADDRESSEE} \\ & \text{CONTACT} & \\ & \text{CODE} & \end{array}$$

Most of these are functions are self-explanatory: a message is sent from addresser to addressee in a certain context—and if language emphasizes the context, it is "referential" language. The message is composed in a code; an emphasis on the code gives language that we call "metalingual," as when we ask what a word means, refer to a lexicon. And the sending of a message requires that there be a contact, a channel of communication established between addresser and addressee: language that emphasizes the contact is what Jakobson calls "phatic"; it includes verifications that the channel is operative, as when we say on the telephone, "Can you hear me?" The telegraph girl, I suggested, presides over the phatic, the emblem of which is "the sounder," literally the key to telegraphic communication. But she comes to think of herself as mastering other functions of language as well.

Everard and Lady Bradeen communicate through codes they have apparently invented: substitute names, various aliases and alibis, and numbers. This makes the telegraphist's participation both all the more exciting and all the more perilous. She invests her own desire into the erotic communications from Everard to his beloved: "the sense of every syllable he paid for was fiercely distinct; she indeed felt her progressive pencil, dabbing as if with a quick caress the marks of his own, put life into every stroke" (321). That "progressive pencil" is engaged (no doubt eraser head down) in counting out Everard's words, and in so doing bringing them to erotic life, endowing them with a meaning in which she participates. It will be only a further step to turn the pencil over and herself write the words of the telegram. This step will soon come.

She has come to believe she masters the code as well as the contact—not only the phatic but also the metalingual function of language, the dictionary function, that which tells us what signs mean. The decisive moment arrives when Lady Bradeen becomes confused about the code, and asks to withdraw a telegram in order to alter a word. "There was a word wrong, but she had lost the right one, and much clearly depended on her finding it again" (343). At this point, it is the telegraph girl who proposes the "right word": "isn't it Cooper's?" "It was as if she had bodily leaped—cleared the top of the cage and alighted on her interlocutress." She makes Juno blush, and forces from her the recognition that she, the telegraphist, is in possession of the keys to their enigma machine: "Oh you know—?" "Yes, I know!"

And the girl then proceeds to make the alteration herself. "People were really too giddy, and if they *were*, in a certain case, to be caught, it shouldn't be the fault of her own grand memory. Hadn't it been settled weeks before?—for Miss Dolman it was always to be 'Cooper's'" (343). The alias Miss Dolman needs the alibi of Cooper's.

This moment of "tampering" with the message on the basis of a superior understanding of the code than that possessed by the putative sender of the message gives the girl a "thrill with the sense of the high company she did somehow keep. She was with the absent [that is, Captain Everard] through her ladyship and with her ladyship through the absent" (342). In other words, she has assumed a *place* in the exchange of messages, become not merely their transmitter but something nearer their editor or ghost-writer. Yet there has been a warning given in passing—so much in passing that I find readers can neglect it, despite its great importance: that Cocker's telegraph office is merely a small one (though in a chic part of Mayfair) that only sends messages and does not receive them. So that when the girl has sent out a message from Lady Bradeen to Everard, from Everard to Lady Bradeen, she does not see the actual answer to the message sent. She has to infer it from the next message originating from Cocker's. She finds merit in this: "there were yet ways in which, on the whole, she pressed the romance closer by reason of the very quantity of imagination it demanded and consumed" (322). Like the reader according to Wolfgang Iser, she finds her pleasure in filling in the gaps, the *Leerstellen*, of the text. Yet obviously this high tightrope act of the imagination presents problems. Imagination here is untethered—as in James's famous description of the balloon of romance in the preface to *The American*—it floats a bit too free of the earth.

Yet if she comes to participate more and more imaginatively in the romance of her two Mayfair idols, and in particular to see herself as a more intelligent substitute for the somewhat dim Lady Bradeen, her generic fictional models don't give full instructions on the role she is to play. Knowing all that she believes she does about the illicit loves of the pair:

> She quite thrilled herself with thinking what, with such a lot of material, a bad girl would do. It would be a scene better than many in her ha'penny novels, this going to him in the dusk of evening at Park Chambers and letting him at last have it. "I know too much about a certain person now not to put it to you—excuse my being so lurid—that it's quite worth your while to

buy me off. Come, therefore: buy me!" There was a point indeed at which such flights had to drop again—the point of an unreadiness to name, when it came to that, the purchasing medium. It wouldn't certainly be anything so gross as money, and the matter accordingly remained rather vague, all the more that she was not a bad girl." (339)

Her vicarious erotic relation to Everard reaches this impasse, in that she cannot figure any erotic role in reference to him that would not cast her as "bad girl," whereas she classifies herself as a lady. The issue of social class reasserts itself here. When finally she does meet Everard out of the cage, and wonders whether people of his sort might be unfaithful to their beloved, "She already had a vision of how the true answer was that people of her sort didn't, in such cases, matter—didn't count as infidelity, counted only as something else: she might have been curious, since it came to that, to see exactly as what" (347).

What we begin to understand here is the extent to which the romance fictions she nourishes and vicariously participates in may indeed be expensive, and not simply because the messages of rendezvous cost so many shillings. Her "reward" for participation in the communicative web between Everard and Lady Bradeen comes when she finally does meet him one evening before the steps of Park Chambers, and they wander off together, eventually to sit on a bench in the park. She finally gains the precious recognition that he has recognized her, that he has been aware of her participation in his drama: that the role of Hermes has been visible. Now the question becomes what difference this will make. When she melodramatically declares, "I'd do anything for you. I'd do anything for you," the result is to create the Victorian equivalent of a lovers' bower: "She bravely and magnificently left it, and little by little she felt him take it up, take it down, as if they had been on a satin sofa in a boudoir. She had never seen a boudoir, but there had been lots of boudoirs in the telegrams" (351). On this metaphorical satin sofa in the legendary boudoir, she reaches her nearest approach to entry into the world of the dreams she has both indulged and censored. Everard places his hand on hers. She is able to make clear to him how fully she knows his story, how much she understands and participates in the danger of his liaison. "All I get out of it is the harmless pleasure of knowing," she tells him. "I know, I know, I know!" (351).

Her choice of the purely cognitive pleasures of her position—what she knows—rather than those that might result from *acquaintance* (recall the first paragraph of the novella) signals a decision to refuse Everard's somewhat inarticulate demand for more—his implicit offer to dine with her, with its postdinner implications. And yet, this decision becomes difficult to sustain. She has awakened to less mediated erotic possibilities, the chance to discard Hermes in order to take the place of Juno. And when this happens, her caged position becomes both imprisonment and protection against a life outside that both threatens and beckons: "to be in the cage had suddenly become her safety, and she was literally afraid of the alternate self who might be waiting outside" (364). Everard comes in to tempt her out of the cage, writing—but not sending—a telegram to Lady Bradeen that reads "Absolutely impossible," as if to demonstrate that the girl at Cocker's has for now trumped the great lady at Twindle or Brickwood. She, not Lady Bradeen, is the true addressee of this particular message. But Everard can do nothing unambiguous—the tie to Lady Bradeen remains, the telegraph girl never fully assumes the role of bad girl—and she cannot risk leaving the cage. Everard leaves, without so much as a good-bye.

What brings him back is crisis. A telegram has miscarried, been intercepted, and needs to be retrieved. At this point, the girl recognizes "how much she had missed in the gaps and blanks and absent answers" (369): how much her fictionalized participation in the liaison has been at the price of an uncertain understanding of its events. It becomes apparent that the missing telegram is in fact the one she corrected for Lady Bradeen. What we know about it is that "she put in by mistake something wrong," but the referent of the "she" hovers ambiguously: Was the mistake Cissy's or her own? We know further that what's in it "*may* be all right. That is if it's wrong, don't you know? It's all right if it's wrong" (371). Now we are at the remarkable moment of climax. The girl is thrust into the role of key witness: she sees in Everard's eyes "a great place like a chamber of justice where, before a watching crowd, a poor girl, exposed but heroic, swore with a quavering voice to a document, proved an *alibi*, supplied a link. In this picture she bravely took her place" (372). She can't immediately retrieve the telegram from the archives; but she can rewrite it from memory. Since the official thrift of the post office has provided no writing paper, she asks Everard for his calling card, but it is not to pay attention to its engraved name and address:

She gave no glance at the name on it—only turned it to the other side. She continued to hold him, she felt at present, as she had never held him; and her command of her colleagues was for the moment not less marked. She wrote something on the back of the card and pushed it across to him.

He fairly glared at it. "Seven, nine, four—"

"Nine, six, one"—she obligingly completed the number. "Is it right?" she smiled.

He took the whole thing in with a flushed intensity; then there broke out in him a visibility of relief that was simply a tremendous exposure. He shone at them all like a tall lighthouse, embracing even, for sympathy, the blinking young men. "By all the powers—it's wrong!" And without another look, without a word of thanks, without time for anything or anybody, he turned on them the broad back of his great stature, straightened his triumphant shoulders and strode out of the place.

She was left confronted with her habitual critics.

"'If it's wrong it's all right!'" she extravagantly quoted to them.

The counter-clerk was really awestricken. "But how did you know, dear?"

"I remembered, love!"

Mr. Buckton, on the contrary, was rude. "And what game is that, miss?"

No happiness she had ever known came within miles of it, and some minutes elapsed before she could recall herself sufficiently to reply that it was none of his business. (372–73)

Her triumph here comes in the exercise of her phatic function, as the one firmly in control of the transmission of messages, of knowledge, and it brings a moment beyond happiness, a moment of bliss. But note that if she can repeat, rewrite the telegraphic message from memory, she can't otherwise *read* it, cannot interpret it. As no more can we as readers. James is famously attracted to blanks that both contain and efface central meanings, as in *The Figure in the Carpet* or *The Beast in the Jungle*. Here, that blank is at the heart of the communicative system itself, the very language that Everard and Lady Bradeen use to carry on their affair. The girl at the last fails in the metalingual function. She merely copies the code, she cannot crack it. And since we cannot crack it either, we appear to be thrown back into her position of hermeneutic bafflement. Her "I know, I know, I know" to Everard now seems to have a somewhat hollow ring, and our implication in a cognitive drama—something akin to a detective story—seems to have led us to a blank wall. We don't even know in what the "mistake" of the faulty telegram consists, and how it has misfired so as to create and then resolve this crisis. Furthermore, Everard leaves without a word of thanks—and never comes back. On the affective level, she is left forlorn. And we are left frustrated. Which is of course the point.

For the rest of the novella will supply some elements of missing information—but they will come not from interpretive games and cognitive dramas but from what the butler backstairs picks up. It is knowledge that comes freighted with the limitations of social class and a lesson in the strict restrictions on freedom of movement imposed by socioeconomic conditions. As much as with Emma Bovary, romance is subject to brutal correction by reality—all the more so in that the correction works on the language of romance, indeed on language itself, deconstructing the very possibility of a cost-free use of language. It's almost James's version of Flaubert's house-wreckings in *Bouvard et Pécuchet*, and a reassertion that the counting of words referred to in the first paragraph of the novella, and the charging of language by the word, is in fact the ultimate reality. The words of romance are expensive, like the telegrams. And if you can't pay for them, you not only are excluded from the communicative code, you are cast out from any further possibility of dreaming.

What happens at the end, briefly, is that the telegraph girl learns from Mrs. Jordan—who learns it from Mr. Drake, Lord Rye's butler, who is going to Lady Bradeen in the same capacity, and becoming Mrs. Jordan's husband—that Lord Bradeen has died, that Everard and Lady Bradeen are going to marry, but that Everard didn't want to, that she saved him by retrieving something lost, and then "nailed him": made him marry her. The something that was lost and retrieved may well be the telegram, in which case it wasn't at all Lady Bradeen who saved Everard, but our telegraph girl (who would then be the person he ought to marry). But what the telegram meant is still wholly unclear: all we learn is that Everard "was in something" (382)—which may give a more sinister shade of implication to his numeric telegrams (a gambling racket, perhaps?), but hardly explicates them. The near-scandals of high life remain vague and unspecified—indeed unspecifiable, given the sources of knowledge available to Mrs. Jordan and the telegraph girl. At the same time comes her gradual understanding that what Mrs. Jordan knows—in many specifics superior to what she herself knows—comes from Mr. Drake the butler, and that Mrs. Jordan's long flirtation with Lord Rye and his world has ended in a considerable social fall, to the servant class.

Mrs. Jordan has maintained that her flower arrangements for the gentry opened a door to romance, and urged the telegraphist to quit the postal service and join her in the floral approach. Hence when the telegraphist learns that Mrs. Jordan has netted not Lord Rye but his servant, she says with a kind of reproach:

> "Only, you know, you did put it to me so splendidly what, even for me, if I had listened to you, it might lead to."
> Mrs. Jordan kept up a mild thin weak wail; then, drying her eyes, as feebly considered this reminder. "It has led to my not starving!" she faintly gasped. (379)

And this stark truth leads at once to the telegraph girl's drop into the very similar reality of her own situation, "the vivid reflexion of her own dreams and delusions and her own return to reality. Reality, for the poor things they both were, could only be ugliness and obscurity, could never be the escape, the rise." Those fictions of escape, of social rise, are prohibitively expensive. She will have to settle for the little home offered by Mr. Mudge, the grocer.

She recalls, after this, sitting on the park bench while Everard put his hand on hers, and then the scene in which he stood before her cage "with supplicating eyes and a fever in his blood," and she in turn "hard and pedantic, helped by some miracle and with her impossible condition, only answered him, yet supplicating back, through the bars of the cage." What is difficult to accept is not only the end of the romance—which she has refused as well as desired—but the way she has lost it, and the necessity to accept a mediated knowledge of her lost lover: "That is what it had come to . . . simply that she might hear of him, now for ever lost, only through Mrs. Jordan, who touched him through Mr. Drake, who reached him through Lady Bradeen." Lady Bradeen has evicted her from the role she came close to filling.

The last paragraph of the novella is brilliant. Mrs. Jordan's "good-bye" comes out of the thick fog as the telegraph girl stands at the foot of the stairs from her flat:

> "Good-bye!" went into it. Our young lady went into it also, in the opposed quarter, and presently, after a few sightless turns, came out on the Paddington canal. Distinguishing vaguely what the low parapet enclosed she stopped close to it and stood a while very intently, but perhaps still sightlessly, looking down on it. A policeman, while she remained, strolled past her; then, going his way a little further and half lost in the atmosphere,

paused and watched her. But she was quite unaware—she was full of her thoughts. They were too numerous to find a place just here, but two of the number may at least be mentioned. One of these was that, decidedly, her little home must be not for next month, but for next week; the other, which came indeed as she resumed her walk and went her way, was that it was strange such a matter should be at last settled for her by Mr. Drake. (383–84)

The low parapet of the Paddington Canal may suggest the temptation to be another poor unfortunate driven to suicide—as the policeman may believe. The presence of the policeman here at the end is significant: a reminder of the whole system of policing of society that makes the escape and the rise impossible. But her own thoughts apparently are not on suicide. The two reported by the narrator concern her decision to settle promptly for what Mr. Mudge has to offer, and, at the last, her reflection "that it was strange such a matter should be at last settled for her by Mr. Drake." We return in this final phrase to the problem of knowing, and the strange humiliation represented by knowledge coming by way of what the butler saw and heard. To have the matter settled by Mr. Drake is more than a comeuppance of her Bovarystic imagination, since it strikes at the very bases of her cognition, at her hermeneutic role. In some ultimate sense, she has known nothing about her hero and putative lover. Yet this is not to say that she hasn't been used by him. On the contrary, she has turned out to be part of a language that he owns. There are no fictions that are not expensive, and if you want to engage in them, you'd better be ready and able to pay. Language doesn't belong to everyone. It belongs to those who hire the policemen.

"Realism" in In the Cage is cruel in form, as in Madame Bovary: what the girl calls "the harmless pleasure of knowing" turns out to be far from harmless. It turns out to be ignorance as much as knowledge, and to be exploitative, and finally it casts her out, back to recognition of her caged position in social hierarchies, the limits to action as to imagination, the antiromance necessary to avoid starving. Narratives may be transformative—but then, they are not for everyone. The impression of cruelty in James's tale is not lessened by his preface—written for the New York Edition of his works—where he speaks of "speculation—prone as one's mind had ever been to that form of waste" set to work by observing London's telegraph service: "the question of what it might 'mean,' wherever the admirable service was installed, for confined and cramped and yet considerably tutored young officials of either sex to be made so free, intellectually, of a range of experience otherwise quite closed to them." James reproaches the "artist" and his "morbid imagination" for reading too much into the situation of the telegraph girl—as she herself reads too much (yet not enough) into the messages she transmits. The "rash" and "idle" faculty of the imagination leads to the "vice of reading rank subtleties into simple souls and reckless expenditure into thrifty ones"—which seems to dismiss the girl of In the Cage following her humiliation, to make of her whole story a kind of "waste." James ascribes the vice of reading too much, and expending too much, to what he calls the "extravagant and immoral interest" of the writer. The self-accusation of immorality is interesting here. It suggests a kind of hardening of the heart toward his character—rather more so than the novella itself suggests about authorial attitude. This is perhaps most of all a declaration of the realist's principle: it is not morality that guides his quest but extravagant and immoral interest. It is a costly kind of speculation.

James's story about hermeneutic uncertainties and vicarious fictions at the end is also very much about social class, economic constraint, and the policing of the imagination. These are issues of central concern in most of James's later fiction. In the Cage gives them particularly concise and brilliant form, in a narrative that itself concerns communication, writing, reading, and imaginative construal. It would be tempting to follow through on these concerns in a number of late novels, including The Sacred Fount, The Ambassadors, The Wings of the Dove, and, most of all, The Golden Bowl. That is too vast an enterprise. I will conclude rather by a brief mention of a late novella, The Jolly Corner (1908), which tells the story of Spencer Brydon, who as a very young man gave up his interests, and his putative career, in New York, and went to live a life of dilettantish leisure in Europe. He returns to New York after some thirty-three years abroad in order to take care of property he has inherited. One is a building he can without compunction sell to builders of the rapidly developing city, and in the process he discovers that after all he has a native capacity to act the capitalist, even the developer and investor. The other is the house of his childhood, on Fifth Avenue, where he was born and raised. This he can't bring himself to turn over to the wrecker's ball. Instead, he takes to entering the house late at night, and prowling through its dark rooms, apparently in search of the ghost of the person he might have become had he stayed in New York and pursued the capitalist imperative rather than slipping off to Europe.

In this parabolic tale, New York and its development come to stand for a certain hard "reality" that Spencer Brydon has largely avoided. He expresses to his friend Alice Staverton the sense of the self he may have missed in abandoning the New York career to which he was born:

> "It comes over me that I had then a strange *alter ego* deep down somewhere within me, as the full-blown flower is in the small tight bud, and that I just took the course, I just transferred him to the climate, that blighted him for once and for ever."
>
> "And you wonder about the flower," Miss Staverton said. "So do I, if you want to know, and so I've been wondering these several weeks. I believe in the flower," she continued. "I feel it would have been quite splendid, quite huge and monstrous."
>
> "Monstrous above all!" her visitor echoed; "and I imagine, by the same stroke, quite hideous and offensive."
>
> "You don't believe that," she returned; "if you did you wouldn't wonder. You'd know, and that would be enough for you. What you feel—and what I feel for you—is that you'd have had power."
>
> "You'd have liked me that way?"
>
> She barely hung fire. "How should I not have liked you?"
>
> "I see. You'd have liked me, have preferred me, a billionaire!"
>
> "How should I not have liked you?" she simply again asked. (557–58)

The conversation appears to figure his potential New York capitalist self as something huge, splendid, monstrous, possibly hideous and offensive, but especially potent. The imagery of the bud become huge and monstrous flower is unavoidably phallic, and Alice Staverton's interest in this more virile and dominating Brydon leads to her admission that she has seen such a figure, twice, in her dreams.

It is this exchange between Brydon and Alice Staverton that appears to trigger his obsessive searches in the dark house in the late-night hours. He figures himself as a hunter in search of his prey. Yet it comes to him one night that his quarry has "turned," has decided to stand his ground: "he's the fanged or antlered animal brought at last to bay," as Brydon expresses it to himself (563). This antagonist takes on greater and greater reality, and at last becomes a potentially threatening specter: when Brydon finds closed a door in the upstairs servants' quarter he is sure he's left open, fear begins to come upon him, and the idea that discretion would be a course better than confrontation. So as the sky outside is beginning to pale, he makes his way to the main staircase and begins his descent, intent on leaving the house as quickly as possible. But as he descends the final flight to the front hall, paved in the black and white marbled squares he so well remembers from childhood, he perceives that the inner door of the vestibule, which he is certain he left closed, now stands wide open. And in the shadowy light the occult presence of "his adversary" begins to take shape and substance: "Rigid and conscious, spectral yet human, a man of his own substance and stature waited there to measure himself with his power to dismay" (571). The figure's hands at first cover his face—and one of these hands has lost two fingers, "reduced to stumps, as if accidentally shot away." But then the hands drop from the face:

> Horror, with the sight, had leaped into Brydon's throat, gasping there in a sound he couldn't utter; for the bared identity was too hideous as his, and his glare was the passion of his protest. . . . Such an identity fitted his at no point, made its alternative monstrous. A thousand times yes, and it came upon him nearer now—the face was the face of a stranger. It came upon him nearer now, quite as one of those expanding fantastic images projected by the magic lantern of childhood; for the stranger, whoever he might be, evil, odious, blatant, vulgar, had advanced as for aggression, and he knew himself give ground. Then harder pressed still, sick with the force of his shock, and falling back as under the hot breath of the roused passion of a life larger than his own, a rage of personality before which his own collapsed, he felt the whole vision turn to darkness and his very feet give way. His head went round; he was going; he had gone. (571–72)

The encounter thus ends in Brydon's loss of consciousness, in a hysterical conversion, a fall from reality. As with James's best ghostly tales, the ontology of Brydon's adversary is thoroughly ambiguous. What is clear is that the specter, from whatever psychic or other realm, threatens the man who would deny any resemblance between it and him. His denegation of any connection to "the stranger" is strong and repeated—and yet the encounter makes him faint dead away.

He awakens in Alice Staverton's arms—she has tracked him down the following afternoon, alerted by her dream in which the monstrous alter ego appeared to herself as well. To Brydon's denegations of any resemblance or connection between the specter and himself—"this brute's a black stranger. He's none of me, even as I might have been"—Alice Staverton demurs: "Isn't the whole point that you'd have been different?" (575). And she claims that her own version of the specter seemed to tell her that "'you somehow wanted me. . . . So why,' she strangely smiled, 'shouldn't I like him?'" Alice accepts the monstrous and potent other of Brydon, indeed she appears to entertain an affection for this other because he tells her—in a way that Brydon apparently never can—that he wants her. The specter, hideous or genial, of the power Brydon has renounced in his life, does appear, in its very spectrality, to unlock the censored erotic potential between Brydon and the woman who here speaks a love that he has not been able to. The tale ends with Brydon drawing Alice Staverton to his breast. It is almost uncharacteristically "happy" as a Jamesian ending—though it may also remind us of the embrace that ends its near contemporary, The Golden Bowl, erotic certainly but fraught with undecidable other emotion. Brydon's encounter with his alter ego appears to be terrifying, bringing horror and loss of consciousness, but also curative, releasing some version of the phallic potential represented by his other.

The specter impresses Brydon, just before his loss of consciousness, by its expressed "rage of personality before which his own collapsed." Brydon resembles many other Jamesian gentlemen, such as Lambert Strether, who can make no claim to a "rage of personality," and indeed often seem to have renounced any phallic claims as well. They are mainly gentlemen who have renounced worldly and erotic power in the cultivation of the artistic sensibility and the contemplative stance toward life. Here at the end of his career —he was not to write much more following The Jolly Corner—James seems to perform some shadowy allegory of the aesthetic self in relation to the executive self. And that executive self can be said to stand for a kind of engagement with the world that James found represented in the work of such as Balzac and Zola and Gissing. The Wall Street capitalist is certainly evoked in Christopher Newman of The American, Adam Verver of The Golden Bowl, and a number of other American figures—but whom we catch up with usually when they have already given up New York, San Francisco, or American City, to discover alternative selves in "Europe." James was painfully aware that there was "not enough of the City" in his novels, an insufficient attempt to represent directly the socioeconomic realities that underpin his characters' lives—The Princess Casamassima standing, I think, as his most persuasive attempt to match Zola on his own ground. Yet the product of the City, money, is everywhere present in James's novels, as the token and medium of power and freedom. It could be said to typify Jamesian indirection of representation that the sign-system itself becomes foregrounded, the medium in which the messages are made. This is true of the making of the telegrams of In the Cage, true also of money as the medium of social relations. It is as if he wanted in The Jolly Corner to remind us—as Spencer Brydon must be reminded—where that money comes from, what Fifth Avenue is made from. Behind the Jamesian drama of consciousness there is a realist drama, often more latent than dramatized, presupposed rather than blatant.

For all his subtlety and indirection, that is, James never falters in his belief that the business of the novel is to represent life, and the novelist is above all else what he frequently calls "the historian." It is this sense of the responsibility of the novelist to the real that comes back again and again in his criticism, as, for instance, in this passage from his essay of 1902 on Balzac: "The novel, the tale, however brief, the passage, the sentence by itself, the situation, the person, the place, the motive exposed, the speech reported— these things were in his view history, with the absoluteness and the dignity of history. This is the source both of his weight and of his wealth. What is the historic sense after all but animated, but impassioned knowledge seeking to enlarge itself?" The telegraph girl, Spencer Brydon, like so many other Jamesian protagonists, however limited in their field of vision and however frustrated by social circumstances, are themselves represented examples of the "historic sense" on such a definition. Their quest for an enlarged knowledge is above all a quest to know more about a real both seductive and overwhelming.

CHAPTER II

Modernism and Realism
Joyce, Proust, Woolf

My main text in this chapter is Virginia Woolf's Mrs. Dalloway. But I want to approach Woolf by way of two great near-contemporaries who, like her, reshaped the novel and in the process created what we now think of as modernism: James Joyce and Marcel Proust. What I want to try to come to terms with, in brief span, is the relation of these three great innovators to the realist tradition in which they grew up, and learned their trade. I can't of course do justice to such complex authors in this way. Instead, I want to make forays into their work.

Joyce is to my mind unthinkable without Flaubert, in his essentially ironic stance toward life, and his adoption of Flaubert's doctrine of impersonality, which Stephen Dedalus cites in his own version toward the end of *Portrait of the Artist as a Young Man*: "The artist, like the God of the creation, remains within or behind or beyond his handiwork, invisible, refined out of existence, indifferent, paring his fingernails." This ideal is realized in a narrative technique that is also essentially Flaubertian, in Joyce's use of free indirect discourse in the presentation of a distanced and ironized view of the world that is nonetheless intimate with perspectives and the language of his characters, without quotation for attribution, so to speak. It is, as with Flaubert, a technique of studied irresponsibility: the narrator does not speak in his own name, and does not quote the characters directly, but rather speaks through them without taking responsibility for what is said—a technique in which we have the impression that the "story tells itself." The debt to Flaubert is perhaps most obvious in the stories of *Dubliners* (1916). Take, for instance, these two paragraphs from the story entitled *Grace*:

Mr. Cunningham was the very man for such a case. He was an elder colleague of Mr. Power. His own domestic life was not very happy. People had great sympathy with him, for it was known that he had married an unpresentable woman who was an incurable drunkard. He had set up house for her six times; and each time she had pawned the furniture on him.

Everyone had respect for poor Martin Cunningham. He was a thoroughly sensible man, influential and intelligent. His blade of human knowledge, natural astuteness particularized by long association with cases in the police courts, had been tempered by brief immersions in the waters of general philosophy. He was well informed. His friends bowed to his opinions and considered that his face was like Shakespeare's. (157)

This is a kind of writing that we have become used to—that they teach in the writing programs. But you don't find it in abundance before Flaubert in French, and Joyce in English. The narrator refuses to be identified, to speak in his own voice. One could imagine his protestations of innocence if one tried to suggest that his portrait of Martin Cunningham is high satiric comedy. He could plead his utter good faith, convincingly since all he has done is rearrange the clichés that circulate in Cunningham's society, the commonplaces used to describe him by "the others." It is only our sense, as readers, of slight incongruities—"blade of human knowledge"; "considered that his face was like Shakespeare's"—that install an attitude of ironic distance on our part. The text itself can claim to have regurgitated the world's clichés with perfect fidelity.

I want to look at one more passage from *Dubliners*, from the story *A Painful Case*, which tells of a repressed man, James Duffy, who draws back in shock from the love offered by a woman, returns to his solitude—then learns from the newspaper of the woman's alcoholic death, and realizes, to an extent, what he has done. It's Joyce's version of Henry James's *The Beast in the Jungle*, far shorter and terser. This passage interests me in part because it reprises the vision of the city from high ground, as in Rastignac's view of Paris from Père-Lachaise cemetery at the close of *Le Père Goriot*, as in Nancy Lord's view of London from the Monument, and so many painterly cityscapes. In the Joyce story, the vision is bleak:

When he gained the crest of the Magazine Hill he halted and looked along the river towards Dublin, the lights of which burned redly and hospitably in the cold night. He looked down the slope and, at the base, in the shadow of the wall of the Park, he saw some human figures lying. Those venal and furtive loves filled him with despair. He gnawed the rectitude of his life; he felt that he had been outcast from life's feast. One human being had seemed to love him and he had denied her life and happiness: he had sentenced her to ignominy, a death of shame. He knew that the prostrate creatures down by the wall were watching him and wished him gone. No one wanted him; he was outcast from life's feast. He turned his eyes to the grey gleaming river, winding along towards Dublin. Beyond the river he saw a goods train winding out of Kingsbridge Station, like a worm with a fiery head winding through the darkness, obstinately and laboriously. It passed slowly out of sight; but still he heard in his ears the laborious drone of the engine reiterating the syllables of her name. (117)

One could write a whole chapter in analysis of this brilliant paragraph. Note how it takes Duffy's own stilted language—expressive of a pretentious, defended self constructed over a gulf of repression—and turns it against him, so to speak. "He gnawed the rectitude of his life": the yoking here of the abstract, pompous, and stilted "rectitude" with the brute physicality of "gnawed"—like a dog with a bone—suggests the transvaluation of values brought by his realization, too late, of what he has missed. (Joyce's love of Dante suggests there is also an allusion to Ugolino, in the Inferno, gnawing on the bones of his children.) Repetition of the phrase "outcast from life's feast" intimates that it must be Duffy's own phrase—the language in which he expresses his regret and bitterness that in its very choice of words and stilted phraseology suggests what is wrong with him, why he has never been able to partake of this feast. Note also the repetition of "winding," for the river and for the "worm with a fiery head" of the train. As in Flaubert, if we live by language we also are destroyed by it.

The controlled Flaubertian narrated monologue of Dubliners of course leads to something further in Ulysses, to what is usually called "stream of consciousness," which by no means accurately describes all the stylistic modes of Ulysses but does apply to the final "Penelope" sequence, Molly Bloom's interior monologue. Just a brief sample here:

I kept the handkerchief under my pillow for the smell of him there was no decent perfume to be got in that Gibraltar only that cheap peau despagne that faded and left a stink on you more than anything else I wanted to give him a memento he gave me that clumsy Claddagh ring for luck that I gave Gardner going to South Africa where those Boers killed him with their war and fever but they were well beaten all the same as if it brought its bad luck with it like an opal or pearl must have been pure 16 carat gold because it was very heavy I can see his face clean shaven Frseeeeeeeeeeeeeeeeeeefrong that train again weeping tone once in the dear deaead days beyond recall close my eyes breath my lips forward kiss sad look eyes open piano ere oer the world the mists began I hate that istsbeg comes loves sweet ssoooooong Ill let that out full when I get in front of the footlights again Kathleen Kearney and her lot of squealers Miss This Miss That Miss Theother lot of sparrow-farts skitting around talking about politics they know as much about as my backside anything in the world to make themselves someway interesting Irish homemade beauties soldiers daughter am I ay and whose are you bootmakers and publicans . . . (762)

I won't dwell on the passage, which is in some paradoxical sense the simplest kind of narration there is — the simulation of the random reactions of one consciousness to the play of memory, anticipation, and the stimuli of the moment. I don't mean to suggest that this simplicity is not a very artful creation — it of course is. When first unleashed on the world it was considered by most to be unreadable, though now it seems to us pellucid. With such a tour de force as Molly Bloom's interior monologue, Joyce takes kinds of narrative conditions that came to the fore in realism — particularly the attention to the world of sensations — and brings them to a more radical realization. For all the radical innovation of Ulysses, there are certainly perspectives in which it is not a repudiation of realism but its further development. It develops techniques for a better matching of writing to experience of the world, to the transitory but crucial sense perceptions that more traditional forms of writing tended to censor or summarize.

Joyce's evolution from Dubliners through Portrait of an Artist as a Young Man to Ulysses and then the postnovelistic Finnegans Wake is there to see. It's comparable to Picasso's passage from figuration to abstraction. Possibly less obvious is Proust's evolution because he published so little before undertaking the novel that was wholly published only after his death. But Proust's relation to the realism he grew up reading is evident from his scattered but substantive commentary on those he sees as his precursors, especially Balzac.

One of Proust's fictional aristocrats, Mme de Villeparisis — a member of the Guermantes clan — reproaches Balzac for having had the pretension of portraying a society "where he wasn't himself invited," and having committed many implausibilities in doing so (2:82) [2:411]. Proust himself at times echoes this critique, quite similar in fact to Henry James's: great ladies of the Faubourg Saint-Germain don't talk and act with the excess and over-the-top snobbery of Balzac's Marquise d'Espard or Louise de Bargeton. And yet, the most aristocratic of all the Guermantes, and the best literary judge, the Baron de Charlus, loves Balzac. The trouble with Mme de Villeparisis's judgment is that it confuses life and art. She is in this manner similar to the famous nineteenth-century critic Sainte-Beuve, who argued that a personal acquaintanceship with a writer, and a knowledge of his or her biography, were the surest bases for sound literary judgment. Proust made himself into a writer against Sainte-Beuve, in a passionate argument that art is not life, and that the "I" of fiction is not the same as the "I" of everyday life. (This in an essay entitled *Contre Sainte-Beuve* that interestingly keeps wanting to become a novel.) Proust in fact wrote the first version of his immense novel in the third person (called *Jean Santeuil*), and was able to come back to the first person only when he could treat it as an I not himself.

Like the Baron de Charlus, like Henry James, Proust adored Balzac, knew his work virtually by heart. Mentions of Balzac within the *Recherche*—they are numerous—serve a number of functions, one of them the evocation of homosexuality, which Proust sees Balzac as treating with rare boldness (especially in the figure of Collin or Vautrin, alias Carlos Herrera who, you recall, makes his appearance at the end of *Lost Illusions*, to save Lucien from suicide, and then sets himself up as his mentor and protector). A more complex function devolving on the Balzac allusions has to do precisely with the relation of the real and the fictional. Madame de Villeparisis's, and Sainte-Beuve's, critiques of Balzac as implausible in his portrayal of certain sectors of society presuppose a kind of correspondence of the real and its literary representation that is immediate and unmediated: like making someone's acquaintance, having them to dinner, belonging to the same world. Balzac's implausibilities become in Proust something of a touchstone, an indicator of the way fiction, even fiction that wants to be realist, needs to produce symbols and representations of the real, not a would-be photographic reproduction of the real. But it is true also that Proust's real affection for Balzac has a touch of condescension as well: Balzac sometimes remains too close to an untransformed real, he is at times "preliterary," he offers us pleasures that are more those of the real-life dinner table than its literary representation. Proust has in mind an art where the transformation of base elements would be more thorough, where the artistic crucible would melt the real into one sensitive perception of it. The story of the *Recherche* is above all that of a vocation: the central character's discovery that he is a writer, and that only as a writer can he make sense of reality. In fact, what most people call the real is a distraction. The true life is elsewhere, says the narrator; it is inward, it is the life of the shaping spirit that will produce a book that will have the "shape of time."

Proust was among other things an exceptional literary critic, whose comments on his predecessor novelists are always of interest. His essay on Flaubert's style—originally a letter to the editor of the newspaper *Le Figaro* in reaction to an essay there—is absolutely one of the best and most profound things ever written about Flaubert, and about the meaning of stylistic details, such as verb tenses, in general. In addition to such occasional literary commentary, Proust wrote a series of *pastiches*, literary parodies of his favorite authors, presenting the same subject—a famous criminal affair—in the style of Balzac, of Flaubert, and others. These parodies are among the most brilliant criticism ever conceived: they demonstrate an extraordinary ability to get inside other writers' styles and visions of the world. They capture the characteristic detail or tic, and exaggerate it just enough to be howlingly funny.

The parodies and the literary criticism are important steps along to way to Proust's becoming a novelist—which occurs only after a long apprenticeship. In other words, he seems to move from reading—of a particularly acute, analytic sort—to writing. It's a movement that absorbs and digests those past writers who matter the most to him—perhaps especially Balzac and Flaubert—so that what we may think of as his creation of the maximal high modernist art novel includes as it passes beyond the realist tradition. This is more apparent if one has read the whole of the *Recherche* rather than just the first volume, *Swann's Way*, that most readers content themselves with, since as it progresses the novel becomes more resolutely engaged with social issues and indeed political ones as the Dreyfus Affair comes to play a central demarcating role in French society, creating two passionate camps. And from Proust's preoccupation with society, including the old aristocrats who seem to belong to Balzac's world, emerges a principal focus on figures of the outsider: the Jew, the homosexual, the artist, those who dissent from the largely corrupt social consensus. The protagonist of the *Recherche* discovers at the end—after some three thousand pages—that he must become a writer in order to capture and explain the meaning of life in time. The book he proposes to write, under the shadow of impending death, is not, I think, the book we have just read. For his future book proposes to be the book of truth, of revelation, of joyous discovery. Whereas the book we have just read is the narrative of error, of wandering, of getting things wrong and achieving only glimpses of a truth to come. In this sense, too, Proust's novel works through the matter of the realist novel in order to come out on something else. It wishes, I think, to be transformative of the realist tradition—which is not to say that it discards that tradition but, on the contrary, includes it and moves beyond it.

I sense that Proust's relation to the realist tradition is more serene than Virginia Woolf's. It takes a yet greater effort on Woolf's part to break with realism and create the kind of novel that we now see as modernist, and in so many ways comparable to Proust's, perhaps especially in its attention to consciousness and its understanding of character as something fluid, without rigid contours, subject to change over time and elusive of analysis. Recall Woolf's almost anguished reaction to the tools and techniques of the Edwardian realist novelists in her essay *Mr. Bennett and Mrs. Brown*, first delivered as a lecture in 1924. These novelists, she says, have never looked directly, searchingly at Mrs. Brown—the mysterious woman Woolf has imagined, who sits in the corner of the railway carriage:

> They have looked very powerfully, searchingly, and sympathetically out of the window; at factories, at Utopias, even at the decoration and upholstery of the carriage; but never at her, never at life, never at human nature. And so they have developed a technique of novel-writing which suits their purpose; they have made tools and established conventions which do their business. But those tools are not our tools, and that business is not our business. For us those conventions are ruin, those tools are death.

A very strong statement in which one senses Woolf's anxiety about the weight of a realist tradition become particularly formulaic and oppressive in Edwardian writers such as Arnold Bennett. In particular, the notion that one can get at character though description of the external world seems to her a debilitating premise. In lines that immediately precede those quoted above she says:

> What can Mr. Bennett be about? I have formed my own opinion of what Mr. Bennett is about—he is trying to make us imagine for him; he is trying to hypnotise us into the belief that, because he has made a house, there

must be a person living there. With all his powers of observation, which are marvelous, with all his sympathy and humanity, which are great, Mr. Bennett has never once looked at Mrs. Brown in her corner. There she sits in the corner of the carriage—that carriage which is travelling, not from Richmond to Waterloo, but from one age of English literature to the next, for Mrs. Brown is eternal, Mrs. Brown is human nature, Mrs. Brown changes only on the surface, it is the novelists who get in and out—there she sits and not one of the Edwardian writers has so much as looked at her.

This is a complex plea, for on one hand Woolf claims that she represents a new age of English literature, and that the presentation of Mrs. Brown changes utterly because new generations of novelists come to observe her. But on the other hand she rejects the claim of the Edwardian realists to have truly observed Mrs. Brown at all: the very premises of their techniques of knowing are seen as faulty. And yet Woolf does not claim that the most underlying premise of all—that of attempting to capture characters from the real world—has changed or should change. (It is notable, for instance, that in 1912 she published a warm appreciation of Gissing's novels in the *Times Literary Supplement*.) Her critique is not that of the French "new novelists" of the 1960s, for example, who wanted to see the whole notion of "character" as outmoded, a kind of illusion of bourgeois culture.

Mr. Bennett and Mrs. Brown raises the question of what place the realist vision may occupy in Woolf's work, and more generally how she subsumes realist concerns within her new age of English literature. Let me try to address this question through one of the sequences—that may be the best word for the way the narrative unfolds—of *Mrs. Dalloway*. The sequence is initiated during Lady Bruton's luncheon party, where she has invited Richard Dalloway, among other important people, to help her write her letter to the *Times*.

> "But let us eat first," she said.
> And so there began a soundless and exquisite passing to and fro through swing doors of aproned white-capped maids, handmaidens not of necessity, but adepts in a mystery or grand deception practised by hostesses in Mayfair from one-thirty to two, when, with a wave of the hand, the traffic ceases, and there rises instead this profound illusion in the first place about the food—how it is not paid for; and then that the table spreads itself voluntarily with glass and silver, little mats, saucers of red fruit; films of brown cream mask turbot; in casseroles severed chickens swim; coloured, undomestic, the fire burns; and with the wine and coffee (not paid for) rise jocund visions before musing eyes. (104)

206   Despite the echoes of *Madame Bovary* in its title, we don't think of *Mrs. Dalloway* as primarily a realist text, especially since we know that Virginia Woolf
has thrown Arnold Bennett and the other Edwardian social novelists out the
window of her railway carriage. And yet the transpersonal Woolfian narratorial consciousness—evident in the passage quoted—is very sensitive to
class difference, to money, to objects, to social imposture and its weight.
The "mystery or grand deception practiced by hostesses in Mayfair" is predi-
cated on the hiding, indeed the unmentionable status of the servant class and
the money that supports a life where tables are spread with glass and silver,
turbot and severed chickens. The repeated "not paid for" may be a critique
of a certain form of the novel of manners that ignores the reality of class
division and economic exploitation. But it is really an assertion of realism,
nearly in the Balzacian sense: the reminder that everything has a price tag.

The privileged life of Clarissa and her society is threatened along its margins, by Miss Kilman in her green mackintosh, who has converted Clarissa's
daughter Elizabeth to her oppositional view of the world, if not to the profound *ressentiment* she displays toward privilege; and, more radically, by Septimus Warren Smith and his hyperrational discourse of madness; by the Great
War, now over but leaving death in its wake; and of course by death itself.

There would be much to say about Septimus and his voices, as brilliant
an evocation of schizophrenia, provoked by shell shock, as any novelist has
created. The inclusion of Septimus in the novel gives it a certain twist or
torque away from the standard Edwardian cast of characters: Septimus contests, puts into question, comfortable assumptions about character and narrative point of view. Without offering a full discussion of Septimus, I want
to focus on his antagonist, Sir William Bradshaw, doctor and exponent of
"proportion." I give the following long passage only in part:

> Worshipping proportion, Sir William not only prospered himself but made
> England prosper, secluded her lunatics, forbade childbirth, penalised de-
> spair, made it impossible for the unfit to propagate their views until they,
> too, shared his sense of proportion . . . .
> But Proportion has a sister, less smiling, more formidable, a Goddess
> even now engaged—in the heat and the sands of India, the mud and swamp
> of Africa, the purlieus of London, wherever in short the climate or the devil
> tempts men to fall from the true belief which is her own—is even now en-
> gaged in dashing down shrines, smashing idols, and setting up in their place
> her own stern countenance. Conversion is her name and she feasts on the

wills of the weakly, loving to impress, to impose, adoring her own features stamped on the face of the populace. . . . But conversion, fastidious Goddess, loves blood better than brick, and feasts most subtly on the human will. For example, Lady Bradshaw. Fifteen years ago she had gone under. It was nothing you could put your finger on; there had been no scene, no snap; only the slow sinking, water-logged, of her will into his. (99–100)

One could find versions of Bradshaw in Zola, in social Darwinian claims that progress entails crushing the marginals, those of weak will, and especially those, like Septimus, whose lack of "proportion" puts them in contest with the ideology of progress. But you of course find nothing like the ironic, satiric, and pointedly dissenting voice of the Woolfian narrator here.

Woolf's dissent from realism, I want to suggest, is of a piece with her dissent from the kind of "proportion" urged by Bradshaw, the definition of "human nature" that he represents and enforces—as in Septimus's reflection: "Once you fall . . . human nature is on you. Holmes and Bradshaw are on you. . . . The rack and the thumbscrew are applied. Human nature is remorseless" (98). Now, Mrs. Brown in Woolf's essay was also "human nature," the kind of thing the novelist needs to capture. But Bradshaw's kind of human nature is totalitarian. He is prime representative of a system of policing that runs through the novel, the imposition of social and ideological conventions that Woolf protests on ethical grounds, and also deconstructs in her technique. Recall her stricture on the Edwardian realists: "For us those conventions are ruin, those tools are death." Bradshaw brings death and ruin in his wake—he brings them even into Clarissa's party. He must be combated, not with Edwardian tools, not through the realist presentation of milieu, detail, character, but in a fluid narrational style that negates the kind of Edwardian fixity and solidity of "character" in which Arnold Bennett and Sir William Bradshaw both believe. As Clarissa's consciousness formulates it early in the novel: "she would not say of Peter, she would not say of herself, I am this, I am that" (8–9). Indeed, the whole opening sequence of the novel works to prevent us from attaching such defining labels to people. Those who, like Bradshaw, claim to know and to represent human nature are purveyors of ruin and death.

Clarissa's maid, Lucy, provides another kind of critique of realism as a mimetic art as she looks forward to Clarissa's party: "They would come; they would stand; they would talk in the mincing tones which she could imitate, ladies and gentlemen" (38). Imitation is easy, and impertinent. More to the point is Peter Walsh's reflection: "For this is the truth about our soul, he thought, our self, who fish-like inhabits deep seas and plies among obscurities threading her way between the boles of giant weeds, over sun-flickered spaces and on and on into gloom, cold, deep, inscrutable; suddenly she shoots to the surface and sports on the wind-wrinkled waves; that is, has a positive need to brush, scrape, kindle herself, gossiping" (161). Such a view of "character" underwrites and is validated by a use of free indirect discourse, or "narrated monologue" as it has also been called, that has learned from Flaubert and James but claims a fluidity of movement in time and space that Flaubert and James could not allow. It is in fact closer to Proust's time-traveling narration, hovering between different temporal moments. Clarissa's consciousness can plunge from the present moment back to childhood mornings at Bourton without any overt "shifters"; and the narrated monologue can move without transition from her consciousness to that of Scrope Purvis waiting next her on the curb; and then it can evoke this June day in a view transcending any single consciousness: "(June had drawn out every leaf on the trees. The mothers of Pimlico gave suck to their young. Messages were passing from the Fleet to the Admiralty . . .)" (7)— all these examples from the first few pages, which are teaching us how to read the novel. And the narration can then even reach into an unimaginable future, evoked on account of the closed motor car bearing its important personage: "the enduring symbol of the state which will be known to curious antiquaries, sifting the ruins of time, when London is a grass-grown path and all those hurrying along the pavement this Wednesday morning are but bones with a few wedding rings mixed up in their dust and the gold stoppings of innumerable decayed teeth. The face in the motor car will then be known" (16). That is, consciousness transcends and deconstructs persons as well as chronological time, and with them the Edwardian novel.

This redefinition of the novel contains a critique of the valuations of the realist novel, for instance in Clarissa's "things." Peter Walsh on his visit to Clarissa—after so many years away in the outposts of empire—reflects on his own lack of accumulation of things as a sign—as in a Balzac novel—of social failure: "he was a failure, compared with all this—the inlaid table, the mounted paper-knife, the dolphin and the candlesticks, the chair-covers and the old valuable English tinted prints—he was a failure!" (43). Her definition by things then modulates to an image of her imprisonment, in the manner of Sleeping Beauty, lying "with the brambles curving over her," and she must summon to her aid "the things she liked," as in refusal of Peter's claim to awaken her from her state of insentience. But it is too late for her, as she often reflects. "Narrower and narrower would her bed be. The candle was half burnt down" (31). What lies in wait, what repeatedly obtrudes in the novel, is death, as in the repeated lines from Shakespeare's *Cymbeline*: "Fear no more the heat o' the sun / Nor the furious winter's rages."

Thematically, the problem in *Mrs. Dalloway* is frequently stated as one of communication: the problem of reading the skywriting over London, for instance, and Septimus's communications with the dead Evans. Septimus offers a parody of knowledge and communication, as if he were the omniscient narrator of the universe: "He knew all their thoughts, he said; he knew everything. He knew the meaning of the world, he said" (66). Richard Dalloway stands at the other end of the spectrum, too self-conscious and abashed to tell Clarissa he loves her. He buys her flowers with the intention of taking them to her and saying, "I love you." But when he does present them, "he could not bring himself to say he loved her; not in so many words" (118). The most effective communication seems to be the most impersonal, the commonplace: Bradshaw's "human nature," Lady Bruton's letter to the *Times*, Peter Walsh's authoritative tone in ordering "Bartlett pears" at the hotel dining room. When Septimus's suicide, reported by the Bradshaws, comes to inhabit Clarissa's party, her first reaction is a kind of imaginative imitation and completion of his act, as if she herself were falling onto the rusty spikes of the railing. She then reads his suicide as an attempt to communicate: the writing of a desperate message to the world. "Death was defiance. Death was an attempt to communicate; people feeling the impossibility of reaching the centre which, mystically, evaded them; closeness drew apart; rapture faded, one was alone. There was an embrace in death" (184).

Clarissa reflects on the old woman in the room visible through the window: "And the supreme mystery which Kilman might say she had solved, or Peter might say he had solved, but Clarissa didn't believe either of them had the ghost of an idea of solving, was simply this: here was one room; there another. Did religion solve that, or love?" (127). Significantly, the old woman in the window recurs just before the end of the novel, going to bed as Clarissa's party unfolds—and the clock starts striking. The joining of two rooms, two disparate subjectivities, does not seem to be soluble by religion, or even love. It is only the frail work of narrative consciousness that can transcend, momentarily, the bounds of definition and naming, the Bradshaw-like view of the world. As in Proust—far more than in Joyce, I think—in Woolf's fiction the play of shaping narratorial voice and consciousness seems to offer the only solution—provisional, time-bound, threatened by impending death—to an otherwise intractable problem of human subjectivity. To say that is to attach a tremendous importance to art and its shaping of the world (and certainly Proust and Woolf could be accused of an excessive valuation of the aesthetic). And to the extent that they foreground and celebrate the role of the artist they move beyond the margins of the realist tradition, which always claimed, I think often with a genuine humility, that the artist was there only as the lens on the outer world.

The realist vision is alive in Woolf but as something inadequate, something rigid and exteriorizing. Its hard outlines must be broken down. The exterior world dissolves in the chemistry of consciousness. Persons lose their protective envelopes to become quivering subjectivities open to anyone peering through the bramble hedge. Yet the real offers its resistance, as in Woolf's enigmatic short story entitled *Solid Objects*. In particular, the real maintains its policing function, through money, social class, things, and through the final limit set by death. And here we return to the crucial importance of the Great War. It has just ended when the novel opens, but its effects are very much felt by way of the missing and the damaged. The great divide marked by the First World War is more explicitly marked in some of Woolf's other works—*Jacob's Room*, for instance—but it is nonetheless there in *Mrs. Dalloway*, and it menaces everything because it represents, in cataclysmic form, the death that lurks everywhere in the novel.

If we look back at the realist tradition through the lens provided by Woolf, we can see its "parti pris des choses," to use the poet Francis Ponge's phrase: its taking the side of things. That seems to me irreducible in the realist project: to register the importance of the things—objects, inhabitations, accessories—amid which people live, believe they can't live without. The realist believes you must do an elementary phenomenology of the world in order to speak of how humans inhabit it, and this phenomenology will necessarily mean description, detailing, an attempt to say what the world is like in a way that makes its constraints recognizable by the reader. Note that Woolf—and also James, and Joyce, and Proust—don't really reject this premise: their work is full of significant things. Clarissa's parasol, the roses Richard Dalloway buys for her, Miss Kilman's mackintosh, Peter Walsh's pen-knife: all these are objects from the real world, the world of commerce and manufacture, that become part of a human semiotic system. But providing a house for Mrs. Brown, says Woolf, does not of itself provide a scrutiny of her human nature. What is different in the modernists is most of all the selectivity of consciousness applied to the phenomenal world, and the establishment of a perspective resolutely within consciousness as it deals with the objects of the world.

Woolfian consciousness may appear to obliterate the world in its desire to get at "Mrs. Brown" from the inside, rather than through the description, à la Bennett, of circumstance and setting. The world is nonetheless there, undergirding consciousness, as in the "not paid for" fiction, as in the telegram Lady Bexborough holds, announcing the death of her son in the war. And as with Flaubert, it is there in the title, *Mrs. Dalloway,* on which Clarissa reflects early on in the novel: "She had the oddest sense of being herself invisible; unseen; unknown; there being no more marrying, no more having of children now, only this astonishing and rather solemn progress with the rest of them, up Bond Street, this being Mrs. Dalloway; not even Clarissa any more; this being Mrs. Richard Dalloway (14)." This being Mrs. Richard Dalloway: I think you could express at least some of the dramatic action of this novel in terms of how much Clarissa is able to escape being merely Mrs. Richard Dalloway, and in what realm that escape is allowed to take place. Peter Walsh's "terror" and "ecstasy" at the end of the novel as he waits for Clarissa to manifest herself at the end of the party—for all the world as if she were a Greek goddess appearing on the ramparts of the city—seem real enough. But are they only in the realm of nostalgia? Can he, can anyone, find Clarissa under the guise of Mrs. Dalloway? Can she? I'm not sure that the novel answers these questions. But the very fluidity of presentation of character is such that I am not sure they are quite the right questions. Life, the soul, as in Peter Walsh's image, is submarine and elusive.

CHAPTER 12

The Future of Reality?

I BEGAN THIS BOOK BY TALKING ABOUT THE HUMAN INTEREST IN MODELING reality: the apparent pleasure we take in making and playing with scale models, at once reproductions and reductions of the world around us. Friedrich Schiller long ago spoke of the *Spieltrieb*, the instinct or drive to play, as inherent to human beings, and crucially important in defining the space of individual autonomy within the constraints of society and the world. The play instinct manifests itself nearly from birth, in animals as well as in people. In humans, it early on often takes the form of imitation of the rituals and gestures and things of the surrounding environment: somehow the game seems more worth playing if it has rules that mime observed realities. (Mimesis itself, we can surmise, is a tool for survival: the principal way human infants learn to cope with the world, for instance.) The realist novel may offer the most faithful version of this kind of play within the spectrum of verbal artifacts we call literature—the most faithful, perhaps the most ploddingly literal, least imaginative in some ways, yet in other ways admirable because of its commitment to the rules it has set for itself. Recall Gissing's realist Harold Biffen, and his novel *Mr. Bailey, Grocer*, devoted to the tedium of the everyday. You don't have to be so boring as Biffen, and you don't have to end in suicide, but you do have to work out of a basic commitment to the constraints of the real.

Consider in this context a short story by Jorge Luis Borges entitled Tlön, Uqbar, Orbis Tertius. Borges regularly writes what one might call metafictions, fictions that comment on the nature of fictions. In the preface to the collection generally referred to as *Ficciones*, Borges expresses a postmodern world-weariness with the comment: "The composition of vast books is a laborious and impoverishing extravagance. To go on for five hundred pages developing an idea whose perfect oral exposition is possible in a few minutes! A better course of procedure is to pretend that these books already exist, and then to offer a résumé, a commentary"(15). Instead of books, Borges says, he offers us "notes on imaginary books." There is a nested set of imaginary books and worlds in Tlön, Uqbar, Orbis Tertius. The discovery of Uqbar comes about originally from "the conjunction of a mirror and an encyclopedia" (17). If the "mirror held up to nature" is a standard description of the realist enterprise, the mirror held up to the encyclopedia suggests the vertiginous opportunities, and possible problems, of a literary representation born from the reflected image of a text that claims already to have ordered reality, as knowledge. Bioy Casares at this point in the tale recalls the memorable state-ment of one of the heresiarchs of Uqbar, that mirrors and copulation are abominable, since they both multiply the numbers of man. Yet: what and where is Uqbar? The narrator never has heard of it. Bioy, however, insists he has read about the country.

Multiplication by way of mirrors continues, as Bioy and the narrator then find an article describing Uqbar in some pages apparently appended to the forty-sixth volume of an edition of The Anglo-American Cyclopaedia (itself a reprint of the tenth edition of The Encyclopaedia Britannica). There is, though, "beneath the superficial authority of the prose, a fundamental vagueness": real geographical regions such as Armenia are "dragged into the text in a strangely ambiguous way"; the one recognizable historical figure (a sorcerer) is "invoked in a rather metaphorical sense" (19). It may then come as no sur-prise that the article notes that "the literature of Uqbar was fantastic in char-acter, and that its epics and legends never referred to reality, but to the two imaginary regions of Mlejnas and Tlön": still another fictional creation from the mirror that has been tilted toward the book rather than the real.

The interpolated article of the forty-sixth volume of The Anglo-American Cyclopaedia is only the beginning of the vertiginous creation of imaginary worlds. Two years later comes the discovery of the eleventh volume of A First Encyclopaedia of Tlön: beyond the "brief description of a false country," now we have "a substantial fragment of the complete history of an unknown planet." It is merely logical that the philosophy and belief systems of this planet must be "congenitally idealist," and its languages devoid of nouns—the names for things—relying instead, in the southern hemisphere, on verbs and adverbs, in the northern hemisphere on the monosyllabic adjective. In fact, there is only one intellectual discipline in Tlön: psychology. All thinking is in the mode of the as-if; the metaphysicians search not for truth but for "a kind of amazement" (25). In Tlön, "Centuries and centuries of idealism have not failed to influence reality" (29). Objects, things, can be reproduced mentally, as hrönir, at first the product of absent-mindedness, later systematically produced. The hrön is a product of expectation; stranger and even more perfect is the ur, a "thing produced by suggestion, an object brought into being by hope" (30).

The story of the "third world" of Tlön is thus about the shaping of the real world by the imagination, the triumph of idealism over science and the verifiable real. This jeu d'esprit might seem harmless enough, but Borges wants to draw a more overt and sinister lesson from his tale. The tale was published in May 1940, as Europe and Latin America were falling to the mirage of ideologies that claimed to reorder the world in more perfect form. The original publication (in the review Sur) included a proleptic postscript dated 1947, which accurately forecasts the horrific consequences of an attempt to reformulate the world according to one's beliefs. This postscript finally reveals the origins of Tlön in a multigenerational conspiracy originating in the American Ezra Buckley's wish "to demonstrate to the nonexistent God that mortal men were capable of conceiving a world." Like Balzac's Comédie humaine or Zola's Rougon-Macquart, the First Encyclopaedia of Tlön aims to create a totalized representation of reality—on a yet vaster scale. But starting in 1942, according to the postscript, something else started to happen: the invasion of the real world by objects from the fantastic world of Tlön. "Almost immediately, reality gave ground on more than one point. The truth is that it hankered to give ground" (34).

Reality cedes its place to fantasy because the fantastic represents "a labyrinth plotted by men, a labyrinth destined to be deciphered by men." That description could stand for many of the more facile forms of entertainment —detective stories, soap operas—with which we amuse ourselves, and give ourselves the momentary illusion that the world is ordered in accordance with human desire and intelligence. As Borges writes further: "Contact with Tlön and the ways of Tlön have disintegrated this world. Captivated by its discipline, humanity forgets and goes on forgetting that it is the discipline of chess players, not of angels." Borges is of course presenting an explicitly political allegory, an image of how the world was taken over by fascism, in particular, and other ideologies that claimed a falsely totalizing explanation of the world, and in the process reduced human beings to pawns in an inhuman chess game. I think he may also—in a story from the volume *Ficciones*—be urging the difference between fictions on one hand and myths on the other. Myths can be seen as fictions that have been totalized, lost their self-conscious fictionality, hardened into belief systems that claim to explain the entire world. Myths—the master race, supremacy of the state, truth as revelation—lead to fanaticism, to crusades, to extermination camps. Fictions are different. They maintain a sense of their as-if quality, of their lack of provable truth, of their provisionality. Fictions are made-up to try out versions of understanding. They are aware of their made-upness.

I think it is part of Borges's point here that fictions that separate themselves wholly from the real, that close themselves hermetically in a realm of fantasy, risk becoming the most totalitarian of fictions: risk degrading into myths. Everywhere in his work, Borges is a pedagogue of reading, teaching us to read critically, skeptically, and to resist the claims of any system to explain all. Borges's wit and playfulness are antidotes to fundamentalist belief systems. And part of the apparent paradox he presents is that fictions must maintain a testing relation to the real. This is not to dismiss the role of fantasy and the fantastic—Borges after all owes much to the Surrealists—but rather to argue that taking chess players for angels is dangerous. There is in *Tlön, Uqbar, Orbis Tertius* what I see as an endorsement of the concern for such as Balzac, Dickens, Flaubert, Eliot, Zola, James, Woolf to maintain an accurate relation to the real—to make their imaginative reformulations of reality recognizably a "criticism of life."

I dwell on Borges's tale because I think we need to beware of the fantasies that are marketed to us as realist. Reality may suffer from fictions of the real that have degraded into myths. I will not connect the political dots on this statement, but it's not hard to do. As W. B. Yeats wrote in a time of civil war: "We had fed the heart on fantasies, / The heart's grown brutal from the fare." But consider such as "reality TV." I think there is a certain fascination in the concept of reality TV as I first heard it explained, when it first hit the screen in the Netherlands, I believe. Then it was supposed to be the unedited record of the lives of a group of people in one house—something like what Zola claimed to be doing in his novel *Pot-Bouille*, which concerns the lives of all the apartment dwellers in one building. It sounded like some of Andy Warhol's experimental films, such as *Sleep*, which trained the camera on a sleeping man for many hours. But what "reality TV" has come to mean is something quite different: the recruitment of nonprofessional actors (who after all come cheaper than professionals) who then are submitted to the rules of a contest that is more or less brutal and degrading, resulting in a Darwinian struggle to survive and win some prize, which may be as real as a husband or a wife. It's no different from sitcom or soap opera except that it leaves a bit more room for the chance occurrence, the individual riff. Reality TV then invaded the cinema with *The Real Cancún*, which chose sixteen college-age men and women from auditions, then put them in a carefully staged and erotically charged environment in a beach hotel, and turned on the cameras to see what "stories" might develop. It used only a selection from those stories, assigning the majority of the original sixteen characters to penumbral status, and editing hundreds of hours of digital tape down to a two-hour product.

The producers' description of *The Real Cancún* is not unlike Zola's claim in *Le Roman expérimental* that he composes his novels on the model of the scientific experiment, taking a certain temperament, a certain bundle of psychosocial traits, then putting it into a certain socioeconomic situation—and standing back to observe and record the inevitable results. Zola's description of method needs to be taken for what it is, another publicity claim on his part, another semiserious attempt to enroll his novelistic practice under the banner of "science." And like Zola's novels, *The Real Cancún*, and no doubt its planned sequels as well, may rather provide confirmation that life imitates art—or, more accurately, that life represented appeals broadly only when edited, only when its "story lines" have been given shape. That "reality TV" and its spawn have managed to make that label stick, made it an accepted category of our entertainments, may substantiate Borges's perception that reality wanted to give ground: that we prefer fantasies of reality to the real thing.

How to explain the real if limited fascination of representations that do come close to keeping a record of the everyday, that claim a largely unedited version of experience? We have a thirst for reality even as we suffer a surfeit of reality. Perhaps more accurately, we have a thirst for the reality of others, which may be paired with boredom or pain in our own. Literature as a whole, and the novel certainly, responds to this thirst, offering what we sometimes call "vicarious experience," living through others, through substitutes for ourselves. The vicarious has not had a particularly good press over the centuries: it's been seen as escapist, the stuff of poets and madmen, and as morally corrupting. The censorship of novels, and of the theater—recurring episodes in the history of both genres—always had much to do with the idea that simulation of experience, especially emotional experience, and most of all amorous experience, was dangerous: dangerous to the state because it promoted idleness and amusement and turned subjects away from productive labor, dangerous to the church because it offered imaginative satisfactions that distracted attention from the official myth. Where realist fictions are concerned, vicarious experience often comes by way of voyeurism, looking at the normally hidden lives of others, as at normally covered bodies (an issue often represented in novels themselves: see the opening of *Daniel Deronda*, for example). Recall that emblematic gesture from early in the history of the novel, from Lesage's *Le Diable boîteux*, where the devil Asmodée lifts off the rooftops of buildings in Madrid to show the private lives being played out under them. This is a source of our fascination with the novel, and it has continuities with other forms of voyeurism, including the explicitly erotic forms.

At times a thin and uncertain line separates realism from pornography. In *Hard Core*, a scholarly study of visual pornography, Linda Williams uses the phrase of a French filmmaker and theorist, Jean-Louis Comolli: the "frenzy of the visible," as characteristic of our times. We do appear to live in a culture where we want to make everything visible, to witness it—though at the same time we may be made uncomfortable by what is seen, want to censor it. Pornography may in this sense be a kind of literalistic—and not finally very imaginative—outcome of the realists' desire to see and tell all. Certainly Zola was aware that his novels, and *Nana* most of all, would be accused of pornography, and he is able to respond—in reasonably good faith—that the accusation is inevitable if he has done his task honestly. Flaubert of course was put on trial for *Madame Bovary*, and Zola's English publisher served a time in prison for bringing out *The Earth*, translation of *La Terre*, an earthy novel about the world of peasants and their animals.

In evoking the concepts of vicarious experience and voyeurism, I am trying to get at our fascination with the visual reproduction of the banal. Realism tends to reassert its claims after long periods of time when it has been out of fashion. Hence we may want to say that realism is both a period concept—as I have used it in discussing largely the nineteenth-century novel —and also one continuing tendency of the imagination. The history of the novel often appears to take the form of successive generations claiming their work is "more real" than that of their predecessors. Then you have a phenomenon such as the "photorealism" or "hyperrealism" that came to the fore for about a decade, from the late 1960s into the 1980s, in Western art, particularly in the United States and Britain. It was related to Pop Art, particularly in its choice of subjects from the everyday commercial landscape, and some sort of a reaction against Abstract Expressionism, claiming an interest in surfaces and simulacra, for instance in the work of Richard Estes. In such as *Parking Lot*, Estes brilliantly renders enameled sheet metal surfaces, seemingly for their sensuous presence as surface, and as cultural icon (fig. 32). In the well-known sculptural work of Duane Hanson, life and art live together in a kind of uneasy crossover. Hanson's figures are of course created from life-casts—they are plaster reproductions of "real people"—and then clothed in the typical real clothing of their life roles, in this case the "typical" janitor (fig. 33).

More unsettling, I find, is the work of John DeAndrea, who also works from life casts, and constructs his human bodies—typically naked—from a polyester resin that he finishes, and details, so that figures are uncannily life-like. The two figures of *Couple Against Wall* seem to shut the mouth of interpretative commentary, a bit in the manner of Flaubert's Bouvard and Pécuchet (fig. 34). They may represent most of all the banality of nudity. DeAndrea may make us want to ask: When does reproduction become so literalized that it hardly seems right to speak of *representation* any more—if representation appears traditionally to involve re-presenting in a sign-system, translating into a certain set of conventions. This was a question posed originally by the invention of photography—and these sculptures resemble what a three-dimensional photograph might be. DeAndrea interests me because he is an artist who seems to beg all the questions relating to representation-reproduction-reduplication. It's significant that he often seems to gesture toward the legend of Pygmalion and Galatea, the artist's creation of a sculpture so perfect that it comes alive in response to his desire (fig. 35). Yet of course DeAndrea's bodies—perfectly reproduced, with high and patient artistry—are patently unalive. As such they pose the question of why we want or need such artistic dummies. DeAndrea produces work that is an interest-

Fig. 32. Richard Estes, Parking Lot, n.d., oil on composition panel. National Academy of Design, New York (1987.5)

Fig. 33. Duane Hanson, *Janitor*, 1973, polyester and fiberglass. Milwaukee Art Museum, Gift of Friends of Art

Fig. 34. John DeAndrea, *Untitled*, polyvinyl, polychromed in oil. ACA Galleries, New York

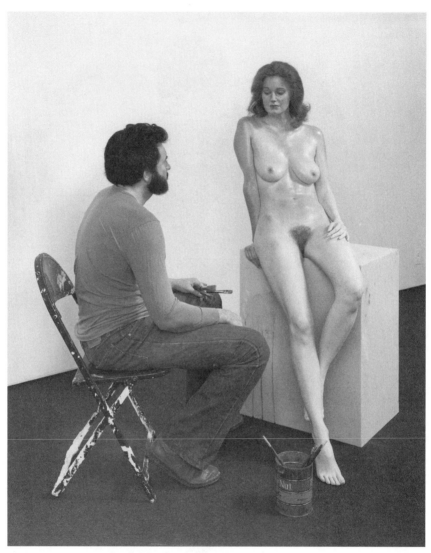

Fig. 35. John DeAndrea, *Artist and Model*, polyvinyl, polychromed in oil. ACA Galleries, New York

ing kind of tautology. This, it seems to say, is the body. It's a bit like another Borges tale, about cartographers who made a map so perfect that it was as big as the country it was supposed to represent. It doesn't answer the question of why it is worth making or looking at such perfect replications, and it may disturbingly make us think about the possible tautological status of all artistic representation.

I glanced, in my first chapter, at the work of the painter often considered our greatest contemporary realist, Lucian Freud. If you set his work next to the photorealism of Estes or DeAndrea, you may have to ask whether Freud is truly a realist. There is a strong expressionist element in his work, a heightening and even exaggeration of certain contours of the real (fig. 36). It lacks the cool of Estes or DeAndrea; it is tormented, seemingly wishing to *say* something through its splayed and twisted bodies, whereas hyperrealism seems to be saying nothing more than: this is the real. Is Lucian Freud realism, or rather expressionism? I'm not sure. But I think it's worth noting the parallels to kinds of expression we find, in different modalities, in Balzac and Zola: moments where the seemingly objective registering of the surfaces and forms of the world can give way to something else, release an intenser vision, often metaphorical in Balzac, allegorical in Zola. Things, streets, persons speak of large-scale dramas. Freud is I think rather like that, a realist in the expressionist mode for whom the world viewed is not enough unless it can be made to release a vision. Whereas the hyperrealists belong more in Flaubert's camp, with the implication that surface, rightly viewed, studied, and represented, is full of interest in itself—and perhaps all we have, since any putative depths behind may be sheer wishful thinking.

It has been one of my central contentions that realism is highly visual, invested in the faculty of sight, in a viewing of the things and the milieux that people move amid, rub up against. Speaking in vague and megaceptual terms, this is a legacy of empiricism, from new understandings of human perception in the world deriving from John Locke and his followers. It is a conception of human subject and world that pervades almost all our disciplines of knowledge and social institutions. The law, for instance, very much depends on what one legal scholar recently characterized as a "ground-zero theory of evidence": that is, the belief that you had to be there to see. Conversely, if you can produce a convincing description of the circumstance, you *were* there, you have validated your claim to eyewitness status. Except that

Fig. 36. Lucian Freud, *Nude with Leg Up (Leigh Bowery)*, 1992, oil on canvas. Hirshhorn Museum and Sculpture Garden, Smithsonian Institution, Joseph H. Hirschhorn Purchase Fund, 1993. © Lucian Freud. Photo: Lee Stalsworth

recently the accuracy of even eyewitness testimony has come under question in studies that show how inaccurate most people's observations and recollections of observations really are. Experiments done in recent years, by psychologists and criminologists, often make one wonder if we can trust eyewitness accounts at all. We have discovered also that a suspect's confession, based apparently on the most intimate knowledge of the person in question—the person him- or herself—can be unreliable, the product of various motives and pressures urging toward confession that may not conduce to an accurate account of what the person has, or has not, done. Sometimes in reading legal materials one is reminded of Dickens's views of the law. I am thinking in particular of a moment in *Great Expectations* when Mike, the clerk to the great lawyer Jaggers, comes to say he's produced a needed witness. Jaggers asks: "What is he prepared to swear?" "Well, Mas'r Jaggers," Mike replies, "in a general way, anythink."

To evoke Dickens and issues of eyewitness and evidence here raises the question of the relation of the novel to the law. It is a close relation, and one related to the realist novel, since law and criminology respond, in the nineteenth century, to the same phenomena and problems as the novel does. It's no accident that some prominent early English novelists, notably Daniel Defoe and Henry Fielding, were professionally involved in the law (and in Defoe's case clearly fascinated by the outlaw), and the annals of crime provided material for the novel from early in its history. Balzac proudly arranged a luncheon party with Vidocq, former criminal become police chief, and author of his memoirs, who was the model for Vautrin–Jacques Collin–Carlos Herrera; and in *Splendeurs et misères des courtisanes* and a host of other novels he explored the underworld, its social organization and its languages, and the culture of prisons. The detective story, "invented" in the early 1840s by Edgar Allan Poe, parallels the rise of the modern police force, the creation of Scotland Yard, and a large social concern with identifying criminal elements in society. Modern urban life, with its vast working-class and underclass populations, created in the bourgeoisie a sense of anxiety about identity, the need to classify "deviant" social elements (such as prostitutes), and particularly to find a means to identify clearly and accurately the recidivist, the habitual criminal. Balzac was fascinated by *la marque*, the branding of criminals that meant they bore the mark of their criminal identity forever—but fascinated in part because the practice was abolished for humanitarian reasons in 1832, which provoked an increased anxiety about finding accurate observational and recording techniques for the criminal population. Almost as soon as it was invented, photography was put to use in the recording of criminal faces and bodies. Bertillon's systematic classification of criminals used photographs along with descriptive notations of characteristic physical marks and cranial and bodily measurements. *Bertillonage* had a long career in criminology, but it was a painstaking and awkward business, and required careful training of its operatives, who had to take both measurements and photos with exacting precision.

If identifying the malefactors of European societies was difficult, dealing with the indigenous peoples of the colonies was far worse: to European eyes, they all looked alike. Eventually, an official of the British Raj in Bengal "discovered" a technique that the Bengalis had probably been using for generations, what they knew as *tip sahi*, a kind of signature by way of the fingerprint. Fingerprinting at once made its way back to England and the rest of Europe, and quickly established itself as the queen of proofs. Western cultures accepted the claims that fingerprints were unique (no two people had identical ones) and permanent (aging did not change them). Societies accepted these claims, it turns out, with virtually no testing of the hypotheses: they wanted to believe, they needed fingerprint evidence. Very recently, a federal district judge in a hearing on evidence cast doubt on the accuracy of fingerprint analysis and matching, suggesting that it did not meet the test of scientific evidence. This is currently a distinctly minority view in the law, but one might hazard a prediction that as DNA testing evolves—and other analytic scientific procedures are possibly invented—fingerprints may come to seem as quaint and approximate as Bertillonage. (It always seemed to me that belief in the uniqueness of fingerprints for all the population the world has ever held was, like the claim that no two snowflakes are alike, more an article of faith than a verified truth.) We needed to believe that our unique identity was at our fingertips, legible from the impress of our bodies. This may belong to an Enlightenment and Romantic identity paradigm that we may eventually need to give up.

We may have to—maybe we already have—let go of the belief that identity is apparent to visual inspection alone, as it generally is to the realist novelist and to the law. The future probably belongs more and more to the analysis of the hidden. Already, courts are facing cases that deal with more and more sophisticated types of invasion of private space, seeing in the dark, seeing through walls, detecting hidden movements. Does this mean that the novel of the future will be less resolutely visual than it has been in the realist tradition? That seems plausible, and one could already cite many kinds of turning away from the visible toward the invisible in modernism (and of course even earlier—none of these developments is linear): a nice emblem would be in Thomas Mann's *The Magic Mountain*, where for the tubercular patients in the sanatorium, it is not the photograph that counts but the X-ray. The patients exchange X-rays as mementos instead of photographs. And an extraordinary highpoint of the novel comes when Hans Castorp views the "pulsating shadow" that is the beating heart of his cousin Joachim in the X-ray machine. Here is a central mystery unveiled, a vital hidden organ made visible. But then: you could argue that the X-ray precisely continues the realist vision, claiming the conquest of sight and the visual image in realms where they could not hitherto penetrate.

When we indulge in what is no doubt idle speculation about the future of reality and realism in the novel, I think we may want to keep in mind two apparently contradictory phenomena. One is the inward turn of the novel with the coming of modernism, its increasing concern with states of consciousness. Even the popular novel today tends toward a good deal of psychologizing, and has taken up Joycean streams of consciousness as entirely natural and ready to hand. On the other hand, postmodern culture tends to be predominantly visual, indeed wedded to that "frenzy of the visible" identified by Comolli. Certainly the most influential medium of our time is television, and in many ways the cultural stylistic standard is defined more by MTV than by anything literature does. Perhaps it's really the comic strip that lies in the future of the novel—and in Europe now you find far more adults publicly reading comic-strip books, graphic novels, than in the United States. There are whole bookstores in Paris that sell nothing but *bandes dessinées*. There are also many cultures in which the *photoroman*—the novel played out through photos—is the most popular genre. Whereas Americans seem to prefer the televised daytime soap.

I intend this idle speculation simply to suggest that, while the realist novel that has been my subject here is part of history, a history that had a beginning and reached an end, the impulse that created realism in the novel still goes on, and no doubt will in the future. The realist novel belongs to the projects of human curiosity, a way of knowing and modeling the world. I suggested at the outset that the pleasure human beings take in scale models of the real—ships in bottles, lead soldiers, model railroads—has something to do with the sense they provide of being able to play with and therefore to master the real world, a way to bind and organize its energies. The scale model—the *modèle réduit*, as the French call it—allows us to get both our fingers and our mind around objects otherwise alien and imposing. The realist novel similarly offers us a reduction of the world, compacted into a volume that we know can provide, for the duration of our reading, the sense of a parallel reality that can almost supplant our own. And the realist novel gives us something of the same sense of playing as the model, entertaining a view of the world, functioning in the mode of the as-if.

I suggested earlier that we postmodernists (as I suppose we inevitably are) appreciate a certain eclecticism of styles, in which the realist discourse of things—its interpretation of realism in the etymological sense of *res*-ism, thing-ism—can again be enjoyed and valued. Of course in rereading the works of such consummate fiction-makers as the great realists, we discover that any label such as "realism" is inadequate, and that great literature is precisely that which understands this inadequacy, which sees around the corner of its own declared aesthetics, sees what may make its house of cards come tumbling down. Reading these novelists we are ever discovering both what it is like to try to come to terms with the real within the constraints of language, and how one encounters in the process the limits of realism, and the limits to representation itself. For these are among the most intelligent, inventive, aware—as well as the most ambitious—novelists in our history. And they are still—they are more than ever—part of our history, part of how we understand ourselves.

James, I noted, says that of all novelists, Balzac pretended hardest. This may be taken as typically elusive Jamesian praise, praise with a slight edge of condescension, praise of the sophisticate for the simpler soul caught up in the web of his own fictions. But James consistently insists that the serious novelist must play seriously and fully the game of pretending, must not ever give the impression of not believing in his created life. This may strike us postmoderns as a bit naive but it could be seen as definitional of the work of the realist. The realist needs to believe that fictional worlds, people and things represented in language, are seriously important. They are not, except in the most self-deluded realism, simple reflections or reproductions of their counterparts in the world, but rather tokens in a game played in earnest with the world. Whatever the particular rules of the game, it is important that there be no cheating, that the game board simulate conditions of the real, that it create a good model of its economies. How do you find the perspectives necessary to give a sense of a world viewed and understood? From Balzac's descriptive insistence to James's radical perspectivism and beyond, that is the question that has preoccupied novelists for whom giving an account of the real world has been a challenge and an imperative. There is no way out of pretending: you are writing fiction. It is how you pretend that counts.

References and Bibliographical Notes

Quotations from Novels

I have given page references to the novels studied within the body of my text. With novels originally written in French, I have provided my own translations, often more literally faithful to the original than would be desirable in an easily readable version. I have given page references to a current French edition in parentheses ( ), and to what I consider the best available English translation in square brackets [ ]. Editions used:

Honoré de Balzac, *Illusions perdues* (Paris: Garnier/Flammarion, 1990); *Lost Illusions*, trans. Herbert J. Hunt (Harmondsworth: Penguin, 1971)

Charles Dickens, *Hard Times* (Harmondsworth: Penguin, 1995)

Gustave Flaubert, *Madame Bovary* (Paris: Gallimard/Folio, 2001); *Madame Bovary*, trans. Geoffrey Wall (Harmondsworth: Penguin, 1990)

George Eliot, *Daniel Deronda* (Harmondsworth: Penguin, 1995)

Emile Zola, *Nana* (Paris: Livre de Poche, 1984); *Nana*, trans. Douglas Parmée (Oxford: Oxford World Classics, 1998)

Emile Zola, *Au Bonheur des Dames* (Paris: Livre de Poche, 1990); *The Ladies' Paradise* (Berkeley: University of California Press, 1992): this is a reprint of the translation published by Henry Vizetelly in 1886; a new translation is much needed

George Gissing, *New Grub Street* (Oxford: Oxford World Classics, 1993)

George Gissing, *In the Year of Jubilee* (London: Everyman, 1994)

Henry James, *Selected Tales*, ed. John Lyon (Harmondsworth: Penguin, 2001)

James Joyce, *Dubliners* (New York: Viking, 1963)

James Joyce, *Ulysses* (New York: Modern Library, 1961)

Marcel Proust, *A la recherche du temps perdu*, 4 vols. (Paris: Bibliothèque de la Pléiade, 1987); *In Search of Time Past*, trans. C. K. Scott Moncrieff, rev. Terence Kilmartin and D. J. Enright, 6 vols. (New York: Modern Library, 1992–93)

Virginia Woolf, *Mrs. Dalloway* (New York: Harcourt Brace/Harvest Books, 1981)

Jorge Luis Borges, *Ficciones*, trans. Anthony Kerrigan (New York: Grove, 1962)

232   Chapter 1: Realism and Representation

Bibliographical note: The classic work on the emergence of realism in Western literature is Erich Auerbach, *Mimesis*, trans. Willard R. Trask (Princeton, N.J.: Princeton University Press, 1953). Of continuing lively interest is Georg Lukács, *Studies in European Realism*, trans. Edith Bone (London: Hillway, 1950). The single most useful study of nineteenth-century realism, in the visual arts and literature, may be Linda Nochlin, *Realism* (Harmondsworth: Penguin, 1971). Other helpful studies include Harry Levin, *The Gates of Horn: A Study of Five French Realists* (New York: Oxford University Press, 1963); Lilian Furst, *All Is True: The Claims and Strategies of Realist Fiction* (Durham, N.C.: Duke University Press, 1995); Franco Moretti, *The Way of the World* (London: Verso, 1987); Fredric Jameson, *The Political Unconscious: Narrative as a Socially Symbolic Act* (Ithaca, N.Y.: Cornell University Press, 1981); Lionel Trilling, *The Opposing Self* (New York: Viking, 1955); and Bernard Weinberg, *French Realism: The Critical Reaction* (Chicago: University of Chicago Press, 1937). A number of interesting manifestos and declarations on realism can be found in George Becker, ed., *Documents of Modern Literary Realism* (Princeton, N.J.: Princeton University Press, 1963). A recent, thoughtful engagement with visual realism is Michael Fried, *Menzel's Realism: Art and Embodiment in Nineteenth-Century Berlin* (New Haven and London: Yale University Press, 2002). For those interested in a persuasive analytic approach to description in the novel, see Philippe Hamon, *Introduction à l'analyse du descriptif* (Paris: Hachette, 1981).

1   Sigmund Freud, *Beyond the Pleasure Principle*, in *Standard Edition of the Complete Psychological Writings*, 24 vols. (London: Hogarth, 1953–74), 18: 3–64.

1   Claude Lévi-Strauss, *The Savage Mind* (Chicago: University of Chicago Press, 1966), 22ff.

1   Friedrich Schiller, *Letters on the Aesthetic Education of Mankind*, trans. and ed. Elizabeth M. Wilkinson and L. A. Willoughby (Oxford: Clarendon, 1982).

2   Wallace Stevens, *Notes Toward a Supreme Fiction*, in *Collected Poems* (New York: Random House, 1954), 383.

3   On Greek philosophy and the visual, see Hans Jonas, "The Nobility of Sight: A Study in the Phenomenology of the Senses," in *The Phenomenon of Life* (New York: Harper and Row, 1966), 135–56.

6   On Plato on *mimesis* and *diegesis*, see Gérard Genette, *Narrative Discourse*, trans. Jane E. Lewin (Ithaca, N.Y.: Cornell University Press, 1980), 162–66.

7   Erich Auerbach, *Mimesis*, trans. Willard Trask (Princeton, N.J.: Princeton University Press, 1953).

12   Parliamentary debate on Zola: see George Becker, *Documents of Modern Literary Realism* (Princeton, N.J.: Princeton University Press, 1963), 363.

12   Ian Watt, *The Rise of the Novel* (Berkeley: University of California Press, 1957).

13   Edmond and Jules de Goncourt, Preface to *Germinie Lacerteux* (1865; Paris: Garnier/Flammarion, 1990), 55.

13   See Benjamin Disraeli, *Sybil, or The Two Nations* (London: Henry Colburn, 1845).

14   Karl Marx, *Manifesto of the Communist Party*, in *The Marx-Engels Reader*, ed. Robert C. Tucker (New York: Norton, 1978), 476.

14   Ferdinand de Saussure, *Course in General Linguistics* (New York: McGraw-Hill, 1966).

14   C. A. Sainte-Beuve, "De la littérature industrielle," in *Portraits contemporains*, vol. 2 (Paris: Michel Lévy, 1870), 444–71.

16   On Balzac's inventory of his house in Passy, see Didier Maleuvre, *Museum Memories: History, Technology, Art* (Stanford, Calif.: Stanford University Press), 1999.

17   Virginia Woolf, *Mr. Bennett and Mrs. Brown* (London: Hogarth, 1924), 18.

18   See Alain Corbin, "Backstage," in *The History of Private Life*, ed. Philippe Ariès and Georges Duby, vol. 4: *From the Fires of the Revolution to the Great War*, ed. Michelle Perrot, trans. Arthur Goldhammer (Cambridge, Mass.: Harvard University Press, 1990), 451–667.

19   Henry James, "The Future of the Novel," in *Literary Criticism*, vol. 1 (New York: Library of America, 1984), 108.

Chapter 2: Balzac Invents the Nineteenth Century

Bibliographical note: The critical literature on Balzac in French is vast; in English there is far less of note. Henry James's essays on Balzac (he wrote five) are still of great interest: see James, *Literary Criticism*, vol. 2: *French Writers, Other European Writers* (New York: Library of America, 1984). On Balzac's technique and vision, see the chapter on Balzac in Harry Levin, *The Gates of Horn: A Study of Five French Realists* (New York: Oxford University Press, 1963); and Peter Brooks, *The Melodramatic Imagination* (1976; rpt. New Haven and London: Yale University Press, 1995). See also D. A. Miller, *The Novel and the Police* (Berkeley: University of California Press, 1988). A recent biography is Graham Robb, *Balzac: A Biography* (London: Picador, 1994).

Readers of French have a plethora of material; of special note may be Albert Béguin, *Balzac visionnaire* (Geneva: Skira, 1946); Michel Butor, "Balzac et la réalité," in *Répertoire* (Paris: Editions de Minuit, 1960); André Allemand, *Unité et structure de l'univers balzacien* (Paris: Plon, 1965); and Pierre Barbéris, *Le Monde de Balzac* (Paris: Arthaud, 1973).

21   Oscar Wilde: see "The Decay of Lying," in *Intentions* (1891; Garden City, N.Y.: Dolphin Books, n.d.), 31.

22   a dangerous urban underclass: see the classic study by Louis Chevalier, *Labouring Classes and Dangerous Classes*, trans. Frank Jellinek (London: Routledge and Kegan Paul, 1973).

22   Dickens's London and Dostoevsky's Saint Petersburg: see Donald Fanger, *Dostoevsky and Romantic Realism: A Study of Dostoevsky in Relation to Balzac, Dickens, and Gogol* (Chicago: University of Chicago Press, 1967).

23   See Georg Lukács, "Illusions perdues," in *Studies in European Realism*, trans. Edith Bone (London: Hillway, 1950).

36   See Marcel Proust, in *Contre Sainte-Beuve* (Paris: Bibliothèque de la Pléiade, 1971), 273–74.

Chapter 3: Dickens and Nonrepresentation

Bibliographical note: See the rousing defense of *Hard Times* by F. R. Leavis in *The Great Tradition* (London: Chatto and Windus, 1948). See also George Gissing, *Charles Dickens: A Critical Study* (1898; New York: Haskell House, 1974); J. Hillis Miller, *Charles Dickens: The*

234   *World of His Novels* (Cambridge, Mass.: Harvard University Press, 1965); Steven Marcus, *Dickens: From Pickwick to Dombey* (London: Chatto and Windus, 1965); Sylvère Monod, *Dickens the Novelist* (Norman: University of Oklahoma Press, 1968); Alexander Welsh, *The City of Dickens* (Oxford: Clarendon, 1971) and *Dickens Redressed: The Art of Bleak House and Hard Times* (New Haven and London: Yale University Press, 2000); Catherine Gallagher, *The Industrial Revolution of English Fiction* (Berkeley: University of California Press, 1994); and the essays collected in the Norton Critical Edition of *Hard Times* (New York: Norton, 1966). For background, see Raymond Williams, *Culture and Society, 1780–1950* (New York: Harper and Row, 1958).

42–43   Quoted from *The Marx and Engels Reader*, ed. Robert C. Tucker (New York: Norton, 1978), 580–81.

50   See Walter Benjamin, "The Storyteller," in *Illuminations*, trans. Harry Zohn (New York: Schocken, 1968), 83–109.

52   G. B. Shaw, "Introduction to *Hard Times*" (1912), in *Hard Times*, ed. George Ford and Sylvère Monod (New York: Norton, 1966), 336.

Chapter 4: Flaubert and the Scandal of Realism

Bibliographical note: The most interesting books on Flaubert in English (which offer very different views of him) are: Victor Brombert, *The Novels of Flaubert* (Princeton, N.J.: Princeton University Press, 1966), and Jonathan Culler, *Flaubert: The Uses of Uncertainty* (Ithaca, N.Y.: Cornell University Press, 1974). See also chapters on Flaubert in Harry Levin, *The Gates of Horn: A Study of Five French Realists* (New York: Oxford University Press, 1963); Hugh Kenner, *Flaubert, Joyce and Beckett: The Stoic Comedians* (Boston: Beacon, 1962); Naomi Schor, *Reading in Detail: Aesthetics and the Feminine* (London: Methuen, 1987); Evelyne Ender, *Sexing the Mind* (Ithaca, N.Y.: Cornell University Press, 1995); Peter Brooks, *Reading for the Plot* (1984; rpt. Cambridge, Mass.: Harvard University Press, 1994). A detailed study of the trial of *Madame Bovary* is Dominick LaCapra, *Madame Bovary on Trial* (Ithaca, N.Y.: Cornell University Press, 1982).

Flaubert did not write critical essays; most of his comments on his craft are to be found in his letters: there exists a two-volume selection in English translation by Francis Steegmuller, *The Letters of Flaubert* (London: Picador, 2001). For the French reader, there is a fine collection of classic essays on Flaubert in Raymonde Debray-Genette, ed., *Flaubert* (Paris: Firmin Didot, 1970), including the essay by Gérard Genette, "Silences de Flaubert." See also Jacques Neefs and Claude Mouchard, *Flaubert* (Paris: Balland, 1986).

57–58   See Roman Jakobson, "Two Aspects of Language and Two Types of Aphasic Disturbances," in *Language in Literature*, ed. Krystyna Pomorska and Stephen Rudy (Cambridge, Mass.: Harvard University Press, 1987), 95–119.

65   See Gérard Genette, "Silences de Flaubert," in *Figures* (Paris: Editions du Seuil, 1966), 223–43; in English: *Figures of Literary Discourse*, trans. Alan Sheridan (New York: Columbia University Press, 1982), 183–202.

66   "Que le lecteur ne sache pas . . .": letter to Louis Bouilhet, 4 September 1850.

68   Sartre on the *lieu-commun*: see his Preface to Nathalie Sarraute, *Portrait d'un inconnu* (Paris: Gallimard, 1956), 7–14.

68   See T. S. Eliot, "Tradition and the Individual Talent," in *The Sacred Wood* (London: Methuen, 1920), 53.

69   "it is a delicious thing to write": letter to Louise Colet, 23 December 1853.

69   See Roland Barthes, discussing Alain Robbe-Grillet, in "Objective Literature," in *Critical Essays*, trans. Richard Howard (Evanston, Ill.: Northwestern University Press, 1972), 13–24.

69   See Henry James, "Gustave Flaubert," in *Literary Criticism*, vol. 2 (New York: Library of America, 1984), 326.

French text for certain key quotations:

59   Jamais madame Bovary ne fut aussi belle qu'à cette époque ; elle avait cette indéfinissable beauté qui résulte de la joie, de l'enthousiasme, du succès, et qui n'est que l'harmonie du tempérament avec les circonstances. Ses convoitises, ses chagrins, l'expérience du plaisir et ses illusions toujours jeunes, comme font aux fleurs le fumier, la pluie, les vents et le soleil, l'avaient par gradations développée, et elle s'épanouissait enfin dans la plénitude de sa nature. Ses paupières semblaient taillées tout exprès pour ses longs regards amoureux où la prunelle se perdait, tandis qu'un souffle fort écartait ses narines minces et relevait le coin charnu de ses lèvres qu'ombrageait à la lumière un peu de duvet noir. On eût dit qu'un artiste habile en corruptions avait disposé sur sa nuque la torsade de ses cheveux : ils s'enroulaient en une masse lourde, négligemment, et selon les hasards de l'adultère, qui les dénouait tous les jours. Sa voix maintenant prenait des inflexions plus molles, sa taille aussi ; quelque chose de subtil qui vous pénétrait se dégageait même des draperies de sa robe et de la cambrure de son pied. Charles, comme aux premiers temps de son mariage, la trouvait délicieuse et tout irrésistible. (269–70)

60   Il s'était tant de fois entendu dire ces choses, qu'elles n'avaient pour lui rien d'original. Emma ressemblait à toutes les maîtresses ; et le charme de la nouveauté, peu à peu tombant comme un vêtement, laissait voir à nu l'éternelle monotonie de la passion, qui a toujours les mêmes formes et le même langage. Il ne distinguait pas, cet homme si plein de pratique, la dissemblance des sentiments sous la parité des expressions. Parce que des lèvres libertines ou vénales lui avaient murmuré des phrases pareilles, il ne croyait que faiblement à la candeur de celles-là ; on en devait rabattre, pensait-il, les discours exagérés cachant les affections médiocres ; comme si la plénitude de l'âme ne débordait pas quelquefois par les métaphores les plus vides, puisque personne, jamais, ne peut donner l'exacte mesure de ses besoins, ni de ses conceptions, ni de ses douleurs, et que la parole humaine est comme un chaudron fêlé où nous battons des mélodies à faire danser les ours, quand on voudrait attendrir les étoiles. (265–66)

62   Elle songeait quelquefois que c'étaient là pourtant les plus beaux jours de sa vie, la lune de miel, comme on disait. Pour en goûter la douceur, il eût fallu, sans doute, s'en aller vers ces pays à noms sonores où les lendemains de mariage ont

236   de plus suaves paresses ! Dans des chaises de poste, sous des stores de soie bleue, on monte au pas des routes escarpées, écoutant la chanson du postillon, qui se répète dans la montagne avec les clochettes des chèvres et le bruit sourd de la cascade. Quand le soleil se couche, on respire au bord des golfes le parfum des citronniers ; puis, le soir, sur la terrasse des villas, seuls et les doigts confondus, on regarde les étoiles en faisant des projets. Il lui semblait que certains lieux sur la terre devaient produire du bonheur, comme une plante particulière au sol et qui pousse mal tout autre part. Que ne pouvait-elle s'accouder sur le balcon des chalets suisses ou enfermer sa tristesse dans un cottage écossais, avec un mari vêtu d'un habit de velours noir à longues basques, et qui porte des bottes molles, un chapeau pointu et des manchettes ! (91)

65   Il était seul, dans sa mansarde, en train d'imiter, avec du bois, une de ces ivoireries indescriptibles, composées de croissants, de sphères creusées les unes dans les autres, le tout droit comme un obélisque et ne servant à rien ; et il entamait la dernière pièce, il touchait au but ? Dans le clair-obscur de l'atelier, la poussière blonde s'envolait de son outil, comme une aigrette d'étincelles sous les fers d'un cheval au galop : les deux roues tournaient, ronflaient ; Binet souriait, le menton baissé, les narines ouvertes et semblait enfin perdu dans un de ces bonheurs complets, n'appartenant sans doute qu'aux occupations médiocres, qui amusent l'intelligence par des difficultés faciles, et l'assouvissent en une réalisation au-delà de laquelle il n'y a pas à rêver. (396)

Chapter 5: Courbet's House of Realism

Bibliographical note: The essential work on Courbet is to be found in T. J. Clark, *Images of the People* (New York: Graphic Society, 1973); Michael Fried, *Courbet's Realism* (Chicago: University of Chicago Press, 1990); and Linda Nochlin, *Realism* (Harmondsworth: Penguin, 1971). Sarah Faunce and Linda Nochlin, *Courbet Reconsidered* (Brooklyn, N.Y.: Brooklyn Museum, 1988), is the catalogue for the important Brooklyn Museum exhibit of 1988 and contains many plates. I thank my colleague and friend Alan Trachtenberg for helpful discussion on the history of photography.

72   T. J. Clark, *Images of the People* (New York: Graphic Society, 1973).

72   Champfleury, "Sur M. Courbet—Lettre à Madame Sand," in *Le Réalisme* (Paris: M. Lévy Frères, 1857), 271–85.

73   Charles Baudelaire, "Puisque réalisme il y a," in *Œuvres complètes* (Paris: Bibliothèque de la Pléiade, 1954), 991–93.

75   See Michael Fried, *Courbet's Realism* (Chicago: University of Chicago Press, 1990).

76   Prosper Haussard, as quoted by T. J. Clark, *Images of the People*, 138.

76   Françoise Gaillard, "Gustave Courbet et le réalisme. Anatomie de la réception critique d'une oeuvre: 'Un Enterrement à Ornans,'" *Revue d'Histoire littéraire de la France* 6 (1980): 978–96.

76   Linda Nochlin: in addition to her book *Realism*, see Sarah Faunce and Linda Nochlin, *Courbet Reconsidered* (Brooklyn, N.Y.: Brooklyn Museum, 1988).

77   Champfleury, "Sur M. Courbet—Lettre à Madame Sand," 279.

86   See Roland Barthes, *Camera Lucida*, trans. Richard Howard (New York: Hill and
      Wang, 1981); see also Susan Sontag, *On Photography* (New York: Farrar, Straus and
      Giroux, 1977).

90   Delaroche: his remark on the end of painting is cited by Alan Trachtenberg in
      his Introduction to *Classic Essays on Photography* (New Haven: Leete's Island Books,
      1980), ix; for Delaroche's favorable comments, see Dominique François Arago,
      "Report," in *Classic Essays*, 18.

92   Baudelaire, "Le Salon de 1859," in *Œuvres complètes*, 770.

Chapter 6: George Eliot's Delicate Vessels

Bibliographical note: Terence Cave's introduction to the Penguin edition of the novel cited
in this chapter offers a thorough and illuminating study of the genesis and reception
of the novel, a judicious assessment of recent criticism, and suggestions for further
reading. See, among other studies: Barbara Hardy, *The Novels of George Eliot* (London:
Athlone, 1959); Gillian Beer, *George Eliot* (Bloomington: Indiana University Press,
1986); David Carroll, *George Eliot and the Conflict of Interpretations* (Cambridge: Cambridge
University Press, 1992); and discussions of Eliot in Sandra M. Gilbert and Susan Gubar,
The Madwoman in the Attic: The Woman Writer and the Nineteenth-Century Literary Imagination
(New Haven and London: Yale University Press, 1979); Jacqueline Rose, *Sexuality in the
Field of Vision* (London: Verso, 1986); and Evelyne Ender, *Sexing the Mind* (Ithaca, N.Y.:
Cornell University Press, 1995). For Eliot's biography, see Gordon Haight, *George Eliot:
A Biography* (New York: Oxford University Press, 1968).

97   Laura Mulvey, "Visual Pleasure and Narrative Cinema," in *Visual and Other Pleasures*
      (London: Macmillan, 1989), 19.

98   Freud's case history: see Sigmund Freud, *Fragment of the Analysis of a Case of Hysteria*,
      in *Standard Edition of the Complete Psychological Writings*, 24 vols. (London: Hogarth
      Press, 1953–74), 7:91.

104   See Georges Bataille, *The Accursed Share* [*La Part maudite*], trans. Robert Hurley,
      3 vols. (New York: Zone Books, 1988–91).

108   See Freud, "On Narcissism: An Introduction," in *Standard Edition*, 14:73–102.

110   Henry James, "Daniel Deronda: A Conversation," in *Literary Criticism*, vol. 1 (New
      York: Library of America, 1984), 990.

111   Leavis: see *The Great Tradition* (London: Chatto and Windus, 1948), 79–125.

111   William Empson: see "Double Plots," in *Some Versions of Pastoral* (London: Chatto
      and Windus, 1935).

111   See Cynthia Chase, "The Decomposition of Elephants: Double Reading *Daniel
      Deronda*," *Proceedings of the Modern Language Association* 93 (1978): 215–27.

Chapter 7: Zola's Combustion Chamber

Bibliographical note: See Naomi Schor, *Zola's Crowds* (Baltimore: Johns Hopkins University
Press, 1978); the chapter on Zola in Harry Levin, *The Gates of Horn: A Study of Five French
Realists* (New York: Oxford University Press, 1963); on *Nana* and contemporary salon art
in Peter Brooks, *Body Work* (Cambridge, Mass.: Harvard University Press, 1993). Most of

238   the best work on Zola is in French: see in particular Jean Borie, *Zola et les mythes* (Paris: Editions du Seuil, 1971); Philippe Hamon, *Le Personnel du roman* (Geneva: Droz, 1983); Chantal Jennings, *L'Éros et la femme chez Zola* (Paris: Klincksieck, 1977); Michel Serres, *Feux et signaux de brume: Zola* (Paris: Grasset, 1975); and Henri Mitterrand, *Zola: L'histoire et la fiction* (Paris: Presses Universitaires de France, 1990).

113   See Walter Benjamin, "On Some Motifs in Baudelaire," in *Illuminations*, trans. Harry Zohn (New York: Schocken, 1969), 155–200, and *Charles Baudelaire: A Lyric Poet in the Age of High Capitalism*, trans. Harry Zohn (London: Verso, 1983).

114   See Michael Serres, *Feux et signaux de brume: Zola* (Paris: Grasset, 1975).

114   See A. J. B. Parent-Duchatelet, *De la prostitution dans la ville de Paris*, 2nd ed. (Paris: J.-B. Baillière, 1837); see also Alain Corbin, *Women for Hire*, trans. Alan Sheridan (Cambridge, Mass.: Harvard University Press, 1990).

119   "Je sais bien mais quand même": I know it but even so: see Octave Mannoni, *Clefs pour l'imaginaire* (Paris: Editions du Seuil, 1969), 9–33.

123   It is curious to reflect that the "cyclopean" aqueduct near Marseille was probably built by Zola's father, an engineer.

127   See James, "Emile Zola," in *Literary Criticism*, vol. 2 (New York: Library of America, 1984), 878–79; see Naomi Schor, *Zola's Crowds* (Baltimore: Johns Hopkins University Press, 1978).

128   Zola, *Mon Salon. Manet. Écrits sur l'art* (Paris: Garnier/Flammarion, 1970), 373.

Chapter 8: Unreal City

Bibliographic note: On the general topic, see Raymond Williams, *The Country and the City* (New York: Oxford University Press, 1973); Burton Pike, *The Image of the City in Modern Literature* (Princeton, N.J.: Princeton University Press, 1981); Richard Sennett, *The Fall of Public Man* (New York: Knopf, 1977); and David Frisby, *Cityscapes of Modernity* (Oxford: Blackwell, 2001), among numerous other studies. On London, see Asa Briggs, *Victorian Cities* (Harmondsworth: Penguin, 1968); and its suburbs: H. J. Dyos, *Victorian Suburb: A Study of the Growth of Camberwell* (Leicester: Leicester University Press, 1961). More specifically on Gissing and the city, see Carol L. Bernstein, *The Celebration of Scandal: Towards the Sublime in Victorian Urban Fiction* (University Park: Pennsylvania State University Press, 1991). On Gissing, see Virginia Woolf, "The Novels of George Gissing," *The Essays of Virginia Woolf*, vol. 1 (San Diego: Harcourt Brace Jovanovich, 1986), 355–62; George Orwell, "George Gissing," *The Collected Essays, Journalism and Letters*, vol. 4 (New York: Harcourt, Brace and World, 1968), 428–36; Adrian Poole, *Gissing in Context* (London: Macmillan, 1975); John Goode, *George Gissing: Ideology and Fiction* (London: Vision, 1978), and *Geroge Gissing: Grave Comedian* (Cambridge, Mass.: Harvard University Press, 1954); and David Grylls, *The Paradox of George Gissing* (London: Allen and Unwin, 1986).

132–33   Balzac, *Ferragus*, in *Histoire des Treize* (Paris: Garnier Frères, 1966), 39ff.

139   On the new behavioral phenomenon of shopping, see the interesting study by Rachel Bowlby, *Just Looking* (New York: Methuen, 1985).

141   See Henry James, *Literary Criticism*, vol. 1 (New York: Library of America, 1984), 1402.

Chapter 9: Manet, Caillebotte, and Modern Life

Bibliographic note: See especially T. J. Clark, *The Painting of Modern Life: Paris in the Art of Manet and His Followers* (New York: Knopf, 1985); Michael Fried, *Manet's Modernism* (Chicago: University of Chicago Press, 1996); Kirk Varnedoe, *Caillebotte* (New Haven and London: Yale University Press, 1987); Françoise Cachin, *Manet*, trans. Emily Read (London: Barrie and Jenkins, 1991); Beth Archer Brombert, *Manet: Rebel in a Frock Coat* (Boston: Little, Brown, 1996); and Robert L. Herbert, *Impressionism: Art, Leisure, and Parisian Society* (New Haven and London: Yale University Press, 1988). On the transformation of Paris, see David Pinkney, *Napoleon III and the Re-Building of Paris* (Princeton, N.J.: Princeton University Press, 1958). A general work on history and culture is Christopher Prendergast, *Paris and the Nineteenth Century* (Oxford: Blackwell, 1992). The work of Walter Benjamin, which has been crucial in shaping modern interpretations of nineteenth-century Paris, is now appearing in a complete edition; volumes published to date include the *Arcades Project*, trans. Howard Eiland and Kevin McLaughlin (Cambridge, Mass.: Harvard University Press, 1999), Benjamin's unfinished study of Baudelaire's Paris. On this project, the *Passagen-Werk*, see Susan Buck-Morss, *The Dialectics of Seeing: Walter Benjamin and the Arcades Project* (Cambridge, Mass.: MIT Press, 1989).

148   On the transformation of Paris, see David Pinkney, *Napoleon III and the Re-Building of Paris* (Princeton, N.J.: Princeton University Press, 1958).

151   See Baudelaire, *Le Peintre de la vie moderne*, in *Œuvres completes* (Paris: Bibliothèque de la Pléiade, 1954), 892; in English: *The Painter of Modern Life and Other Essays*, trans. and ed. Jonathan Mayne (London: Phaidon, 1995).

151   See Antonin Proust, *Édouard Manet—Souvenirs* (Paris: Librairie Renouard, 1913), 17. See also Beatrice Farwell, *Manet and the Nude: A Study in Iconography in the Second Empire* (New York: Garland, 1981), 39.

152   "cette fille de nos jours": see Zola, *Mon Salon. Manet. Écrits sur l'art* (Paris: Garnier/Flammarion, 1970), 109.

174   See James, "The Picture Season in London," *The Galaxy*, August 1877, in James, *The Painter's Eye: Notes and Essays on the Pictorial Arts*, ed. John L. Sweeney (Cambridge, Mass.: Harvard University Press, 1956), 141.

179   Barthes: see Roland Barthes, "The Reality-Effect" (1968), in *The Rustle of Language*, trans. Richard Howard (New York: Hill and Wang, 1986), 141–54. This well-known essay on the realist detail seems to me more applicable to painting than to literature.

Chapter 10: Henry James's Turn of the Novel

Bibliographical note: There is of course an exorbitant amount of critical material on James; best of all there is James as critic. See in particular the prefaces to the New York Edition, and the literary essays and reviews collected in the two volumes of *Literary Criticism* (New York: Library of America, 1984). Also helpful: F. O. Matthiessen, *Henry James: The Major Phase* (New York: Oxford University Press, 1944); Laurence B. Holland, *The Expense of Vision* (Princeton, N.J.: Princeton University Press, 1964); Peter Brooks, *The Melodramatic Imagination* (1976; rpt. New Haven and London: Yale University Press, 1995); Ruth B. Yeazell, *Language and Knowledge in the Late Henry James* (Chicago: University of

240 Chicago Press, 1976); John Carlos Rowe, *The Theoretical Dimension of Henry James* (Madison: University of Wisconsin Press, 1984); and Sharon Cameron, *Thinking in Henry James* (Chicago: University of Chicago Press, 1989).

180 Henry James, "Emile Zola," in *Literary Criticism*, vol. 2 (New York: Library of America, 1984), 895.

180 James, "The Lesson of Balzac," in *Literary Criticism*, 2:133.

181 James, "Lesson of Balzac."

184 Roman Jakobson, "Linguistics and Poetics," in *Language in Literature*, ed. Krystyna Pomorska and Stephen Rudy (Cambridge, Mass.: Harvard University Press, 1987), 62–94.

192–93 Preface to *What Maisie Knew, The Pupil, In the Cage*, in *Literary Criticism*, 2:1168.

197 *Literary Criticism*, 2:110.

Chapter 11: Modernism and Realism

Bibliographical note: On questions of narrative point of view and ways of narrating, see Dorrit Cohn, *Transparent Minds* (Princeton, N.J.: Princeton University Press, 1978), and Gérard Genette, *Narrative Discourse.* Among the scores of books on Virginia Woolf, see Hermione Lee, *Virginia Woolf* (London: Chatto and Windus, 1998); Maria DiBattista, *Virginia Woolf's Major Novels: The Fables of Anon* (New Haven and London: Yale University Press, 1980); and Rachel Bowlby, *Virginia Woolf: Feminist Destinations* (Oxford: Blackwell, 1988).

198 James Joyce, *Portrait of the Artist as a Young Man* (New York: Viking, 1944), 215.

202 See Marcel Proust, *Contre Sainte-Beuve* (Paris: Bibliothèque de la Pléiade, 1971), 221–22.

204–5 Virginia Woolf, *Mr. Bennett and Mrs. Brown* (London: Hogarth, 1924), 16.

Chapter 12: The Future of Reality?

214 On the "Postscript" of Tlön," see Emir Rodriguez Monegal, *Jorge Luis Borges: A Literary Biography* (New York: E. P. Dutton, 1978), 332.

215 William Butler Yeats, "Meditations in Time of Civil War," from *The Tower* (London: Macmillan, 1928).

217 See Linda Williams, *Hard Core: Power, Pleasure, and the "Frenzy of the Visible"* (Berkeley: University of California Press, 1989).

223 See Kim Lane Scheppele, "The Ground-Zero Theory of Evidence," 50 *Hastings Law Journal* 321 (1998).

169 Charles Dickens, *Great Expectations* (1860–61; Harmondsworth: Penguin, 2003), 169.

226 On fingerprint analysis, see *United States v. Llera Plaza*, 179 F. Supp. 2d 492 (E.D. Pa 2002). In this case, Judge Louis Pollak decided that experts would not be permitted to testify to a "match" between a "rolled" print and a "latent" print left at the crime scene, since fingerprint analysis did not meet the test of scientific evidence; he then reversed himself a few months later, 188 F. Supp.

549 (E.D. Pa 2002). On this question, see also Simon Cole, *Suspect Identities* (Cambridge, Mass.: Harvard University Press, 2001), and Jennifer Mnookin, "Fingerprint Evidence in an Age of DNA Profiling," 67 *Brooklyn Law Review* 13 (2001).

228–29   See James, "The Lesson of Balzac," in *Literary Criticism*, vol. 2 (New York: Library of America, 1984); see also James, "The Art of Fiction," in *Literary Criticism*, 1:44–65.

Acknowledgments

While I have long taught these books and the issues raised by realism, I would not have undertaken to organize my thoughts as formal lectures had it not been for the invitation to serve as Eastman Visiting Professor at Oxford for 2001–2. I am especially grateful to Terence Cave and Malcolm Bowie for their warm welcome, and for assuring that I had an audience at the lectures. I also profited from the collegiality of Ann Jefferson, Adrianne Tooke, Kate Tunstall, Nicola Luckhurst, Jonathan Patrick, Hermione Lee, Diego Zancani, Paul Strohm, Claire Harman, and Marina Warner, among others. For the appointment as William Clyde DeVane Professor at Yale in 2002–3, I am deeply grateful to President Richard C. Levin. The pleasure of teaching the course was greatly enhanced by my four stellar teaching fellows, Brad Anderson, Caroline Fitzpatrick, Aaron Matz, and Bonita Rhoads. They and many other Yale students, both graduate and undergraduate, have over the years taught me more than I can possibly acknowledge.

My interest in realism reaches back to my own days as a graduate student under the guidance of the late Harry Levin, and has been influenced by a number of scholars over the years, notably Victor Brombert, Linda Nochlin, Michael Fried, Richard Brettell, T. J. Clark, Philippe Hamon, and Michael Holquist.

I was fortunate in having my manuscript evaluated by Linda Nochlin, who knows more about the subject than anyone else. At Yale University Press, working with Jonathan Brent and Candice Nowlin was always a pleasure. Laura Jones Dooley was tactful, deft, and altogether admirable as copyeditor.

Thanks, finally, and as ever, to Rosa, Anna, and Clara.

Index

Page numbers in italics refer to illustrations